# *Tudor, Stuart and Hanover*

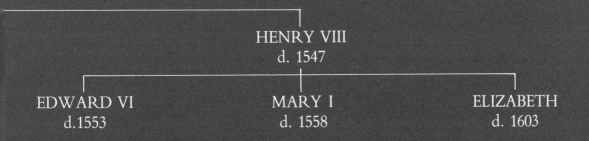

**HENRY VIII**
d. 1547

**EDWARD VI**
d.1553

**MARY I**
d. 1558

**ELIZABETH**
d. 1603

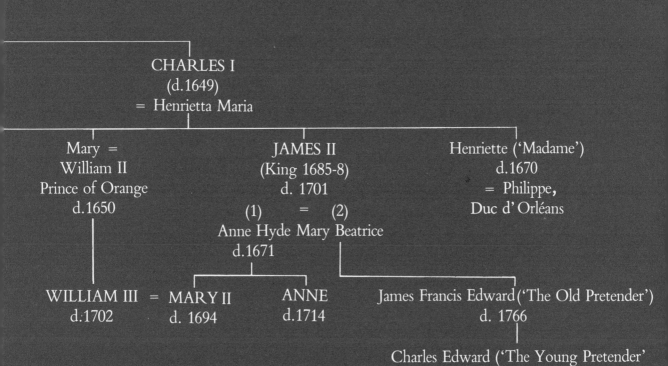

CHARLES I
(d.1649)
= Henrietta Maria

Mary =
William II
Prince of Orange
d.1650

JAMES II
(King 1685-8)
d. 1701
(1)      =      (2)
Anne Hyde Mary Beatrice
d.1671

Henriette ('Madame')
d.1670
= Philippe,
Duc d' Orléans

WILLIAM III = MARY II
d:1702    d. 1694

ANNE
d.1714

James Francis Edward ('The Old Pretender')
d. 1766

Charles Edward ('The Young Pretender'
or Bonnie Prince Charlie)
d. 1788

# BOURBON AND STUART

# JOHN MILLER

# *Bourbon and Stuart*

## Kings and Kingship in France and England in the Seventeenth Century

 Franklin Watts  1987  New York

Library of Congress
Cataloging−in−Publication Data

Miller, John (John Leslie)
  Bourbon and Stuart : kings and kingship in
France and England in the seventeenth
century.
  Bibliography : p.
  Includes index.
  1. Great Britain — Politics and government
  — 1603−1714.
  2. Great Britain — King and rulers.
  3. Stuart, House of.
  4. France — Politics and government —
  17th century.
  5. France — Kings and rulers.
  6. Bourbon, House of.
  7. Monarchy.     I. Title.
  DA 375.M48   1987   941.06   86−26764
  ISBN   0-531-15052-6

Printed in Hong Kong

*Illustration acknowledgements*

*Albertina Museum, Vienna* plate 4; *British
Library* plates 10 and 18; *British Museum*
plates 13 and 19; *English Heritage* plate 3;
*A.F.Kersting* plates 1, 8 and 9; *Musée Condé*
plate 12 (courtesy of Photographie Giraudon);
*Musée de Versailles* plates 6, 14 and 15; *Museo
del Prado* plate 16; *National Galley* plate 5;
*National Portrait Gallery* plates 2, 7, 11, 17,
20 and 21.

# Contents

*FOR MY PARENTS*

# Preface

The idea for this book came from an article I wrote a few years ago, comparing English and French government in the late seventeenth century. In it I questioned the usefulness of the concept of 'absolutism', once it is removed from the French institutional set-up which it was coined to describe. My aim here is to attempt a similar comparison, embracing the whole century and devoting more space to the major personalities than was possible in a twenty-page article.

I have tried throughout to keep technical terms to a minimum. While appreciating that there was a difference between the offices of *surintendant des finances* and *contrôleur-général des finances*, it seems sufficient in a book such as this to refer to both as 'finance ministers'. My aim throughout has been to produce a synthesis that will appeal to as wide a readership as possible, not just to students and specialists, and to ask some broad questions about the nature of monarchy. While I have set out both to discuss the personalities of the various monarchs and to place them in a wide historical context, I have not set out to write a general history of the two countries in this period.

In the seventeenth century, England adhered to the 'old style' of dating, ten days behind the 'new style' in use on the continent. I have used 'old style' dating for events in England and 'new style' for those on the Continent, unless otherwise stated.

I am very grateful to Richard Cust for allowing me to make use of his important thesis; to Lydia Greeves and David Starkey for their help in the shaping and production of this book; and to my wife and sons for their forbearance during its preparation and writing — not least in helping me to fight my way, on crutches, through the crowds at Versailles on an August afternoon.

*John Miller, November 1986*

# 1
# Introduction

If someone were to travel back in time to the Europe of the early seventeenth century, he would find a world vastly different from his own. The majority of people lived in villages, scratching a precarious living from unproductive soil. Industry, as we know it, scarcely existed: manufactured goods were produced by hand, by craftsmen working in their own homes. Disease and squalor were ever-present; harvest failure, famine and plague constantly cast a shadow over the lives of people far more familiar with death than their modern counterparts. Life, in the words of the philosopher Thomas Hobbes, was 'nasty, brutish and short', but most people lacked the leisure or the education to indulge in philosophy. Few could read, fewer could write. The lives of men, women and children were taken up with grinding labour, in the fields or at the loom, interspersed with periods of enforced idleness and the all-too-rare feast days and carnivals, when they forsook their meagre diet and workaday tedium for a bout of frenetic eating and drinking, sexual licence and violent amusements. In so far as historians can reconstruct it, the mental world of peasants and craftsmen contained a mixture of Christian teachings, folk tales and magical beliefs, transmitted partly by the churches and partly by oral tradition. Families and village communities clung together, ignorant and suspicious of the outside world: even people from a few miles away were seen as 'foreigners'.

Our time-traveller would certainly be struck by the poverty all around him, by the cripples, vagrants and beggars. He would also, however, see that poverty was not universal. Alongside the hovels of the poor he would see splendid churches and monasteries, testimonies to the piety of countless generations. In the larger towns he would see the elegant dwellings of merchants, lawyers and officials, with glass windows, fine hangings and costly furnishings. Here lived people with a very different perception of life, who were literate, often widely read, and whose knowledge embraced far-flung parts of the globe, the intricacies of law and the rich philosophical and theological heritage of Christendom. A few town houses would stand out from the rest: not so much mansions as palaces, the dwellings of bishops, nobles and kings, whose primary residences would be well away from the crowds, smells and smoke of the town. There, in their castles and country houses, they indulged their fondness for building, for gardens and for hunting and created a refined, opulent environment, far removed from the crudity and misery of plebeian life.

Just as the wealth of the few contrasted starkly with the poverty of the many, so political power was concentrated in a few hands. The bulk of the population lacked the leisure, the knowledge or the inclination to take an active part in government. The peasant trudged through his yearly round, largely oblivious of the functioning of government: when it did impinge upon his life, it was usually for the worse, and took the form of predatory tax-collectors or brutal soldiers. Sometimes peasants and townsmen reacted violently against such intrusions, but they generally showed little interest in public affairs, except when these involved a direct threat to themselves and their families. Ignorance, parochialism and inertia were the dominant themes of popular political behaviour, except in major cities, where a higher level of literacy and political awareness prevailed and sheer numbers made 'the people' a force to be reckoned with. In general, however, few seem to have questioned openly what their superiors and the churches said were the major elements of the natural order of things: inequality, the Christian religion and monarchy.

Most educated Europeans took it for granted that monarchy was the best form of government. It was the form chosen by God, as shown by the kings of the Old Testament, and it was the most natural: the corollary, on a larger scale, of a husband's authority over his wife, servants and children. It seemed common sense that, in war or diplomacy, ultimate responsibility should be concentrated in one person and that only a king, raised above the rest of the population, could provide impartial justice and protect the weak against the strong. Over the centuries, churchmen, seeking protection against predatory laymen, had magnified the power of kings and the sanctity of monarchy; they had also tried, not always successfully, to bend kings to the church's will. Across Europe, monarchy was the norm, from the kings of England and France in the west to the tsar of all the Russias in the east. Many monarchs ruled small territories. What we now know as Germany was

**FRANCE AND HER FRONTIERS**

——— 1715
········· 1598

Dunkirk

Brussels

Lille
SPANISH NETHERLANDS

GERMANY

Rhine

Amiens

Rocroi
Sedan

Seine

Versailles

Paris
Melun

Philippsburg

DUCHY OF LORRAINE

Strasbourg
Kehl

ALSACE

Breisach

Belle Ile

Blois

Loire

F  R  A  N  C  E

FRANCHE
COMTÉ

TYROL

SWISS
CONFEDERATION

Rhône

Adda

THE
VALTELLINE

Ile de Ré

La Rochelle

SAVOY

A  L  P  S

MILAN

VENICE

Lyons

Turin

PIEDMONT

Po

MONTFERRAT

Privas

Pinerolo

Montauban

Alais

BÉARN  Toulouse

Montpellier

Tarascon

Castelnaudary

NAVARRE

P  Y  R  E  N  E  E  S

Narbonne

ROUSSILLON

S  P  A  I  N

a mosaic of some 300 principalities, bishoprics and city-states; Italy was under a dozen different rulers. At the other extreme there were great multinational empires. The Turks controlled vast tracts of southeastern Europe, including modern-day Greece, Romania and much of Yugoslavia and Hungary. In the west, the dominant empires were those ruled by the two branches of the house of Habsburg. The Austrian branch, based in Vienna, ruled directly over a motley array of lands, including modern-day Austria, much of Czechoslovakia and parts of Hungary, Yugoslavia and Italy. They were also invariably elected to the title of Holy Roman Emperor, which gave indirect, frequently challenged but still substantial powers in Germany and beyond, including Alsace and Lorraine. The Habsburg kings of Spain ruled not only Spain and its vast empire in the New World, but large parts of Italy and what we now call the Low Countries. Throughout the first half of the seventeenth century, Spain was locked in a bitter struggle for control of the Low Countries, which ended with her retaining the southern part (roughly modern Belgium) but conceding independence to the Dutch, in what is now usually known as Holland.

In this world of monarchies, republics (apart from petty city-states) were few and far between: Venice, Switzerland, the Dutch Republic. Yet despite the overwhelming prevalence of monarchy, it has rarely been systematically studied. One reason must be that many historians would claim that the history of 'kings and queens' is irrelevant or peripheral, that historians should concentrate on the 'real' social and economic forces behind historical change. Such a viewpoint is especially prevalent in France, where the influence of the 'Annales school' has made political history unfashionable, so that much of the best work on early modern French government and politics has been produced by American or British scholars. In Britain, recent work on the seventeenth century has seen a reaction against this approach, with more stress on the importance of political and religious factors, on personalities and chance, in determining historical development. After all, while accepting that it is necessary to understand the economic and social bases of political power, it surely does not follow that political change *must* reflect underlying economic and social change: politics can have a momentum of its own. Moreover, however much the study of kings may offend some historians' egalitarian scruples, their actions (and especially their wars) could have a major impact on their subjects' lives.

The aim of this book is to investigate the nature and working of monarchy in England and France in the seventeenth century. This was a time when kings were far more than ornate figureheads or 'burlesque Jupiters', when they were expected to govern their kingdoms. Although the legitimacy of monarchy, as an institution, was seldom challenged, its precise powers were often a matter for debate and it underwent dangerous vicissitudes in both countries, notably in the 1640s. Charles I of England was faced, in 1640, with a Parliament which made unprecedented attacks on his authority. Rioting Londoners forced him to agree to the execution of his chief minister, the Earl of Strafford, and drove him out of his capital city. For four years King and Parliament fought a bloody and bitter civil war. Charles was defeated and early in 1649 he was tried by a special court, on a charge of making war on his people. The verdict of guilty came as no surprise; he was executed and the monarchy was abolished.

The French royal court watched these events with a mixture of bewilderment, at the unpredictability of the English, and anxiety, that the contagion of rebellion might spread to France. Their fears proved well founded. In 1648 Queen Anne of Austria, regent for the young Louis XIV, and Cardinal Mazarin, her leading adviser, faced open defiance from the Parlement of Paris. Unlike the English Parliament, this was not a representative body but a law court; its prestige and authority, however, made it a formidable adversary. It quickly won support from other law courts and put forward demands which, in the eyes of the Queen and Mazarin, threatened the very foundations of the monarchy. The Parlement found support among the citizens of Paris, who proved as ready to riot as their counterparts in London, and the great military nobility. Soon much of France was engulfed in a civil war which became known as the Fronde. Like Charles I's seven years earlier, the French royal family fled from its capital city, in January 1649, and Anne, like Charles, was forced to sacrifice her chief minister: in April 1651 Mazarin went into exile.

In the middle of the seventeenth century, then, the English monarchy was abolished and it seemed that the French monarchy would soon suffer a similar fate. Yet the monarchy survived, in France until the Revolution, in England until the present day. What, then, were the strengths which enabled the monarchies to emerge from their respective crises and to go from strength to strength in the latter part of the century? What were the weaknesses which brought about civil wars in the two countries? Were contemporaries right to stress the parallels between them?

Such questions are not easy to answer. The two countries had very different institutions and constitutions. One was part of an offshore island, the other a continental power surrounded by potentially hostile territories. One was Protestant, one Catholic. There were also similarities, however. Both monarchies had to control extensive and diverse territories: the Stuarts were also kings of Scotland and Ireland. Both possessed powers of coercion insufficient for their needs and feeble compared with those of a modern state. Each had difficulty controlling the officials who nominally served it. Both had the perennial problem of raising money from subjects who were not keen to part with it. Both had the problem of religious minorities, who provoked fear and hatred among the majority. Above all, both were personal monarchies. Bourbon and Stuart kings ruled as well as reigned. Their success depended on their ability to use their powers within a given political and institutional framework. Being a king could be hard work. It also required an understanding of one's subjects' attitudes and, above all, a sense of what was politically possible. This political sense, or the lack of it, distinguished an unsuccessful king, like Charles I, from Louis XIV, regarded by all Europe as the epitome of successful, 'absolute' monarchy.

'Absolutism' is a term which historians are liable to use without attempting to define or explain it.[1] Its roots lay in a theory of monarchy in which the king had unlimited power to act for the nation's good, as he saw it. How far the reality approximated to the theory was open to question. It seemed to many that Louis XIV ruled alone, maintaining total personal control over all aspects of government and that his will was translated into action instantly by a multitude of ministers and officials. It seemed, too, that his power over his subjects was 'absolute': that he could make laws and levy taxes without their consent and that their lives, liberty and property were wholly at his disposal. These were appearances that Louis XIV worked hard to sustain, but they were in many respects misleading, as the upheavals of the Fronde showed all too clearly. The major aim of this book is to distinguish between, on one hand, the theories and myths elaborated by monarchs and their apologists, and, on the other, the practical realities of monarchy, of kings struggling, with inadequate resources, to tackle difficult and sometimes insoluble problems. It is, in short, a study of how monarchy worked.

# 2
# Beginnings

On the morning of 24 March 1603 a meeting of privy councillors and peers was hastily convened at Whitehall Palace, in London. A few hours before, the death of Queen Elizabeth I had brought the Tudor dynasty to an end. To prevent uncertainty and to forestall rival claims, her successor had to be proclaimed at once, so at ten o'clock it was announced that King James VI of Scotland was to be King James I of England. The proclamation came as no great surprise — James himself had approved its wording — but it was not a foregone conclusion. There were other claimants (including the daughter of the King of Spain) but James' claim was the strongest and as a Protestant he was well suited to a mainly Protestant kingdom.

The proclamation was greeted with widespread and apparently unfeigned rejoicing. For the first time in fifty years England was to have a king, who, moreover, was an experienced ruler and had two sons to guarantee a secure succession. Many were not sorry to see the end of Elizabeth's reign. Later generations may have seen it as a golden age of national harmony and self-confidence, symbolized by Drake's circumnavigation of the globe and singeing of the King of Spain's beard, but that was not the way it seemed at the time. For much of the reign English Protestants had good reason to feel anxious about the future. When Elizabeth became Queen, the Protestants were probably a smaller minority in England than in France or the southern Low Countries, both of which were to remain Catholic.

To win over hearts and minds and to establish Protestant convictions, over and above mere conformity, was a slow process. It required years of pastoral and evangelical effort, backed up by the full power of the State and its laws. The success of Protestantism thus depended on Elizabeth's having a Protestant successor, but she resolutely refused to provide one, even though she nearly died of smallpox in 1562. Whereas her subjects took it for granted that she should marry and have children — they saw breeding as a woman's primary function — she knew that whatever choice she made would be unpopular with an important section of her subjects. She remained single, dangling the carrot of her marriage before unlikely and unprepossessing foreign princes, until even the greatest optimists accepted that she was past childbearing age. Her failure to marry meant that the strongest claim to the succession remained that of James' mother, Mary Queen of Scots. As she was a Catholic, it seemed that when Elizabeth died there would be either another Catholic regime, like that of 'Bloody Mary' Tudor, or a religious civil war, like those raging in France. To make matters worse, Mary was the focus of several Catholic plots against Elizabeth's life, but despite her transparent guilt only in 1587 did Elizabeth bow to the pressure of her councillors and Parliament and have her rival executed. James now had the best hereditary claim to the succession, but Elizabeth refused to acknowledge any successor, fearing that that person would be the centre of a dissident 'reversionary interest', as she herself had been under her half-sister Mary.

Elizabeth may have had plausible, if selfish, reasons for refusing to settle the succession, but her conduct could be seen as irresponsible. In their different ways, Henry VIII, Louis XIII and Louis XIV all tried to provide for an orderly transfer of power after their deaths. Elizabeth did nothing and so added to the anxieties of her last years, when England was at war with Spain. That three armadas failed owed more to the weather than to English naval skill. If the Spaniards had landed, the part-time soldiers of the militia would have been no match for the finest infantry in Europe.

The war years also saw a growth of divisions and bitterness at home. For much of the reign, rulers and ruled had been in broad agreement about the ends and means of government, about the need to encourage Protestantism and suppress Catholicism, to enforce the laws and to promote the general well-being of the realm. Such agreement was necessary because English government depended on the consent and co-operation of the governed. The crown lacked effective powers of coercion. It could not afford a standing army or a large professional bureaucracy, with which to impose its will on the localities, so it made use of the leading figures in each community.

In the counties, wealthy gentlemen served as Justices of the Peace (JPs), who investigated crime, punished petty offenders and enforced social and economic legislation; a select few, as deputy lieutenants, organized the county in its military capacity and commanded the militia. In corporate towns these tasks were performed by elected councillors, chosen from among the leading families. In villages, the humbler offices of churchwarden and overseer of the poor were filled by the more substantial farmers or craftsmen.

In much the same way, law enforcement depended more on the individual citizen in England than in France, where it was largely controlled by professional judges. These sought out and punished offences, using procedures far more inquisitorial than those used in England (including torture, which ceased to be used in England in the early seventeenth century). In England, most disputes were settled within the village or town without coming to court: restitution and communal harmony took precedence over punishment. Crime was seen as an offence against the individual and not (as in France) against the State. Grand juries used their local knowledge to assess the plausibility of a charge, trial juries often acquitted the accused or brought in a verdict which limited his punishment. JPs often tried to appease quarrels, although a minority followed the example of their French counterparts, waging war on sin and disorder as they understood them and trying to impose their standards of conduct on the people.[1]

In general, then, English local government and law enforcement depended on the crown's ability to secure the co-operation of its subjects and especially those with the leisure, education and local standing to involve themselves in local government. This system of reliance on unpaid amateurs (vestiges of which survive in the use of lay JPs) had the great advantages of being cheap and of tapping the local knowledge and influence of those involved. Local notables, for their part, valued the prestige and power which local office brought. On the other hand, to appoint officials on the basis of status rather than ability could cause problems. Some were idle or incompetent, others proved uncooperative. They might feel that national legislation was inappropriate to their locality or seek to protect local vested interests. The privy council, which supervised their activities, was overburdened with business and lacked reliable agents in the localities, so had to rely on persuasion rather than coercion. It dismissed officials who were openly recalcitrant, but its field of choice was limited to men of sufficient status and in general it had to trust in the good sense of those on the spot. It explained carefully the reasons for its orders, by letter or through personal contacts. Parliament provided a particularly useful medium of communication. A majority of members of both Houses were involved in local government, so could inform councillors of the problems they encountered, while councillors could explain and justify their policies. Much of the legislation which emerged was based upon practical experience in the localities, reflected the give and take of debate and so was shaped by the sort of men who were to enforce it.

For much of Elizabeth's reign, the reality of government was not too removed from this ideal image of harmonious co-operation. In its dealings with local governors, the council showed tact and a willingness to listen and to change its mind. The Queen's government was frugal, the country was at peace and taxes were low. With the war against Spain the crown's financial needs increased dramatically. Parliament voted extra taxation, but not nearly enough. Crown lands were sold off, sacrificing future income to present need, and still more was needed. The council was always pestered by 'projectors', with clever schemes for making money for the crown (and themselves). Some involved reviving long-forgotten royal rights over land, others administrative tasks or the regulation of some trade. Many involved monopolies or the charging of fees, from which the crown might derive some profit, but which also enabled the projectors to extract money from some section of the public.

Normally these projects met with a cool response from Queen and council, but in the 1590s they were desperate for money and for patronage. The crown needed to reward those who served it, the two to three thousand who really mattered politically : the peers and upper gentry, the top lawyers, churchmen and civil servants. Given its restricted income, many of the crown's rewards had to be at the expense of others. Church livings for the younger sons or nephews of great men cost the crown nothing. Offices usually carried small salaries, the officials relying mainly on fees and gratuities from those who used their services. The crown would also grant away small parts of the royal revenue or administration, to be exploited by others. Some forms of revenue-raising and patronage were seen as extortionate and oppressive, so the crown had to assess the benefits carefully to see if they outweighed the dissatisfaction which they might provoke.

In the 1590s it threw caution to the winds. The war had to be paid for, while competition for rewards became frenetic. Hitherto Elizabeth had maintained a fairly even balance among her ministers, but now court and council polarized into factions as a bitter rivalry developed between Robert Cecil and the Earl of Essex. Cecil was an astute and diligent, if not always scrupulous administrator, trained for high office by his father, Lord Treasurer Burghley. Essex was a military man, young and dashing, with a charm that the hunchbacked and prickly Cecil conspicuously lacked. Resentful of Cecil's dominance of the administration, Essex used his large estates and influence with the Queen to build up a clientele reminiscent of those of the 'overmighty' barons of the fifteenth century; Cecil responded in kind. A ferocious competition for patronage developed, as each tried to extend his following and the restraint and discipline of public life disappeared in an unholy scramble for profit. By the later 1590s Cecil was gaining the upper hand, driving Essex to desperate measures. In 1601 he rebelled against his Queen and was executed.[2]

While the wealthy few profited, provincial England groaned under a multiplicity of rates and taxes and suffered a run of four disastrous harvests. Food prices soared, famine gripped parts of the north and the hungry poor rioted. Meanwhile, in its impatience to mobilize men and money for the war, the council gave more responsibilities to the militia authorities, the lord lieutenant and his deputies. The JPs deeply resented this reduction in their authority, which in some respects made them the mere agents of the lieu-tenancy. There were thus many reasons for local governors to resent the conduct of central government in the 1590s. Earlier councillors and local rulers had shared a sense of common purpose and common peril, agreeing with each other (if not with the Queen) on the need to suppress popery and execute Mary Queen of Scots. Now the councillors imposed new burdens, interfered with established patterns of local government, allowed the favoured few to profiteer at the expense of the many and, in many cases, profited themselves. The council had changed from partner to predator, making it very difficult to reconcile the government's demands with the interests of the local community.[3]

The Parliaments of Elizabeth's last years reflected this growing dissatis-faction. When she entered the Commons in 1601

few said 'God bless your majesty' as they were wont. . . . And the throng being great . . . one of the gentlemen ushers said openly 'Back masters, make room'. And one answered stoutly behind 'If you will hang us we can make no more room', which the Queen seemed not to hear, though she heaved up her head and looked that way towards him that spake.[4]

After a bitter attack on monopolies, the Queen agreed to withdraw many of them. The twilight of the reign was a time of rancour and recrimination, while politicians surreptitiously sought the favour of the Scots King.

As he often said, James was an experienced king, having been proclaimed at the age of two in 1568. His mother had been deposed by the Scots lords amid accusations of adultery and murder. As he grew up James learned how to play the great nobles off against each other and how to manage Parliament and the Kirk. He resisted the claims of the high Presbyterian clergy that he should submit to their direction even in secular matters, manipulated the Kirk's general assembly and reintroduced a limited measure of episcopacy. In all this he had to find his own way, without a parent or preceptor, in a nation where the nobility retained extensive military power and had few scruples about resorting to violence. By 1603 James had emerged as an astute judge and manipulator of men, able to balance individuals and factions, to manage assemblies and to put his case effectively in debate. When he wrote treatises on monarchy, he could claim he knew what he was talking about.[5]

Englishmen who met James before his accession were generally impressed. Sir Henry Wotton found him learned and eloquent, diligent in matters of state and always ready to take advice. His court resembled that of France more than Elizabeth's: anyone could watch the King eat and he chatted familiarly with domestics and gentlemen. When he arrived in England, early impressions were equally favourable. He seemed vigorous and well built, with a fair complexion, square-cut beard and blue eyes. Far less formal and stately than Elizabeth, he eschewed elaborate ceremony and long deliberations. He was quick-witted and decisive, with an excellent memory. His generosity was a welcome change after Elizabeth's parsimony and all who had not prospered under her hoped to do so now.[6]

For his part, James regarded his new kingdom as both richer and more ordered than Scotland. The nobility no longer had private armies or built fortified castles: houses like Longleat and Audley End reflected a peaceful society. Disputes were settled in the courts, or by arbitration, not by violence. The English were still quarrelsome, drawing their swords at the slightest pretext, but their quarrels no longer escalated into bloodfeuds.

Except perhaps for the Scottish borders and parts of Wales, England no longer had 'lawless zones' like those which still existed in parts of Scotland (or France). Kings of England no longer needed to fear aristocratic rebellion. The rising of the northern earls in 1569 had been the last; the earls had had to use Catholicism as a rallying-cry and many of Northumberland's tenants failed to follow him. Essex' rising had been an attempted coup, using part of the royal army.[7] It was thus with good reason that James wrote in 1602 that the Scots were 'a far more barbarous and stiff-necked people' than the English.[8]

In time James learned that if England lacked Scotland's truculent nobles and domineering pastors, its people were no easier to rule and its government required skills different to those he had developed in Scotland. A king of England needed subtlety, deliberation and determination and he had to operate more indirectly and at a greater distance than James was used to. Scotland was a smaller country with a small court; its Parliament was managed through a committee, the Lords of the Articles. James had been able to deal directly with groups and individuals, to put his views in person in the Articles or the general assembly of the Kirk, to counter the arguments of others and to shift his ground when necessary: he revelled in the cut and thrust of debate. In England, his role was more formal and remote. His speeches to Parliament were set pieces — rather too elaborate and theoretical for English taste — and after speaking he withdrew and left the management of Parliament to his ministers. England's laws and institutions were very different from those he was used to and its administration was more complex and burdensome. The ruling élite, too, was larger: there were more names and faces to get to know.

However intelligent and experienced James might be, he was a foreigner. He had to adapt to an alien system, absorb a vast amount of new information and cope with the endless importunities of his subjects. James tried, but found the effort beyond him and delegated responsibility to his ministers. His court, too, was larger than he was used to and Elizabeth had made it formal and elaborate, emphasizing the distance of majesty. James did not see himself as an elegant figurehead, remote from ordinary mortals. Though not yet a shambling old man, he was not very interested in clothes and pomp and ceremony bored him. He hated sitting still and walked around while thinking, much to the discomfort of Cecil, who was rather lame. Called upon to play a static ceremonial role, to dazzle and inspire awe, he rebelled and fled to the hunt.[9]

If James found being King of England less easy and pleasurable than he had hoped, there was still much to enjoy. First and foremost there was hunting. He travelled restlessly from one country house to another, hunting with a ferocity which exhausted his ministers and courtiers. 'We are all become wild men, wandering in a forest from the morning till the evening', one complained. The court lumbered around the countryside, filling the inns, blocking the roads with its carts of provisions and spreading the plague. When James announced his intention of hunting in Northamptonshire, the gentry hastily found reasons to be away from home. Entertaining the King was a costly privilege: it cost the Bishop of Winchester £2000 for three days.[10] For James, however, hunting was a psychological and (he claimed) a physical necessity. He hated London with its crowds and smog and felt happiest in the company of a few close, male friends with whom he could hunt, drink and talk. He was a shy man who 'did not love to be looked on and those formalities of state which set a lustre upon princes in the people's eyes were but so many burdens to him'. He did not appreciate that 'the English adore their sovereigns and if the king passed through the same street a hundred times a day the people would still run to see him'.[11] He was so irritated by the rustics who came to gawp at him as he hunted that he appointed a special official to ensure that his sport was not interrupted.

James' other great passion was scholarly debate. He discussed theology with his chaplains while he ate (and they did not) and hugely enjoyed the Latin disputations at the universities, often joining in: he said that if he had not been King, he would like to have been a university man. When meeting Sir John Harington, he talked much of learning 'and showed his own in such sort as made me remember my examiner at Cambridge', ranging from Aristotle to witchcraft and the evils of tobacco. He was not really the polymath he aspired to be. He compared Bacon's pioneering scientific treatise, the *Instauratio Magna*, to the peace of God, passing all understanding. He often won arguments not because he had the stronger case but because he was king and passed off the ideas of others as his own. Even so, a king capable of producing serious works of controversy was a rare phenomenon. It was one of his many misfortunes that as king he had so few opportunities to display his debating talents.[12]

If hunting and scholarship brought him pleasure, he derived little from his family. With his wife, Anne of Denmark, he had little in common. She did not share his interests and liked dancing, fine clothes and jewels; she played a major part in organizing court masques and took principal roles herself. James' poor opinion of female intelligence was confirmed by his marriage. He became intolerant of feminine fashions and vanities and was bored by masques: he preferred a good farce, with plenty of verbal wit. To make matters worse, Anne became a Catholic. Her conversion owed little to theological conviction and she showed a naïve delight in collecting relics and other consecrated objects. Given their differences of temperament, it was not surprising that James and Anne did not spend much time together, or that they sometimes quarrelled. James, who became increasingly tetchy with age, complained especially of her extravagance, but he always preserved a certain outward respect towards her. He granted many of her requests, indulged many of her whims and usually sought her approval for appointments at court. Sometimes he showed flashes of kindness. When she accidentally shot his favourite hound, Jewel, James was livid but, next day, having calmed down, he sent her a jewel as a 'legacy' from the dog. In the words of Bishop Goodman: 'The King of himself was a very chaste man and there was little in the Queen to make him uxorious. Yet they did love as well as man and wife could do, not conversing together.'[13]

James' relationship with his children was little happier. His elder son Henry was in many respects a model Prince of Wales and offered an embarrassing contrast to his father. He was sober, whereas his father drank increasingly heavily. He kept an ordered household, while James' tended to riot and disorder. He was frugal and paid his bills punctually; James was extravagant and his credit was poor. Henry excelled at military exercises; James, for all his reckless courage while hunting, was in many ways a coward, as he himself admitted. He went in constant fear of assassination and wore a padded doublet to guard against the killer's knife. Henry did not share his father's enthusiasm for either hunting or scholarship. 'It is not necessary for me to be a professor', he said, 'but a soldier and a man of the world. If my brother is as learned as they say, we'll make him Archbishop of Canterbury.'[14] Not surprisingly, Henry became the great hope of those dissatisfied with James' policies and style of government. James complained of the number of people paying court to his son and accused him of prying into his affairs and abusing his servants. When Henry died in 1612, James did not seem greatly distressed. He ordered that Charles, the new Prince of Wales, 'be kept within a stricter compass than the former and not to exceed his ordinary in diet or followers'.[15]

Charles was quite unlike his brother. He contracted rickets as a child, which left his legs short and slightly bowed, and he had a persistent stammer. Where Henry was an extrovert, a natural focus for attention, Charles was shy and withdrawn : it was not so much that he lived in his brother's shadow, more that nobody noticed him. James paid him little attention, nor (despite her claims that he was her favourite son) did his mother. His household was smaller and less grand than Henry's : younger sons always played second fiddle to the first-born. He remained on the periphery of the court, whose crudity must have repelled him — he was a prim and sensitive youth — receiving little comfort from those who should have been closest to him. His father became besotted with his favourites, his mother was preoccupied with her trivial pleasures and his adored brother treated him with condescension or cruel contempt : if Charles was made archbishop, he said, the robes would at least hide his rickety legs.

Of James' three children, only the daughter, Elizabeth, brought him any real pleasure. Vivacious, intelligent and level-headed, she became the darling of the court and of her dashing elder brother, to whom she became very close : Charles, as usual, was left out. In 1613, however, she married one of Germany's leading Protestant princes, Frederick, the Elector Palatine. The young couple turned out to be well suited, fell madly in love and produced a large family. The wedding was celebrated with a magnificence which James could not afford, but once the jollifications were over, Elizabeth left for Germany, leaving the court a sadder place. Time was to show that James had not only lost a daughter, but had acquired a son-in-law whose escapades would plunge Europe into turmoil and bring James much grief and heart-searching.

Despite the crowds which surrounded him, James was in many ways a lonely man. Most of those who thronged the court were seeking favours of some kind. He had few friends, as distinct from servants or companions, and these had mostly come with him from Scotland. James was an affectionate man and needed an outlet or object for his affection. Neither of his sons warmed to him : one was proud and wilful, the other primly disapproving.

Although James showed a prurient interest in other people's sexual activities — he always inquired whether newly-weds had done their duty on their wedding night — he was basically uninterested in women. He was always at least latently homosexual. In his teens he had a crush on his cousin, Esmé Stuart but if other male favourites followed, their names have gone unrecorded.[16] Then, in 1607, one of his pages, Robert Carr, broke his leg while jousting. Carr was a Scot, well-built, 'comely and handsome rather than beautiful', an affable companion. James spent a great deal of time with him as he convalesced. He taught him Latin (some maliciously suggested that he should teach him English too) so that, by adding learning to his innate charm, Carr could become an ideal companion. James soon showed his affection openly, leaning on Carr's arm, smoothing his clothes and looking at him even when talking to others. Naturally the King's fondness for his favourite aroused unfavourable comment, but this was nothing compared to the scandal which was to surround him a few years later.[17]

When James discovered Carr he was over forty. The optimism and self-confidence he had shown in 1603 were wearing thin. He resented his subjects' anti-Scottish prejudices and his constant shortage of money ('this eating canker of want') and was badly shaken in 1605 by the attempt of Catholic extremists to blow up Parliament. By 1610 the jocular tone and raillery of his earlier letters to his ministers had largely disappeared. It was a sadder, lonely man who sought solace in the companionship of Carr. But if James and his subjects had each lost the rosy view of the other which they had had in 1603, where did the fault lie? Was James inadequate or malevolent? Or were his people ungrateful, truculent and even rebellious?

When considering James' kingship, one should first look at his court. This contained some 1500 officers, servants and attendants, who had to be fed and paid, plus throngs of suitors, sightseers and aristocrats who came, with bevies of followers, to see and be seen. The King's London 'home' was Whitehall, a sprawling hodgepodge of buildings which contained lodgings for the royal family and numerous court officers, plus kitchens, pantries and the like. When James was away hunting — as he usually was — many stayed behind at Whitehall, at the King's expense, while many suitors approached his councillors, who remained in London while he disported himself. Whether James was there or not, his court was a centre of aristocratic social life, where the cream of the nobility, in all their magnificence, provided a dazzling setting for the King's majesty. James' courtiers spent ever more unsparingly on clothes and jewels, competing in display as their forebears had competed on the battlefield, while their feasts moved from the gargantuan to the ludicrous. The Earl of Carlisle introduced the double banquet : two meals were prepared ; the first, being merely for show, was taken away and only the second was eaten. For one of his feasts, a hundred cooks worked for eight days at a cost of £3000.

All this lavishness failed to enhance the dignity of monarchy because James refused to play his part as the centrepiece of the display. He disliked the ceremonial role at which Elizabeth had excelled and performed it badly. Despite his great interest in the fashions of the young men at court, James dressed dowdily, even scruffily : in his last years he wore his clothes until they fell to pieces. Ceremonies and long speeches bored him and he found it difficult to be either patient or gracious : the English 'like their king to show pleasure at their devotion, as the late Queen knew well how to do ; but the King manifests no taste for them, but rather contempt and dislike'.[18] Moreover, for the court to enhance the public image of monarchy, it was necessary to maintain a certain dignity and decorum. The Tudors regulated access to the royal person by creating a series of chambers of varying degrees of formality or privacy. Thus the king would receive suitors or dine in the presence chamber, but only his councillors and more intimate servants would be admitted to the privy chamber. Such differentiations enabled the monarch to preserve a certain aloofness and distance and Elizabeth had reinforced the discipline which this imposed by an elaborate code of etiquette.

James, however, lacked either the inclination or the strength of character to maintain such discipline. Despite their fine clothes and the artificial elegance of the court masques, James' courtiers could behave like a gang of hooligans, throwing themselves at a buffet with such ferocity that the tables broke. When James entertained his wife's bibulous brother, Christian IV of Denmark, the allegorical entertainment was somewhat marred by the fact that the ladies and gentlemen taking part were much the worse for drink.

The entertainment went forward and most of the presenters went backward or did fall down.... Hope did essay to speak but wine rendered her endeavours so feeble that she withdrew.... Charity.... returned to Hope and Faith who were both sick and spewing in the lower hall.... Now did Peace make entry and strive to get foremost to the king; but I grieve to tell how great wrath she did discover unto her attendants and much contrary to her semblance made war with her olive branch and laid on the pates of those who did oppose her coming.[19]

Such goings-on highlight a major failing of James' kingship, his lack of any sense of public relations. A king needed to create a sense of majesty and to be gracious to his subjects: James did neither. Kings also needed to conform to some extent to the moral norms of their people. While drunkenness and self-indulgence were not rare in Jacobean England, there was a substantial 'Puritan' element which frowned upon both and which disapproved strongly of James' fawning on his favourites. Finally, if James wished to convince his people that his revenues were insufficient to support his government, he weakened his case by doing nothing to check the extravagance of his court.

The court was not just a gaudy setting for monarchy: it was also a major centre of politics. The king formulated policy, directed the administration and distributed offices and other rewards. All those seeking favours, all those with particular political objectives, sought to influence the king, or those close to him. To discriminate carefully between the innumerable petitioners and pressure groups was not easy. There was a danger that the king would give away more than he could afford or approve projects which were dishonest and unpopular. If he listened to only one group or point of view, he might drive other groups into factious opposition and provoke resentment in the nation at large. In terms of policies and factions, James often proved astute. His instincts inclined him towards moderation[20] and he had learned in Scotland the advantages of balancing opposite extremes. When it came to petitions, however, James found it very difficult to say no, especially if they were well larded with flattery. He may have gone hunting to escape these importunities, but his closest companions profited most of all from his generosity. He probably did not fully understand the value of money. After one lavish grant, Cecil had the sum in question placed before the King, in cash: James hastily reduced the amount. Such self-restraint was rare. James often told his ministers to find ways of curbing his extravagance, only to circumvent the restrictions to which he had agreed. Had his patronage gone only to the deserving or the politically important, it might have been money well spent: 'For the king not to be bountiful', said Cecil, 'were a fault, for that duty is best and surest tried when it is rewarded.' All too often, however, it went to his personal favourites, not least the Scots, while by giving more than he could afford he exacerbated his financial problems and reinforced the impression that those problems were of his making.[21]

In making decisions on matters of government, James depended on advice and information from his ministers, just as a modern cabinet minister depends on his senior civil servants. If he took that advice on trust, he risked being deceived. His ministers had their own interests and ambitions and (like modern civil servants) their own pet policies. In order to maintain personal control over decision-making, the king needed to do his homework: to read the relevant documents and listen to the differing viewpoints of his councillors. All this required time and effort; James, however, was not prepared to work that hard. Perhaps, in his late thirties, it was unreasonable to expect him to learn the intricacies of an alien system of government and law, but the overriding impression is that he simply could not be bothered. He expected the council 'to undertake the charge and burden of the kingdom and foresee that he be not interrupted nor troubled with too much business'. He would take care of his health (and that of the kingdom) by hunting.[22] Apart from foreign policy, which he kept in his own hands, he expected to give general directives, leaving to his faithful councillors the hard work of running the country. When they wished the King to sign letters, answer questions or make decisions, such business had to be fitted around the King's hunting, early in the morning or late at night. 'This tumultuary and uncertain attendance upon the King's sports affords me little time to write', grumbled one official. Never a patient man, James inclined to snap decisions, based on insufficient consideration, and he sometimes berated his councillors for what were really the consequences of his own lack of application and diligence.[23]

In his early years James had two leading councillors. Robert Cecil, later Earl of Salisbury, was Secretary of State and eventually also Lord Treasurer. James called him his 'little beagle, that lies by the fire when the good hounds run in the fields' — an unkind allusion to his lameness and an unjust imputation that he was idle. Despite such taunts, Salisbury served James well, struggling to cope with a huge workload and to curb James' unflagging generosity; he also accumulated a massive fortune. His leading colleague, Henry Howard, Earl of Northampton, became Lord Privy Seal in 1608. Despite the fact that Howard had supported Essex, by 1600 he was acting as an intermediary between James and Cecil. The appointment to the council of Howard and his nephew, the Earl of Suffolk, in 1603 offered the prospect of a lasting reconciliation between the two factions of the 1590s.[24]

James' declared intention was to heal divisions and to avoid extremes, which was seen most clearly in his ecclesiastical policy. Elizabeth bequeathed to James a divided Church. The 1559 settlement preserved the traditional system of Church government, based on bishops, and introduced a form of worship somewhere between Catholicism and full-blooded Protestantism. This continued the use of set forms of service — radical Protestants preferred to be free to improvise — but the liturgy was purged of most aspects of Catholic ceremonial. A few remained, notably the use of the sign of the cross in baptism and of the ring in marriage. The 'priest' was still to wear a distinctive gown, the surplice. For militant Protestants, to retain such 'rags of Rome' was intolerable, the Church was 'but halfly reformed'. Moreover, Elizabeth placed restrictions on preaching: how could they combat the errors of Rome, how could they persuade people to make the Bible the rule of their daily lives, if they were not free to preach the Gospel? Elizabeth was adamant. She feared that uncontrolled preaching might stir up the same spirit of sedition as that seen in the Calvinists of France, the Netherlands and Scotland, all of whom rebelled against established authority. The militants (or Puritans) voiced their views in press and pulpit and mobilized their supporters in Parliament and on the council, but Elizabeth insisted that the liturgy must stay as it was and that the clergy must conform to it.

By 1603 most of the clergy did indeed use the Prayer-Book services, although a minority did so only reluctantly or partially and that minority had supporters even among the bishops. Most laypeople came to accept the Prayer-Book services and many came to love them, as they became familiar: even those who could not read could learn to participate. By contrast, the appeal of Puritanism was limited. With its stress on Bible-reading, it had little to offer to most of the illiterate majority, while among the literate many would not put in the intellectual or spiritual effort which Puritans demanded, or did not share the Puritans' moral inflexibility and rigid sabbatarianism. Many (James included) thought it no sin to play games on Sunday afternoon or to go to the alehouse after divine service. The Puritans were, in fact, an articulate and influential minority within a Church which satisfied the limited spiritual aspirations of most of its members. Meanwhile, some clergymen reacted against Puritanism. They stressed the importance of communion where Puritans stressed the sermon; they exulted in the continuity between the pre-Reformation and Anglican churches, which the Puritans deplored; and they argued that the clergy were spiritually superior to the laity, which to Puritans smacked of 'priestcraft' and popery.

James, after his experience with the Kirk, regarded the radical Puritans as subversive: nonconformity was an affront to the King, who was head of the Church. However, his theology was basically Calvinist and he accepted the need for an effective preaching ministry. Inheriting a Church which included a broad range of beliefs and practices, he spread his patronage widely enough to embrace both the high episcopalian Lancelot Andrewes and the stolidly Calvinist George Abbot. In 1604 he held a conference at Hampton Court in which advocates of further reform confronted defenders of the existing order. James was in his element: he loved theological debate and joined in eagerly. He exploded with rage when one Puritan mentioned 'presbyters', but in general he listened sympathetically to their complaints and acted on some of them, notably their call for a definitive translation of the Bible (the Authorized Version). Despite his waspish description of Puritan nonconformists as rebels or republicans, only the few who would make no pretence of conformity were deprived of their livings. Most continued within the Church and some received high preferment. James sought to separate the moderate majority from the irreconcilable few and largely succeeded. For most of his reign, the Church enjoyed an unaccustomed peace, as James held the balance between its disparate elements.[25]

His policy towards the Catholics was similar. In 1570 the Pope had excommunicated Elizabeth and called upon her Catholic subjects to rise up and destroy her. As a result, Catholics now appeared potential traitors. Catholic extremists (like Calvinist extremists in France or Scotland) argued that the State should be subordinated to the Church and that rulers who did not do the Church's bidding should be resisted and even killed. The Gunpowder Plot of 1605 confirmed James' belief that religious extremism, whether Catholic or Puritan, threatened the monarchy, but he was also aware that most Catholics were loyal subjects, whose religion was a purely personal matter. He therefore denounced the claims of the Pope and Catholic church to temporal power and sought a way to distinguish between the loyal majority and the subversive few, using the oath of allegiance of 1606. Most priests refused to take it, as it described the Pope's alleged power to depose kings as 'impious, damnable and heretical', but many lay Catholics took it, in order to show their political loyalty.

James' quarrel with the Catholic church, as with the militant Puritans, was essentially political. He had no dogmatic views on theology and believed that Puritans who made an issue of what he saw as 'matters indifferent' were motivated by a restless dislike of authority. He had the laws against Catholics enforced to prevent their numbers growing to a point where they might prove politically dangerous. He did not share the virulent anti-Catholicism of most of his English subjects, but hoped that in time the differences between Catholic and Protestant might be solved. This might seem naïve and unrealistic, but it was a vision shared by distinguished people on both sides of the confessional divide throughout the century. In seeking peace and reconciliation with the Catholic church, James lived up to his motto 'Blessed are the peacemakers'. Where religion was concerned, however, most of his Protestant subjects were bent on war.[26]

James also fell foul of his subjects' prejudices when he promoted a union between England and Scotland. He assumed that, as they shared the same king, it would be natural for them to unite as one. The Commons would agree to union only on terms which would, in effect, mean that England would absorb Scotland, rather as it had earlier absorbed Wales. James came to see the Commons' attitude as negative and bigoted and was incensed by the anti-Scottish remarks of some MPs: the chauvinistic English regarded the Scots as an alien and inferior race. The Scots, for their part, would not have welcomed incorporation into England on English terms. As in religion, James' hopes of peace and unity remained unrealized.[27]

For many historians, James' disagreements with his subjects on religion or the union mattered far less than those on the nature of monarchy. James is said to have brought from Scotland alien ideas of divine-right monarchy, whereby the king was above the law, leading to a clash between two views of monarchy. On the one hand, there was the continental view of absolute monarchy, in which the king's power was (in effect) unlimited, in that he could make laws and impose taxes without consent. On the other, under England's tradition of limited monarchy, he could legislate and tax only with Parliament's consent and people could be deprived of liberty or property only with their own consent or after due process of law. In English eyes, the French were slaves, who could be taxed and imprisoned at will, whereas an Englishman's liberty and property were protected by Parliament and the law.

In the early seventeenth century many Englishmen believed that there was a design to convert England into an absolute monarchy. This belief was to some extent mistaken, but was not unreasonable. James told Parliament in 1610 that 'the state of monarchy is the supremest thing upon earth; for kings are not only God's lieutenants upon earth and sit upon God's throne, but even by God himself they are called gods'. He compared God's attributes — 'to create or destroy, make or unmake at His pleasure, to give life or send death, to judge all and to be judged nor accomptable to none' — with those of kings. After this sweeping assertion of royal power, however, James stressed that it must be used for the good of the people and that kings must obey the laws of their kingdoms, as he had sworn to do in his coronation oath. 'A king governing in a settled kingdom leaves to be king and degenerates into a tyrant as soon as he leaves off to rule according to his laws.... Never king was in all his time more careful to have his laws duly observed and himself to govern thereafter than I.'[28]

Thus what seemed to start as an assertion of absolute power ended as a statement of a king's obligation to rule within the law, later quoted with approval by Locke. Before dismissing it as a mere reiteration of conventional platitudes, however, three qualifications should be made. First, some disliked the way James compared kings to gods and were struck more by the stress on kingly power than by the subsequent qualifications.[29] Second, while James accepted that he should rule according to law, he did not suggest that he could be made to do so. Aware that his knowledge of English law was limited, he was ready to take advice, but he bitterly rejected claims that the common law was too technical for laymen to understand and so that he should submit to the direction of his judges. The obligation to keep within the law was a matter for the king's own conscience, knowing that God would punish any transgressions.[30] Third, and most important, it was all very well to promise to rule according to law, but what *was* the law? It was a motley collection of precedents — customs, statutes, decisions by judges — which often conflicted, so there were substantial grey areas where there was scope for differences of opinion. The early Stuarts never claimed to be above the law, but exploited its uncertainties and ambiguities so as to extend their power to raise money without consent and to punish without due process of law. Each extension of power raised fears that worse was to come: precedents, once established, could be developed and extended. This was seen clearly in the case of impositions.

In order to put impositions in their context, one must consider the nature of the royal revenue. The king had three major permanent, or ordinary, revenues. The crown lands had been swollen by the Tudors' plunder of the Church, but subsequently reduced by sales. Feudal dues were a hangover from the medieval past. Many landowners still technically held estates from the king on feudal tenures, which imposed obligations to pay money to the crown when one tenant succeeded another. If an heir succeeded while under age, he became the king's ward and the king could sell his wardship, usually to a near relative. Finally, the customs (or tonnage and poundage) had, since the fifteenth century, been granted by Parliament to each king, for life, at the start of his reign. The yield of all these revenues was eroded by the inflation of the Tudor and early Stuart periods. The crown lands were poorly managed and depleted by sales. Feudal dues were not vigorously exploited under Elizabeth: any attempt to increase them suddenly provoked howls of protest. Customs were levied, not on a percentage basis but at a fixed rate per item and the rates were not revised under the Queen.

The English crown had never been generously endowed. Unlike the French *taille*, it had no permanent tax on the main source of wealth: land. Land taxes had to be voted by Parliament and were usually granted only in wartime. One solution to the crown's financial problems, therefore, would be for Parliament to vote much more in taxation. Under Elizabeth, it voted more 'subsidies' than in the past, but the benefit to the crown was undermined by increasing under-assessment. Taxpayers gave in a figure for their net income, after deducting 'necessary' expenses. They were not on oath, so the more subsidies Parliament voted, or the more the crown raised in other ways, the more grossly they under-assessed themselves. While prices rose, each subsidy brought in less than the last. The Commons would not reform the method of assessment and became increasingly unwilling to vote subsidies at all as James developed other, unpopular ways of raising money.

The crown had never confined itself exclusively to its generally accepted forms of income. It had made money out of its powers of economic regulation (not least through monopolies), it had fined people for infringing archaic statutes, it had raised forced loans (and neglected to repay them), it had sold economic privileges. These methods mostly rested on the king's prerogative: the ill-defined body of powers which enabled him to deal with emergencies and with problems for which existing law made no provision. Usually such methods were used sparingly and more to provide patronage than to raise money. In the 1590s they had been used widely and had provoked a great outcry, but unpopular, immoral and illegal though many of them were, they offered one possible means of solving the crown's financial problems. The opposition which they aroused would make it harder to secure subsidies from Parliament, but, as the yield of subsidies fell, there might come a time when (from the king's point of view) calling Parliament to vote money might not seem financially worthwhile. Parliament might then follow many continental representative bodies into oblivion. Without it, England's traditional constitution was unlikely to last long and the king might become as absolute as that of France.

Such gloomy fears were voiced increasingly often in the early seventeenth century. Were they justified? In his first years, James was sometimes short-tempered in his dealings with Parliament, and claimed that it owed its privileges to his favour, but in general he was willing to consult with those who knew more about English affairs than he did and to consider reforming what was amiss. Worried by some of his remarks, however, the Commons in 1604 produced a statement of their privileges and grievances in which their anxiety was manifest: 'The prerogatives of princes may easily and do daily grow', they declared; 'the privileges of the subject are ... at an ever-lasting stand.'[31]

The tone of this 'Form of Apology and Satisfaction' was defensive, but it cannot have pleased James to be lectured in this way and his closing speech was somewhat petulant. He had little to thank them for, he said; they had been led astray by 'idle heads'. He resented their dilatoriness — they always took on more business than they could handle — and by what he saw as aspersions on his integrity. He regarded himself as honest and was conscious of no malevolent intentions towards Parliament, so was upset that he should be suspected of harbouring any. Reluctant to think that the generality of

MPs distrusted or disliked him, he preferred to believe that a few trouble-makers had misled the rest. The Commons' suspicions, and James' resentment, came to a head in 1610, when they tackled the question of impositions.

In 1606 a Mr Bate refused to pay to the King a duty on currants, which dated back to a trading dispute with Venice in 1575, claiming it was illegal because it had not been voted by Parliament. The judges in the Court of Exchequer ruled that it was legal. Chief Baron Fleming argued that the king had a discretion, to deal with emergencies and with foreign powers, which he should use as he saw fit. If another state imposed new tariffs on English goods, the King needed to be able to retaliate, at once. Fleming went on:

whereas it is said that if the king may impose, he may impose any quantity what he pleases, true it is that this is to be referred to the wisdom of the king, who guideth all under God by his wisdom, and this is not to be disputed by a subject.

At first, the Commons were indeed prepared to trust the king not to abuse these powers, but in 1608 Salisbury announced a new set of customs rates. To the duties granted by Parliament at the start of the reign were added many new duties, whose legal foundation was the judges' ruling in Bate's case. A power which was ostensibly to be used to protect English commercial interests was now being used to raise revenue, without Parliament's consent.[32]

This sudden extension of impositions seemed to mark a major shift from taxation by consent to prerogative taxation, but it was not irrevocable. In the 1610 session of Parliament Salisbury proposed a 'Great Contract', whereby James would abandon wardship and other unpopular feudal revenues and promise that there would be no further impositions, in return for an annual grant from Parliament and a large lump sum to pay off the royal debts. It was a brave attempt, but stood little chance of success. James was lukewarm, MPs were dismayed by the huge sums they were asked for and nobody (not even Salisbury) had any clear idea how to raise the money: indeed, given the falling yield of the subsidy, it is unlikely that the Commons could have delivered anything that they promised.

Meanwhile, MPs attacked impositions. To levy them, said James Whitelocke, 'induceth a new form of state and government', like that which followed the introduction of the *taille* in fifteenth-century France: 'you may there note

the mischiefs that grew to the kingdom of France by the voluntary impositions first brought in by Charles VII and ever since continued and increased,
to the utter impoverishment of the common people and the loss of their free
council of three estates.' If the king's right to levy impositions were conceded,
Parliament's future would be bleak.[33] James bitterly resented such criticism.
'Alas I am your king,' he told the Commons, 'you have a king, not only
one whom I suppose you all have cause to love, but a king whom God
requires you to obey.' 'This Lower House', he wrote, 'by their behaviour
have perilled and annoyed our health, wounded our reputation, emboldened
an ill-natured people, encroached upon many of our privileges and plagued
our purse with their delays.'[34] The optimism and good intentions of 1603
now lay in ruins: James was coming to regard Parliaments as not only
useless but dangerous.

⁂　⁂　⁂

Unlike the accession of the first Stuart king of England, that of the first
Bourbon king of France was neither eagerly anticipated nor enthusiastically
welcomed. With the accession of the childless Henry III in 1584 the Valois
dynasty was doomed to extinction. The heir presumptive was a distant
cousin, Henry, King of Navarre, but Henry was a Huguenot (Protestant)
and France was predominantly Catholic. Since 1562 it had been wracked
by civil wars in which religious divisions played a major part. The dreadful
prospect of a Protestant king increased Catholic fanaticism, which found its
strongest expression in the Catholic League of the 1580s. Initially dominated
by the nobility, the League's conduct was increasingly dictated by the lower
clergy and their supporters among the petty bourgeoisie, minor officials and
artisans, who imposed their will by violence and terror. Fortified by a decree
from the Pope depriving Henry of Navarre of his right to the throne, the
League put forward a rival candidate and denounced Henry III as a tyrant
for refusing to wage all-out war on his heir presumptive, thus betraying the
duty of kings of France to uphold the Catholic religion. Driven out of Paris
by the Leaguers, Henry joined with the King of Navarre to besiege the city.
Just when it seemed that Paris might be starved into submission, Henry III
was stabbed by a monk and died on 1 August 1589.

　　Henry IV inherited the crown the moment his predecessor died, but many Frenchmen refused to recognize him as king and it was nine years before peace was restored. The civil wars had exacerbated the weaknesses of the French monarchy, which differed markedly from those of England. Except in Wales and Cornwall, England had a single language and it had been ruled as a unit for centuries. It had a single basic system of law, justice and local government, which had been extended to Wales under the Tudors. The independent jurisdictions and anomalies of the Middle Ages had been greatly curtailed under Henry VIII, not least by the State's asserting control over the Church, although town constitutions remained almost infinitely various. Even so, the England of James I had one of the most uniform systems of government in Europe. By contrast, much of what we now think of as France came under the rule of the French kings only in the fifteenth and sixteenth centuries. Much, including Normandy and Aquitaine, had to be captured from the English. In 1450 the king ruled a motley group of territories, between which were interspersed those of quasi-independent magnates and princes, owing an allegiance that was often little more than nominal. Gradually, from their heartlands in the Ile-de-France, the kings brought the other territories under their rule. By 1589 the crown ruled a kingdom similar in outline to present-day France, if rather smaller.

Many French provinces thus came under the crown comparatively late, having already developed distinctive institutions and a sense of provincial identity, often focused on a representative assembly or estates. This was true even of provinces which came under the crown much earlier: Languedoc was so far removed from the kings' main power-base as to develop almost independently. There were different languages and patois — Breton, Provençal, Occitan — to which would be added German in Alsace and Catalan in Roussillon. The Pyrenean provinces had more in common with their neighbours on the Spanish side of the mountains than with the government far away in Paris. In frontier areas, 'foreign' coins were used more than French. 'Frontiers', indeed, were often ill-defined; many lands within France were subject to foreign seigneurs. Within the kingdom similar confusions proliferated. Almost invariably, the territorial units used for fiscal, jurisdictional, legal and ecclesiastical purposes did not coincide. 'Everywhere tradition reigned at the expense of simplicity and logic', commented one historian wearily.[35]

In general, customary law was dominant in the north and Roman law in the south, supplemented by royal edicts, decrees of the sovereign courts and a vast array of local customs. The laws were interpreted and enforced by tribunals ranging from the Parlements and other sovereign courts down to private seigneurial courts. There were endless clashes of jurisdiction and disputes between officials, for the crown would often create new officials to perform a certain function without abolishing the old.

This lack of uniformity was universal. There were no standard weights and measures. Different provinces paid different taxes, or the same taxes but at different rates. Over much of France the *taille* was collected by royal officials (*élus*) at rates fixed by the crown, but in some provinces taxation on land was voted by provincial estates, as it was by Parliament in England. Indeed, the difference between their representative bodies typified the contrast between the two countries. The English Parliament had developed as a national institution : there had never been local assemblies. Its legislative powers were formidable — there was nothing which an Act of Parliament could not do — and in the Tudor period had been used greatly to enhance the powers of the crown, most strikingly in the breach with Rome, but more prosaically in a mass of economic and social legislation.

In France, provincial and local estates mostly grew up before the areas in question came under the French crown. Many still functioned in 1589 and some continued until the Revolution. By contrast, attempts to establish a national representative body, the Estates General, to pass laws and vote taxes for the realm as a whole, had failed. There were squabbles between the representatives of different provinces or between the orders — clergy, nobles and third estate (the rest). The Estates General did not meet between 1484 and 1560 and thereafter were called in desperation, to placate opposition, not with any hope of constructive co-operation.[36]

In the seventeenth century, France's population and economic resources were larger than England's, but in order to exploit these assets the crown had to overcome the problems posed by administrative confusion and provincial particularism. It was often not clear which official had the power to do what, or where. There were endless arguments and opportunities for evasion, obstruction and delay. The crown had to deal not with its subjects as a whole but with groups — estates, town corporations, the clergy, bodies of judges or officials, the universities — all of which had vested interests to defend. These groups wanted some freedom to conduct their own affairs and expected benefits from the King in return for their co-operation. Dealing with these bodies individually was time-consuming and inefficient and even when they seemed co-operative they might quietly fail to obey royal commands.

Communications within France were slow and difficult: it might take a fortnight to travel from Paris to Toulouse. The supervision of local officials, never easy, was complicated by the fact that many had bought their offices. On the one hand, as most offices passed from father to son, young men were trained for the job, usually in university law faculties, and so were likely to prove technically more proficient than England's amateurs. They also had a vested interest in extending royal power at the expense of municipal, seigneurial and ecclesiastical authorities: the more business they brought within their orbit, the greater their income from fees. On the other hand, as they owned their offices they were more difficult to remove than English JPs. Family links and traditions created a strong esprit de corps and they were tenacious in defending their interests against the crown. Their salaries cost the crown a great deal and added to the burden of taxation.

Thus France's resources were superior to England's; in mobilizing them the French king faced greater problems, but had at his disposal a more powerful government machine — if he could control it. In other respects, too, the French king's problems were greater. As England was surrounded by sea, an attack on England was far more complex and risky than a cross-border assault on France. Except in Ireland, England's rulers had no need for constant military preparedness. Even the Scottish borders became comparatively peaceful under Elizabeth. France, however, had lengthy land frontiers. Some were well protected by natural obstacles, like the Alps and Pyrenees, but the plains and rolling hills of northern France could do little to deter an attack from the Spanish Netherlands. To the east, Lorraine was independent, its dukes vassals of the Holy Roman Emperor, who also claimed suzerainty over much of Alsace. Franche Comté was under Spanish rule. Much of France's territory thus bordered on that of the hereditary rivals of the French crown, the two branches of the House of Habsburg, Spanish and Imperial (or Austrian). 'Habsburg encirclement' meant that France faced invasion from several directions at any time, so the crown needed to mobilize more men and money than the English kings did, for which it required a larger state apparatus.

One other respect in which French kings faced greater problems was in dealing with the nobility. By the end of the Tudor period the English nobility had virtually lost its military role. The French nobles maintained their skills during the long wars of Valois and Habsburg, which ranged across Italy, Germany and the Low Countries, then put them to good use inside France in the wars of religion which began in 1562. In the confusion of civil war an armed following offered not only a means of survival, but also opportunities for profit. As royal authority crumbled, magnates assumed effective control over provincial administration and appropriated royal revenues. Many towns sought the magnates' protection, although some fell under the control of popular Leaguer dictatorships, like the Sixteen in Paris. Many lesser nobles turned to brigandage or pursued private feuds. Without effective protection, peasants and townsmen suffered appallingly at the hands of the soldiers : 'They were all vagabonds, thieves and murderers, men who renounced God ... riddled with the pox and fit for the gibbet. Dying of hunger they took to the roads and fields to pillage, assault and ruin the people of the towns and villages.'[37] Noble habits of violence did not begin, or end, with the civil wars : examples of noble brigandage can be found, in remote areas, even under Louis XIV. But during the wars they flourished to an extent which in many areas made effective government impossible.

Following a massacre of Protestants in 1572, many Huguenots became convinced that the Catholic King was bent on destroying them. Some, therefore, began to claim that the people — or the leaders of the community, the 'inferior magistrates' — had the right to resist and overthrow a king who failed to fulfil his obligations to his subjects. Some English Protestant writers had developed similar arguments under the Catholic Mary I, but mainstream political ideas in both countries centred on the divine origins of monarchy and the subject's duty to obey established authority. Englishmen were told, in their parish churches, that 'we may not resist, nor in any wise hurt, an anointed king, which is God's lieutenant'. Kingly power was part of a larger hierarchy : 'God hath created all things in heaven, earth and waters in a most excellent and perfect order. . . . In the earth He has assigned kings, princes, with other governors under them, all in good and necessary order.'[38] For Huguenot writers to claim that inferior magistrates could authorize the people to resist the king was to challenge the hierarchical view of creation upon which royal authority so largely depended.

The Huguenot challenge to royal authority did not last long: by 1589 they were again denying the legitimacy of resistance. By now, the main threat to the Huguenots came not from the crown but from the League. When Henry of Navarre became heir presumptive, Leaguer writers abandoned their reverence for royal authority: if the King failed to uphold the Church's interest, he became a tyrant and could be resisted or killed. Some claimed that the pope could depose a heretical prince, others advanced ideas of popular sovereignty which made those of the Huguenots seem timid. The League combined diverse elements — aristocratic particularism, Catholic fanaticism and popular radicalism. All in their own way challenged the traditions of the French monarchy and all drew much of their force from the spectre of a Protestant king, but the League also had its weaknesses. Its leaders could not agree on a Catholic candidate for the throne, while Philip II of Spain, who allied with the League against the French King in 1585, pressed the claims of his daughter, although by French law it could pass only to a male. Leaguer extremism alienated moderate Catholics: officeholders who believed in ordered government, patriots who resented Spanish and papal interference in French affairs, conservatives scared by the popular regimes in some towns, constitutionalists who believed that, whatever his religion, Henry IV was the rightful king.

There was thus a strong reaction against the League even before Henry destroyed the main basis of its appeal by attending mass at St Denis on 25 July 1593. Whether or not he said 'Paris is worth a mass', his conversion was politically essential, although it did not end the wars. It was two years before the Pope absolved him from the sin of heresy. Leaguer propagandists protested that his conversion was feigned and Spanish troops helped to keep their cause alive. Gradually, however, towns and nobles made their peace with the new King, often on generous terms: tax arrears were remitted, pensions granted. In March 1594 Henry unexpectedly entered Paris, to receive an enthusiastic welcome from the citizens. The Sixteen and their leading followers were banished.

Peace came, at last, in 1598. The Treaty of Vervins ended the war with Spain. Mercoeur, the last major Catholic leader, surrendered. There remained the problem of the Huguenots, who had naturally felt betrayed by Henry's conversion. Like the Leaguers the Huguenots included great magnates, with quasi-regal power, and militant town governments, reinforced by national assemblies. Only after stubborn bargaining did King and Huguenots reach the agreement enshrined in the Edict of Nantes and its accompanying documents. It allowed the Protestants full civil rights and the right to worship freely in specified towns and regions and in the fiefs of Protestant nobles. Elsewhere they were not to be molested for not attending Catholic services, but everywhere they were to pay tithes for the maintenance of the Catholic clergy. Protestant worship was prohibited within twelve miles of Paris, at court and in many provincial towns; Catholic worship was allowed everywhere and Protestants were not to seek to convert Catholics.

Two separate letters allowed the Protestants to garrison about a hundred towns, at the King's expense, for eight years (later renewed). The garrisons provided a surety for the execution of the edict and perpetuated the Huguenots' autonomous military power, making them a 'state within a state'. Essentially, however, the edict froze the Huguenots' position as it was in 1598; in some respects it weakened it, notably in restoring Catholic worship in hitherto Protestant towns. Expansion was impossible and Huguenot numbers were probably already dwindling north of the Loire. They made up maybe eight per cent of the population, although in parts of the south and west they were in a majority. With their numerical weakness and vulnerability, they depended on the edict for protection against an aggressive, resurgent Catholicism. Many Catholics saw it as a shameful concession to heretics and rebels and an obstacle to the national unity which could come only from unity in religion. The Huguenots, for their part, had to trust in the King to maintain their privileges.

Only after nine years of struggle could Henry IV settle down to something approaching normal government. He was now forty-five, small, red-faced, with greying hair and a straggly beard. He shared with James I a passion for hunting and a loathing for sitting still. Like James, his clothes were mostly shabby, although he could dress regally to impress visiting dignitaries, and he was not keen on washing: indeed, Henry smelt so bad that his Queen would douse herself in perfume; but whereas James claimed that water upset his sensitive skin, Henry could not be bothered to wash. Like James, he made decisions while walking around and was bored by long speeches, but there the similarities ended.

Where James was in many ways a coward, Henry was brave to the point of recklessness. He had spent all his adult life as a soldier and had loved it: the discomfort, the comradeship, the bawdy. James knew little of the English people and tried to avoid them; Henry had travelled over more of his kingdom than any other king of France.[39] Unlike James, he had little interest in literature and confined his reading, and his sponsorship of education, to practical matters — cartography, mathematics, engineering, medicine. He had little interest in philosophy. He liked listening to historical epics, but when he wished to send a love-poem to a lady, he got one of the court poets to write it. He enjoyed music and dance and the visual arts — architecture, painting and sculpture. He was always a practical man rather than a theorist. James would not have talked, as Henry did, with the masons working at the Louvre, or installed artists and craftsmen in a royal palace. In Henry's opinion, James was a fool, who talked and published too much.

The two Kings differed also in their attitude to women and to their families. While James became increasingly open in his fondness for young men, Henry was an insatiable womanizer, whose lusts led him into serious political errors. His first marriage, to Marguerite de Valois, was childless and was annulled by the Pope. His mistress, Gabrielle d'Estrées, died before he was free to remarry, so he had to look elsewhere. He was an exacting suitor: 'The woman I need must fulfil seven principal conditions, which are beauty of person; modesty of life; a complaisant nature; a ready wit; a fruitful womb; eminent rank and great estates. But' he added wistfully, 'I think that such a woman is dead, indeed, perhaps is not yet born.'[40] Lowering his sights he chose Marie de Médicis, daughter of the Grand Duke of Tuscany. She was big, blonde and not bad looking; the women of her family had the reputation of being good breeders and (last but not least) Henry owed the Médicis a great deal of money: marriage could reduce his debts.

While Henry was seeking a wife, he found a successor to Gabrielle. Henriette d'Entragues came of a family with experience of royal lusts — her mother had been Charles IX's mistress — and she and her parents were determined to make the most of her attractions. Once she had caught Henry's eye, he pursued her relentlessly, only for her to be whisked away each time he thought he was about to possess her. He offered lands, titles, money: she demanded a written promise of marriage. Consumed with lust, he agreed and the fateful document was hidden in her father's château.

Henry did not find his new love easy to live with. She was intelligent and ambitious, with a sharp tongue and fearful temper. Thanks to his promise, she saw herself as the rightful queen and Marie ('the fat banker') as no more than the King's whore. When Henry recognized Marie's son as Dauphin, Henriette and her family intrigued with Spain and plotted against the King's life. Only after discovering the plot did Henry recover his promise. He resolved to send Henriette to a convent, but soon relented. She resumed where she had left off, taking other lovers and taunting him for his fading prowess. He, for his part, continued to pursue other women, despite his age, his gout and occasional doses of gonorrhoea. Many of these women ensured that he paid heavily for their favours, though the price was never as high as the one which Henriette had demanded.

No wife would have found Henry easy to live with. Marie was twenty years his junior, shy, naïve, rather superstitious (she was fond of astrology) and not very intelligent. She read little — her eyesight was poor — and talked a great deal about trivial things. Brought up to see the French as barbarians, her first meeting with Henry, in December 1600, can only have confirmed her prejudices. He had travelled (with Henriette) to meet her at Lyon, came to her lodgings the day before he was expected and asked if he could sleep there, as he had nowhere else to go. He pronounced her better-looking than he expected, but complained of her poor command of French and the large number of Italians in her entourage. He then returned to Paris with Henriette. When Marie arrived she found the Louvre barely habitable (which she took as an insult) and Henry economized on her ceremonial entry, saying the marriage had cost more than enough already. He introduced Henriette: 'This beautiful person has been my mistress and wishes to be your especial servant.' Henriette curtsied, but not low enough, so Henry forced her to kiss the hem of the Queen's dress.[41]

This incident set the pattern for Henry's strange family life. Queen and mistress were soon pregnant. Marie gave birth first: Henry was delighted and showed her great affection, only to tell her soon after that Henriette's son was much handsomer. He was not playing the two women off against each other, just saying what he thought. In general, the Queen's many pregnancies brought the royal couple closer together. Six of her children survived and Henry took a great interest in her pregnancies and in the children's upbringing. His offspring, legitimate and illegitimate, were brought up together, mostly at St Germain-en-Laye, which Henry fitted out with novelties and amusements for their enjoyment. Pride of place belonged to the Dauphin, Louis, a serious child, very conscious that one day he would be king and that the royal bastards belonged to 'a different race of dogs'. Despite outbursts of petulance and stubbornness, for which he was well beaten, Louis adored his father. Henry spent much time playing with his children, talking to them and cuddling them : he was a very tactile man. He kept his wife away from them, sending terse notes on their health : 'As for our children, the males are well but the girls have colds.'

However, Marie was less concerned about her offspring than about Henry's endless infidelities and Henriette's posturing and bitching. There were many quarrels between the King and Queen : he firmly denied her any role in government and paid little heed to her interests, devoting his energies to hunting and wenching. Small wonder that the Queen felt happiest with her little coterie of Italians, or that the Tuscan ambassador asked rhetorically : 'Has there ever been seen a brothel like this court of France?'[42]

Morally outrageous Henry's court might be, but, like James', it served a definite social and political function. It was of similar size, with a staff of about 1500, including four hundred priests and eighty doctors. The top household offices, as in England, were held by great nobles. Henry appreciated the need to maintain a measure of lavishness, in order to impress foreign dignitaries and to attract the nobility. He also knew that he had to play a central role in court life. Whereas James fled from London and from company, Henry based himself in Paris. He greatly extended the Louvre, his principal residence, adding the long gallery beside the Seine, which linked it to the Tuileries, thus providing a venue for his ambulatory council meetings in bad weather and a discreet escape route to the west in case of trouble.

Although his court was much less formal than that of his Valois predecessors, Henry imparted some ceremonial significance to various parts of his daily routine in order to differentiate between his courtiers. Only the most favoured were present when he got out of bed, others would be allowed in while he dressed and breakfasted, others had to try to catch his attention as he strode round the gallery or the gardens. Despite his concessions to etiquette, Henry's preference was always for informality. He liked to choose his own company, even when he invited himself out to dinner, and if he became bored he would fall asleep. Of the entertainments put on to amuse his courtiers, he most enjoyed the ballets, the most bizarre of which celebrated, in graphic detail, the success of an operation for one of his bouts of venereal disease.[43]

Henry chose to live in Paris because he was well aware of the capital's political importance and the volatility of its inhabitants. With nearly half a million people crowded into a small area, squalor, disease and disorder were constant problems. Unlike the Valois, Henry devoted much time, energy and money to controlling (and feeding) Paris. He intervened in elections to ensure that his nominees were installed in power at the town hall. He increased the funds available for poor relief and had the water supply improved. Sully, the minister responsible for roads, tried to clear the streets of shacks and rubbish: wolves still wandered the city at night. Henry felt that Paris lacked imposing thoroughfares worthy of a capital. He completed the Pont Neuf, which, unlike the other bridges, was not to be covered in houses and shops. While it was incomplete, Henry leapt the gap: others who tried to emulate him fell to their deaths, but (as Henry said) they were not the King. Henry also sponsored major new developments in the Place Dauphine (on the Ile de la Cité) and the Place Royale, now known as the Place des Vosges. In both Henry imposed his own uniform style of architecture. The Place Royale, in particular, marked a new departure in French urban design: a symmetrical square around a large open space, initially reserved for equestrian pursuits. The dwellings were built by individuals, but to a common plan. It was a model widely followed elsewhere, not least in London, in such developments as Covent Garden, or St James's Square.[44]

Henry's treatment of Paris combined the salient features of his kingship: energy, determination, a certain lack of scruple and a fine sense of public relations (he had a Te Deum sung each year to celebrate Paris' deliverance from civil war). By contrast, both James and Charles I were somewhat wary of London. Their main London palace, Whitehall, was well away from the City. While they tried to lay down specifications for new buildings, the main initiative for such developments came from private individuals, notably the Earl of Bedford, who in Covent Garden built a whole new community, including a church and a market. It was perhaps symbolic that one of the first new developments (Long Acre and Great Queen Street) was along the route by which the kings left London for one of their favourite country houses, Theobalds, in Hertfordshire. Their treatment of London was motivated partly by a concern for order — the apprentices were prone to riot on public holidays — and partly by fiscal considerations: the king forbade new buildings and imposed building regulations only to sell exemptions from these restrictions. There was to come a time, in the 1630s, when the crown's predatory attitude towards the capital provoked a breakdown in the relationship of City and court.[45]

In his dealings with London, James I showed the distrust which he felt towards his subjects, whereas Henry set out to assert himself, to impose his authority, but also to win over his people. This was seen clearly in his remarkable speech to France's premier law court, the Parlement of Paris, in 1599. The Parlement was wholly Catholic and was most reluctant to register the Edict of Nantes, and so give it full legal force. Henry told them:

You see me here in my study, where I have come to speak to you, not in royal attire like my predecessors... but dressed like the father of a family in a doublet, to speak freely to his children.... I have secured peace abroad and I desire peace at home. You are obliged to obey me.... God chose me to set me over this kingdom, which is mine both by inheritance and acquisition.... I shall nip in the bud all factions and all attempts at seditious preaching and I shall behead all who encourage it.... Do not use as an argument the Catholic faith. I love it more than you do and I am a better Catholic than you.... Try as you may, I know all you do and all you say. A little devil tells me... I am king now and I speak as a king and expect to be obeyed![46]

Here are none of the scholarly allusions and finely drawn comparisons in which James delighted. Instead, it is the speech of a man of action, confident in his own prowess and demanding obedience. It reflects Henry's awareness of the need to reassert the crown's authority after the civil wars. How did he set about doing so?

It is unlikely that he set out with a grand overall strategy. As a soldier he had had to react to problems as they arose; as king he made decisions quickly and impulsively. He made mistakes, but generally showed shrewdness and common sense; he was an instinctive politician whose instincts seldom let him down. He relied on a small team of ministers. Two, Bellièvre and Villeroy, had served under the Valois kings. Both were Catholics and came from families of office-holding nobility (*noblesse de robe*). Both were conscientious, efficient career civil servants, with a strong preference for established routines and a deep respect for existing laws and procedures. Neither had much sympathy with Henry's military values, his occasional interference with the workings of the law or his caprices and inconsistency. His other leading adviser, Sully, came (unusually for a top administrator) from the old military nobility. He was a Protestant, who had served with Henry in the wars of religion, an administrator of prodigious energy, who accumulated more and more responsibilities: roads, artillery, buildings, fortifications and above all finance. He was also the King's personal friend in a way Bellièvre and Villeroy were not: Henry often visited him in his home at the Arsenal.[47]

Villeroy and Bellièvre believed that the King should always respect existing laws and be guided by his officials and lawyers: they were the experts, who knew how things should be done. Bellièvre, indeed, saw the Parlements as a 'fourth estate', keeping the king from error. Henry respected the expertise of his lawyers and officials and knew that to govern effectively he needed their co-operation, but he also knew that they were tenacious in defending their vested interests and on some issues he disagreed with them politically. He deeply resented the Parlements' reluctance to register the Edict of Nantes: that of Rouen did not comply until 1609. Henry was therefore unwilling to trust implicitly in his officials' wisdom and judgement: sometimes they needed to be overruled, using unorthodox or arbitrary methods. Sully agreed. A tough, abrasive character, he quickly grew impatient at the obstacles raised by organs of government to the implementation of the King's will. He set out to override or circumvent these obstacles and to ensure that the King was obeyed.

Henry did not always follow Sully's advice, which sometimes appeared politically provocative, but from 1605 he did so more and more, not least because Sully's policies worked. The crown emerged from the civil wars heavily in debt; by 1610 many debts had been paid, there was an annual revenue surplus and a modest emergency fund in the Bastille. Sully achieved this without increasing the *taille*, but the means he used were often unpopular. He increased indirect taxation and reduced the crown's debts by delaying repayments to creditors; often he avoided paying them at all. Many accepted a fraction of what they were owed, rather than risk ending up with nothing. Interest was paid at less than the agreed rate, if at all. Some who claimed that the king owed them money were probably lying, but many were not and Sully's 'rough courses' created resentment and weakened the King's credit.

Sully also extorted money from financiers and finance officials through 'chambers of justice'. Many tax officials advanced the King money at interest on the credit of the revenues they were due to receive. Often they loaned the King his own money, doctoring their accounts to conceal this fact. Many revenues were collected by tax 'farmers': contractors, who undertook to pay the King a certain sum and kept as profit anything they raised above that figure. They thus had every incentive to squeeze all they could from the taxpayer. As in England, there were always 'projectors' with bright ideas for new 'farms', or contracts. Many involved the sale of new offices, with purchasers recouping their investment by drawing salaries from the crown and exacting fees from the people. Financiers and finance officials were often accused of fraud and extortion. There were frequent calls to bring them to justice and to make them disgorge their ill-gotten gains. Their relationship with the crown was somewhat delicate. On the one hand, the King needed their expertise in collecting and extending his revenues and in persuading his subjects to part with their money. He also depended on them for advances of ready cash. On the other, they relied on the King's power and protection in carrying out their functions. This reliance, and their unpopularity, left them vulnerable. Four times Henry threatened to charge them with extortion and peculation in a 'chamber of justice': each time proceedings were halted when they paid him a large sum of money. As one Englishman noted, the king 'wringeth them like sponges and ransometh every three or four years'.[48]

Such treatment was typical of Henry's dealings with his officials, from whom he extracted money by threatening the value of the offices they had bought, usually by creating new offices which would eat into the business and profits of the old. This practice never developed in England: although some offices were sold, the purchasers never enjoyed security of tenure. The early Stuarts did sometimes exact money by threatening administrative reforms, which were dropped after a suitable payment from the officials,[49] but the exploitation of sales (or 'venality') of office was on a far smaller scale in England than in France. Henry IV added an important new refinement. Hitherto an office-holder could transfer an office to his heir only if he did so

at least forty days before he died, which sometimes led to unseemly sub-
terfuges whereby families concealed an official's death for several weeks in
order to keep his office. Henry allowed officials to secure exemption from
this restriction in return for an annual payment, nicknamed the *paulette* after
Paulet, who contracted to collect it. Officials rushed to take advantage of
this opportunity, which reinforced the tendency for offices to become
hereditary. The King gained money and made it more difficult for the high
nobility to install their clients in offices, as fewer would now fall vacant.
Moreover, by granting the *paulette* for a limited period the King could
bargain afresh when it came up for renewal and play one set of officials off
against another. On the other hand, the growth of heritability tended, in the
long run, to increase the officials' esprit de corps and independence of the
crown.[50]

While officials welcomed the *paulette*, many of the military nobility
complained that it made offices too expensive, although (as Sully remarked)
many were too idle or illiterate to qualify anyway. Many nobles had been
ruined (or said they had) in the civil wars. Henry granted many pensions
and other rewards, especially to the most powerful and dangerous, but could
never satisfy all their demands and many grumbled at his alleged ingratitude
and injustice. Henry had little choice but to employ the greatest nobles as
provincial governors, although he often did so away from their main power-
base. On the other hand, while he loaded his Bourbon kinsmen, the princes
of the blood, with favours, he dictated their marriages and denied them the
political influence which they claimed as of right. Others, too, complained
of Henry and Sully's rough methods. The Parlements grumbled when
Henry overrode their attempts to scrutinize revenue contracts. Urban élites
resented his interference in local elections and their management of town
revenues.

Sully, and apparently Henry, believed that too many groups put their
interests before those of the State and grew rich at the poor's expense.
Neither, for example, had much respect for the provincial estates. Henry
wrote in 1595: 'Such assemblies ... tend ordinarily to discharge my subjects
of expense rather than to strengthen and aid me in my affairs.' Sully set out
to suppress the small local assemblies in Guyenne and to establish in their
place collection of the *taille* through *élus*. Similar moves in the past had been
dropped when the estates offered large sums of money, but this time Sully

insisted that the crown would not be bought off. Villeroy and Bellièvre argued that it was both politically wiser and morally right to work only through traditional institutions, but Sully got his way. *Elus* were introduced in 1609 and, after some vicissitudes, became permanent. Had Henry lived longer, he might have carried the assault further: Sully's papers include a draft edict to introduce *élus* into Languedoc.[51]

The most serious threats to Henry came not from provincial estates but from magnate conspiracy and Catholic fanaticism. Henry tried to weaken the links between magnates and their provinces, encouraging governors to spend their time at court, while trustworthy deputies carried out their functions. He was wary that his Bourbon cousins might make a claim to the throne, so treated the Prince de Condé with scant respect, questioning his legitimacy, and excluded the Comte de Soissons from the council. In fact, those who proved most dangerous were not former Leaguers (whom he treated generously) but his own kinsmen. Biron, his cousin, ignored a warning from Elizabeth I (who showed him Essex' head on a spike as an illustration of what happened to rebels) and dreamed of making Burgundy an independent principality. He fell in with the Spaniards, who missed no opportunity to destabilize France: they cast doubt on the validity of the annulment of Henry's first marriage and on the legitimacy of the Dauphin. Henry found out about Biron's activities and, when he refused to confess, he was executed. Two years later, Henriette's father and brother were discovered to be intriguing with Spain. In 1606 the machinations of the Duc de Bouillon, who harboured ambitions similar to those of Biron, ended only when Henry captured his power-base at Sedan.

The threat from the militant Catholics was less obvious but equally serious. Many claimed that Henry's conversion had not been sincere and that he had not fulfilled the conditions upon which the Pope had granted him absolution, since he had not waged all-out war on heresy. In fact, although Henry remarked that his religion was one of the great mysteries of Europe, his Catholicism was idiosyncratic, but not insincere. He disliked some 'superstitious' Catholic practices, like the cult of relics, and thought there were too many saints' days, but he attended mass daily with every appearance of devotion. In his discussions with his confessor he showed considerable concern for the salvation of his soul. He helped to equip the French Catholic church to compete more effectively with the Protestants, securing the return of the Jesuits and encouraging many of the new religious orders spawned by the Counter-Reformation.

Some top posts in the church still went to the children of the well-connected (a boy of four was appointed Bishop of Lodève), but in general the quality of the episcopate improved. Henry set up a fund to maintain Protestants who were converted to Catholicism and showed a tasteless glee when his old friend Duplessis-Mornay was worsted in a debate with Cardinal du Perron. There was ample cause, therefore, for the Huguenots to feel that he had deserted them,[52] but many Catholics were not satisfied with his conduct. They saw the Edict of Nantes as a shameful recognition of heresy and resented Henry's turning a blind eye to breaches of its provisions. He allowed the Huguenots to build a church at Charenton, just outside Paris; when angry crowds heckled the worshippers, he erected a gibbet to deter them. His sister, Catherine, organized Protestant services at court. In strongly Protestant areas, Catholics were harassed and even forced to abjure their faith. Many of Henry's companions were Protestants, such as the Duc de Bouillon and Duc de Rohan; others held major offices, not least Sully. The great Protestant families had supported Henry in the wars and he needed to keep their loyalty, but to 'good Catholics' his conduct was intolerable. He was still a heretic, to whom they owed no allegiance; he was a tyrant, who could lawfully be killed.[53]

In 1609, as dissatisfaction with Henry built to a crescendo, he faced crises in both his personal life and his foreign policy. One spring day he slipped in to watch a rehearsal for a ballet and was totally smitten by one of the dancers. Charlotte-Marguerite de Montmorency was delicate, blonde and beautiful. She was also fourteen, and her innocence and modesty only added to his desire for her. She was engaged to marry one of Henry's favourite companions, but he decided that the only fit match would be with Condé, who was not only first prince of the blood but timid, weak and not much interested in women — not the sort of man who would complain too much if his wife became the King's mistress. They were duly married, but Condé showed an unexpected reluctance to hand his bride over to Henry. He withdrew from court and travelled from one château to another, with Henry in hot pursuit. He wrote his beloved long letters, couched in the language of chivalry and courtly love: she responded in kind. He dressed more smartly than usual and rode at the ring in an effort to impress her. He donned strange disguises — he and his companions were arrested wearing ludicrous false beards — and arranged clandestine meetings. His past amours had been earthily physical but now his love was more spiritual, even ethereal, as he acted out the romances he so enjoyed. He had Charlotte appear all dishevelled on a balcony between two torches. 'Jesus,' she said, 'how mad he is !'[54]

There was much that was comic in the spectacle of a gouty, smelly, middle-aged man posturing like a young gallant in pursuit of a girl more than forty years his junior, but his infatuation had serious consequences. It was a time of international tension. Having signed a truce with the Dutch, the Spaniards could turn their attention elsewhere. The princes and states of Germany were becoming polarized, with the Catholics following the lead of the Emperor and the Protestants looking to Henry for support. Then the Catholic Duke of Cleves and Jülich died, leaving rival Lutheran claimants to the succession. These territories occupied a position of vital strategic importance on the Rhine, forming part of the 'Spanish road' along which troops and provisions passed from Spanish Italy to the Netherlands. The Emperor occupied the duchies, pending a decision on the succession, but many Protestants believed that his forces would never relinquish them.

At Henry's court not only Protestants like Sully but also members of the Catholic military nobility called for war against the Habsburgs. Henry had so far avoided a major conflict, while carrying on the 'cold war' with Spain by encouraging the Dutch and the German Protestants. Now, as he wavered, Condé's patience snapped and he took his wife to Brussels, where the Spanish authorities began to put him forward as a rival claimant to the French throne. Henry was furious at Condé's departure and at the Spaniards' refusal to send the couple back. Late in 1609 he resolved to make war the following spring. By attacking Cleves and Jülich he could help his German allies and menace the eastern frontier of the Spanish Netherlands. His decision outraged the 'good Catholics'. How, they asked, could he justify allying with heretics against fellow-Catholics ? Why did he lavish favours on Protestants ? Were not the Huguenots the real enemy ? His conduct showed that he was still a heretic in his heart, not to mention a wicked adulterer. Catholic priests talked wildly of a Protestant plot to murder all Catholics : it was a case of kill or be killed. Henry was denounced as a tyrant, who oppressed the Church and the people. Astrologers prophesied, and others prayed, that he would soon die.

Henry was deeply affected by this highly charged atmosphere, saying that 'they' would kill him, but he still prepared to go to war. On 13 May 1610 the Queen was crowned at St Denis, so that she could act as regent in his absence. Henry had no illusions about her abilities and provided for a strong council to advise her. That night he slept badly. Next morning he told his companions : 'You others do not know me now ; but I shall die one of these days and when you have lost me, then you will realize what I was worth and the difference there is between me and other men.' That afternoon, he decided to visit Sully. From the Louvre his carriage passed down the Rue St Antoine into the Rue de la Ferronnerie, a narrow street made narrower by market stalls on both sides. The horses slowed and stopped, as two carts blocked the way. The footmen who escorted the carriage dropped back : some cut through an adjacent cemetery to rejoin the street further on. In the carriage, the Duc d'Epernon read a letter to the king, who had come out without his glasses. Suddenly a tall, red-haired man leapt onto the wheel and stabbed the king twice through the open window.[55]

After the first blow Henry cried out ; the second killed him. It had happened so fast that no-one in the coach had seen the murderer, who could easily have escaped, but stood, transfixed, with the bloody knife in his hand. While Henry's body was taken to the Louvre, his assailant was arrested and tortured, in an effort to make him reveal his accomplices. His name was François Ravaillac, from Angoulême. Of limited intelligence but great religious zeal, he had failed to become a monk because he kept seeing visions. He had listened to sermons which denounced Henry for failing to make the Huguenots return to the true Church or to punish them for plotting to murder the Catholics. Now that Henry was about to make war on the Pope it was Ravaillac's sacred duty to kill him. He was a simple man for whom the whole issue seemed simple : he was amazed at the hostility shown by the crowd when he was brought for execution. Far from achieving his aim, he had dissipated the hostility to Henry which had built up in recent years and provoked a reaction against the ideas which (in his eyes) legitimated his action. The concept of tyrannicide (and that the Pope could declare kings deposed) was discredited. Royalist writers stressed the sinfulness of resistance to royal authority : God had made kings absolute rulers of their kingdoms. Henry, meanwhile, passed into folk memory as an ideal king, who brought an end to civil war and allowed peasants to till the fields in peace. In fact, his reign benefited the monarchy more than its subjects, marking the beginning of that extension of royal power which historians have called 'the rise of absolutism'.

# 3
# Factions and Favourites

James I reacted with alarm to Henry's assassination. He ordered that all
Catholics should leave London and that priests should leave the country, but
his anxieties were unnecessary. Gunpowder Plot was the last Catholic conspiracy against the House of Stuart and English Catholics (like the Huguenots)
came to look to the crown for protection against those of the majority
religion. For his part, James came to see his Protestant subjects (especially
those in Parliament) as a greater threat to his authority. In 1610 his ministers
tried to persuade the Commons to accept the Great Contract, arguing that if
they wanted the benefits of monarchy — peace, order and justice — they
would have to ensure that the King had a realistic income. MPs were not
impressed by such arguments, nor by Salisbury's threats that the King might
be forced to use extortionate methods.[1] In February 1611 James dissolved
the Parliament which had met, at lengthy intervals, since 1604. Until now
he had tried to govern by persuasion and reasoned argument, in what he
thought was an English manner. He had met with suspicion and (in his eyes)
a bloody-minded refusal to co-operate. For the next decade he made little
effort to be agreeable to his subjects and found solace for his unhappiness in
his favourites.

Even before 1611 James found it difficult to cope with the demands
of kingship and his grip became weaker as he entered middle age. His health
deteriorated. He suffered from kidney infections (exacerbated by drink),
arthritis, which led him to turn his foot in, and gout. He bolted his food and
ate too much fruit, which played havoc with his digestion. He drank more
heavily, often becoming gloomy and maudlin. With so much violent exercise
in inclement weather, he became overheated and caught colds. His dislike of
washing and of changing his clothes meant that he stank. As his health
worsened, he became more ill-tempered, indolent and indecisive. His grasp
of detail and his mental alertness diminished. Always emotional, he became a
prey to sudden surges of enthusiasm, rage or depression. Sir Anthony

Weldon's devastating *Character of King James* describes him, in these later years, as a timorous figure, whose large eyes rolled towards any stranger, who slobbered when he talked and dribbled when he drank. He leaned on others when he walked, because of his arthritis (not, as Weldon claimed, because of a congenital weakness in his legs). 'His walk was ever circular, his fingers ever ... fiddling about his codpiece': with his sensitive skin and aversion to washing he must have itched a great deal. Weldon bore James a bitter grudge for dismissing him from a lucrative office, but others gave a similar picture. 'His timidity increases day by day', wrote the French ambassador, 'as old age carries him into apprehensions and vices diminish his intelligence.' 'All things end with the goblet.'[2]

As James grew older, it became ever more difficult to see in him the godlike attributes which he ascribed to kings. He applied himself less to business, refusing to see his secretaries when he was ill. His faith in Salisbury was undermined by the failure of the Great Contract and by the insinuations of his courtiers that Salisbury took too much upon himself. When he died in 1612 James decided to do without a chief minister and perform the functions of secretary of state himself, with Carr as his amanuensis, to protect him against the importunities of petitioners. His enthusiasm did not last long. The two secretaries were the lynchpins of the administration, handling a large volume of domestic and foreign business: James found the burden too much. Early in 1613 the council complained that he had not prepared the papers it required. No new secretary was appointed until 1614, by which time James' interest had long since evaporated. When one of the secretaries died in 1617, James again said he would take over the job, as he had never been so well served as when he had been his own secretary. This time it was only three months before he appointed a successor.[3] James clearly saw the need to involve himself in government, to supervise the work of his officials and councillors and to deal firmly with petitioners, but lacked the necessary stamina and will-power. He needed someone to help him bear the burden, an alter ego or personal assistant. While his favourites met an emotional need, they also served a political function by helping James to cope with the business of policy-making and patronage. They were not just pretty young men who played on the weakness of a doting old man to seize political power; James *wanted* them to help him rule.

While Salisbury was alive, Carr showed few signs of political ambition. As the King's personal assistant, he received many petitions for favours and opportunities for profit (although, as he sanctimoniously remarked, he never took a bribe without asking James' permission). He prospered mightily, lending the King £24,000 in 1613, and may well have concentrated on making money rather than seeking political power. As a Scot, he perhaps felt it wise not to make enemies; gracious and affable, he was generally well liked. Loaded with wealth and honours, created Viscount Rochester and then Earl of Somerset, he seemed assured of a glittering future, until he fell in love with and later married the Countess of Essex, the daughter of the Earl of Suffolk, a strong-willed and unscrupulous woman, who would stop at nothing to get her man. She secured an annulment of her first marriage on the grounds that her husband, the son of the rebel Earl of Essex, had been unable to consummate it. When one of Somerset's cronies, Sir Thomas Overbury, opposed his marrying the Countess, she had him poisoned. The annulment proceedings and the Earl and Countess of Somerset's trial for murder revealed a sordid tale of necromancy, secret potions and intrigue, which ruined Somerset and did little for the public image of James and his court. James showed flagrant partisanship in the annulment proceedings: when Archbishop Abbot expressed doubts about the Countess' case, James told him that he should trust in his King's judgement, for he was both learned in theology and, he claimed, utterly impartial. When the poisoning came to light, however, James made no effort to intervene on Somerset's behalf. Both he and his wife were found guilty. James spared their lives and they lived out the rest of their days in obscurity.[4]

Even before his disgrace, Somerset's hold on the King's affections was weakening. Despite his efforts to be all things to all men, he made enemies, especially when his marriage linked him to the Howard faction, headed by Northampton and Suffolk. The Howards favoured friendship with Spain and Northampton inclined towards Catholicism. Ranged against them was a 'Protestant' faction headed by Archbishop Abbot and the Earl of Pembroke, who wanted a firm stand against Spain and Popery. Knowing James' susceptibilities they put forward, as a rival to Somerset, George Villiers, a member of a minor gentry family. What he lacked in wealth he made up in good looks, grace and charm. Everyone liked him — except Somerset, whose own looks were not what they had been. He resisted any suggestion that Villiers be made a gentleman of the bedchamber, which would give him constant access to James; he blustered and threatened the King and told Villiers he would break his neck if he could. In the face of Somerset's ferocity, James did not dare install Villiers in the bedchamber, until the 'Protestant' faction found an unlikely ally in the Catholic Queen, who disliked Somerset. On St George's Day 1615, she approached James with a drawn sword, at which he was much alarmed, and asked him to knight Villiers and swear him gentleman of the bedchamber. The gesture seemed so appropriate that James agreed: he also gave Sir George a pension of £1000 a year.[5]

Somerset was furious. James assured him that his affection was undiminished but warned him against trying to hold him by awe rather than by love; if he did 'the violence of my love will in that instant be changed in as violent a hatred.... It lies in your hand to make of me what you please, either the best master and truest friend, or if you force me once to call you ingrate...no so great earthly plague can light upon you.' It was a warning which Somerset would have been wise to heed. James would never again love him as he now loved Villiers, but with a due show of respect Somerset could have remained high in his favour. As it was, his credit declined until the Overbury scandal completed his ruin. James took his leave, 'slabbering his cheeks' and begging him 'For God's sake, give thy lady this kiss for me!' Hardly was he in his coach when James declared: 'I shall never see his face more.'[6]

Many have seen in this incident evidence of James' hypocrisy, but it probably reflected a tangle of conflicting emotions: love, anxiety, resentment. Meanwhile, the emotional needs which Somerset had once met were now satisfied by Villiers. It is likely that Villiers was prepared (unlike Somerset) to give in physically to the King, although it is worth remarking that when, in 1610, James granted a general pardon or indemnity to those guilty of a wide range of offences, cases of sodomy, along with deer-stealing and piracy, were excluded.[7] With Somerset disgraced, the rise of Villiers accelerated. James showed his love more openly than he had with Somerset. He nicknamed Villiers 'Steenie', after St Stephen, who was supposed to have had the face of an angel. In 1617 he told the council:

I, James, am neither a god nor an angel, but a man like any other. Therefore I act like a man and confess to loving those dear to me more than other men. You may be sure that I love the Earl of Buckingham [Villiers had been raised to the peerage] more than anyone else and more than you who are here assembled. I wish to speak in my own behalf and not to have it thought to be a defect, for Jesus Christ did the same and therefore I cannot be blamed. Christ had his John and I have my George.

His favour extended to all Villiers' numerous kindred : he said he wished to advance that family above all others. When Buckingham married, he treated his wife like a daughter-in-law — he signed letters to Buckingham 'your dear dad' — and showed constant concern for her and her children's health : indeed he derived far more pleasure from the Villiers' offspring than from his own. His court 'swarmed' with them 'so that little ones would dance up and down the privy lodgings, like fairies'.[8]

Villiers, who became Earl, Marquis and eventually Duke of Buckingham, was much more than a pretty face. He was quick, intelligent and eager to please. James set out to train him as a private secretary, as with Somerset. At first Buckingham dealt mainly with suits and petitions ; he built up a substantial clientele through the distribution of the King's patronage and boosted his income with suitors' gifts. Later, the King gave him administrative responsibilities. As Lord Admiral he did much to end the inefficiency and corruption which had flourished under his predecessor, the aged Earl of Nottingham (yet another Howard). He also backed Lionel Cranfield's attempts to reduce waste and peculation in the royal household. As an administrator, Buckingham combined an astute brain with diligence and determination. With added responsibility, he grew in political stature. James consulted him more on matters of policy until, in James' last years, Buckingham became the dominant influence in government.

James' love for Buckingham helped make bearable an old age which was often lonely, painful and depressing. He showed 'a kind of morosity that doth argue a great discontent in mind, or a distemper of humours in his body, but he is never so out of tune but the very sight of my Lord of Buckingham doth settle and quiet all'. In 1618 he grew bored with a masque, complaining that nobody danced, whereupon Buckingham sprang forward and danced so gracefully that he appeased the King and won general admiration.[9] If Buckingham ever tired of James' gushing affection and pet names, he never showed it, nor did he try (like Somerset) to dominate his master. As for James, his love never wavered and he showered his 'dog' with titles, offices, lands, jewels and money. The rise of the impecunious Northamptonshire squireen to vast riches and a dukedom was only the most spectacular illustration of the rich pickings to be had at James' court. Along with the Earl of Carlisle, he was also the most spectacular exponent of conspicuous consumption. Even more than in the previous two decades, the court of the 1610s appeared extravagant, predatory and corrupt, while the means by which the crown raised money and rewarded its servants provoked increasing resentment in the nation at large.

After dissolving his first Parliament in 1611, James staggered from one financial expedient to another until, in 1614, he allowed himself to be persuaded that only through Parliament could he secure money. He told MPs of his love for his subjects; he had had bills drawn up remedying known grievances. If they had others, MPs should present them individually: to 'heap them together' would cast aspersions on his government. He would abandon none of his prerogatives, nor would he stretch them further than his predecessors had done. If James thought his attitude reasonable, MPs resented his deciding what constituted grievances, some of which remained unresolved from the last Parliament, notably impositions. 'So do our impositions daily increase in England', said one MP, 'as it is come to be almost a tyrannical government in England.' Another suggested that Henry IV's death was a just retribution for the burdens he had imposed on his people. Most were incensed when the Bishop of Lincoln said, in the Lords, that in discussing impositions the Commons exceeded their power, struck at the King's prerogative and violated their oath of allegiance. Irritated by the lack of progress, James threatened to dissolve Parliament. The Commons became still more excited: one MP called courtiers 'spaniels to the king and wolves to the people', another inveighed against the Scots. James, furious, dissolved Parliament.[10] It had passed no legislation and was called the Addled Parliament. It confirmed all James' prejudices: he told the Spanish ambassador that Parliament was disorganized and disorderly and was amazed that his predecessors had tolerated it. He had the most outspoken MPs imprisoned, following (as he said) the example of Elizabeth. These revealed that they had been incited to make trouble by persons outside the Commons. This evidence of conspiracy seemed to confirm James' belief that a few incendiaries had led the rest astray. He decided to appeal to his loyal subjects to show their affection by a large gift of money. Despite substantial donations from the bishops and a few others, the response was disappointing.[11]

Thrown back once more on non-parliamentary sources of revenue, James sought to marry Prince Charles to the Infanta of Spain, who (he hoped) would bring a huge dowry. The Spaniards proved tricky negotiators, however, raising grave difficulties about religion. James also talked of economizing, but did little about it until, in 1617, he sent to London for money for his journey back from Scotland, after his first and only visit to his native land since coming south in 1603. The treasury cart trundled up to Carlisle, where it was found to contain a mere £400. Shaken, James told the council to cut expenditure as they pleased. Cranfield in the household and Buckingham in the navy economized to such good effect that in 1618 a surplus was expected, although the crown's debts remained substantial. These reforms were not entirely disinterested. Cranfield undertook to run the wardrobe for much less than its current cost — and still made a handsome profit. Buckingham's zeal for reform owed much to his desire to break the power of the Howards : Nottingham was eased out of the admiralty and Suffolk was dismissed from the lord treasurership. He and his wife were later convicted of corruption in the court of Star Chamber and fined heavily. Their trial might seem to resemble a French chamber of justice, a means of clawing back the excessive profits of a financial official, but the fine was later drastically reduced. The real motive was to discredit Suffolk totally, so that he could offer no challenge to Buckingham's power. As Northampton had died and Nottingham had been pensioned off, Suffolk's fall brought the Howards' power to an end.

While Buckingham patronized schemes of retrenchment and reform, the years after 1614 saw a proliferation of projects, 'a sort of idle dreams that vanish away'.[12] Some brought the King large sums, notably the sale of titles, but most made fat profits for favoured individuals. Economic concessions and the delegation of administrative tasks were necessary forms of patronage and could serve a valid purpose, but they needed to be used with care and restraint. On the one hand, it was important that rewards should be granted in return for service. On the other, the crown had to avoid grants which provoked too much public resentment. As Northampton explained :

These ways of sucking satisfaction by private persons out of subjects' fortunes hath been ever so dangerously scandalous in this state.... When the king's power strengthens and enables one subject to cramp and fleece another in the king's right ... all goes to ruin and mischief follows.[13]

When Salisbury renewed his farm of duties on silks, increasing his annual profit from £1333 to 7000, it could be argued that his services merited such a reward and that the only loser was the King: merchants paid no more than before. Other concessions were less defensible. The alehouse patent (in which Buckingham's brother was deeply involved) was ostensibly designed to ensure that only orderly alehouses received a licence. In fact, the patentees and subcontractors granted as many licences as they could and charged as much as they could for them. Alehousekeepers who refused to pay were harassed: about one hundred were outlawed. Similarly, a monopoly on salmon and lobsters from those waters which had not hitherto supplied London was used as a pretext to force fishermen in the Thames estuary to sell their catch to the monopolists' agents, at knock-down prices.[14]

Most monopolies and patents were justified by claims either that they served a necessary regulatory purpose (such as suppressing disorderly alehouses) or that they encouraged a new product or process — the lobster patentees claimed to have discovered a new way of keeping fish fresh. Many monopolies and patents of the late 1610s had three common and disturbing features. First, they involved a large measure of dishonesty. Second, they depended on an unholy alliance between well-placed courtiers and unscrupulous entrepreneurs. The latter (typified by Buckingham's kinsman Sir Giles Mompesson) dreamed up the projects and exploited the patents, which the courtiers secured for them; Buckingham's brothers Kit and Edward were very active in this. Finally, many patents delegated wide and arbitrary powers to the patentees' agents, who hauled those who defied them before the court of Star Chamber.

Star Chamber consisted of the privy council together with the two chief justices. The council had always received petitions and redressed grievances, but under the Tudors its meetings for judicial purposes became distinct from its other meetings and it became recognizably a court. It dealt mainly with cases between subjects, supplementing the work of the common law courts, and punished breaches of proclamations. Its procedures were quicker and simpler than those of the other courts and with its reputation for fairness it became popular with litigants. However, once the King started to establish monopolies and patents by proclamation, this speed and simplicity seemed less attractive; defendants enjoyed far less protection than in the common law courts (there was no jury), for now the King (and those licensed by him) was an interested party. One contemporary wrote in 1620:

The world is now much terrified with the Star Chamber, there being not so little offence against any proclamation but is liable and subject to the censure of that court. And for proclamations and patents they are become so ordinary that there is no end, every day bringing forth some new project or other.[15]

It seems unlikely that James consciously set out to make Star Chamber into an instrument of oppression. He had a strong sense of justice: he remarked that if those who rioted against enclosure were punished, those whose illegal enclosures provoked the riots should be punished too. He insisted that justice be done against Somerset and lost much of his belief in witchcraft after several fraudulent cases were exposed. When he was uncertain of the legality of an action he consulted the judges, but he did not slavishly follow the letter of the law. He felt, with some justification, that the common law was unnecessarily complicated, that lawyers kept it so for their own ends and that they greedily sought to enlarge their competence at the expense of others' jurisdictions.[16] He disliked the claim of the great lawyer, Sir Edward Coke, that the king possessed only such powers as the common law gave him and that therefore only the judges, with their years of legal training, were truly qualified to say what those powers were. As James said, to accept this would be to subordinate the king to the judges.

In many respects, indeed, James' approach to law showed a solid common sense, but he was not always as impartial or objective as he liked to think. He could be swayed by personal predilections (as in the Essex divorce case) or by those close to him. He sometimes did not grasp the full implications of documents he endorsed, or did not see how seemingly beneficial powers might be misused: he cancelled many patents in 1621. In the last analysis, however, there was much in James' use of the law to alarm those who saw in the growth of non-parliamentary taxation evidence of a move towards absolute monarchy. In 1610 MPs denounced the council's powers of arbitrary arrest. James' brushes with Coke, his high-flown talk of prerogative and his increasing use of Star Chamber to enforce proclamations all suggested that he was claiming wider discretionary powers than his predecessors and using them to threaten liberty and property. James may have believed he was acting only as his predecessors had done : others did not and they were not reassured when several were imprisoned for disobeying a proclamation forbidding discussion of state affairs.[17]

It may seem paradoxical that the reforms and retrenchments of the later 1610s coincided with an efflorescence of patents (backed up by Star Chamber) and of corruption : nothing, it was said, could be achieved without gold. If one common factor linked these developments, it was not the King's financial need (for the patents brought him little profit), but the interests of Buckingham. The reforms both served the King and drove out the Howards, while the patents helped Buckingham to build a very extensive patronage network. As yet, he did not confine his favours to any political, religious or factional group, but his use of patronage still provoked resentment. It may be that attitudes to standards of conduct in public life were changing : what was once seen as normal was now labelled 'corrupt'. In addition, however, many disliked the predatory conduct of those he favoured, the showering of rewards (not least glittering marriages) on his own relatives and the concentration of so much power in the hands of a young man of humble origins.[18] At first, his critics focused on 'corruption' rather than political or religious issues. That was soon to change.

On becoming King, James had ended Elizabeth's war with Spain. Unlike many of his subjects, he never saw European affairs simply as a struggle to the death between Protestantism and Catholicism. He regarded Calvinists as inherently antimonarchical and once referred to the Huguenots as 'rascals'. He dreamed that Christendom would one day be reunited and his innate aversion to war was reinforced by his awareness that he had no army and could not afford one. He regarded the French as 'fiddling and giddy', but thought the Spaniards serious and steady, and hoped for a fat dowry from a Spanish marriage. The Spaniards craftily dangled this prospect in front of James and sought to drive a wedge between the English and the Dutch.

Then, in 1618, the situation was transformed. The Calvinists of Bohemia revolted against Habsburg rule and invited Frederick to be their king. In 1620 his forces were routed by the Emperor's and the German Catholic League overran much of his hereditary principality, the Palatinate, forcing

Frederick and Elizabeth to flee to the Dutch Republic. James was filled with distress and perplexity. He could not condone Frederick's usurping the Bohemian crown, which rightfully belonged to the Emperor, but felt rather flattered that his beloved daughter was now a queen. Their expulsion from Bohemia and the Palatinate resolved that moral dilemma, but left him no surer of what to do. Many councillors called for war against Spain, but that would mean calling Parliament, which he had no wish to do. He hoped that the long-projected Spanish marriage could be linked to the restitution of the Palatinate: he always greatly overestimated the influence of the Spanish Habsburgs over their Austrian cousins. To the many Englishmen who saw the war in stark religious terms, the subtleties of James' policy were incomprehensible and played into the Papists' hands. There was thus general relief when James finally agreed to call Parliament in 1621.

James hoped that Parliament would grant money and declare its support for action to recover the Palatinate. The Commons did both, but showed more interest in redressing grievances (especially patents) and revived the device of impeachment, whereby the Commons acted as prosecutors and the lords as judges, to proceed against those responsible. When they reconvened after a summer recess, war seemed much more likely and James pressed for a firm commitment of support. At last the Commons urged James to make war if Spain would not agree to his demands concerning the Palatinate, which is what James had wanted, but also called for Charles to marry a Protestant. To MPs, it seemed logical that Charles should not marry the Infanta when England was threatening war against Spain, but James was furious at what he saw as an insolent interference in the royal family's affairs. Taking advantage of his absence and ill health, he wrote, some 'fiery and popular spirits' had dared to debate 'matters far above their reach and capacity, tending to our high dishonour and breach of prerogative royal'.[19]

Hitherto, the Commons had behaved circumspectly, but they could not ignore this challenge to their traditional privilege of freedom of speech: to say nothing would be to concede that they should discuss nothing displeasing to the King. They asserted, in a 'protestation', that they had a right to discuss foreign policy and other matters. James disliked this talk of 'rights'. He had told them that Parliaments and their privileges had been brought into being by past monarchs: 'kings and kingdoms were long before Parliaments, contrary to the fond opinion of some that thought otherwise'.[20]

After proroguing Parliament, he tore the 'anti-monarchical' protestation out of the Commons' journal — a petulant gesture which achieved nothing. The chance to unite King and Parliament for a war against Spain had gone — if it had ever existed. James' attitude had been equivocal — he made no real effort to guide Parliament's proceedings — while MPs had been readier to make bellicose noises than to vote the money needed for war.

Although the Commons behaved far more moderately in 1621 than in 1614, there were signs of a growing polarization, seen most clearly in religion. Hitherto, James had skilfully balanced the 'High Church' and 'Puritan' elements in the Church, but this balance came under intolerable strain with the outbreak of what many saw as a religious war on the Continent. Puritan preachers exhorted James to rush to aid Frederick and the German Protestants against the forces of Antichrist. Their conduct drove James to concentrate his favour on those whose religious views allowed them to support his foreign policy: High Churchmen, soon to become known as Arminians. Influenced by the Dutch theologian Arminius, many divines who stressed the importance of the liturgy, the sacraments and episcopacy and who sought to revive the authority of the clergy, also began to challenge Calvinist theology, which had hitherto been generally accepted. They argued that God had not determined irrevocably who should be saved or damned: people could, by faith and virtuous living, accept the grace that God offered them.

To Calvinists, Arminian theology, like the stress on ritual and clerical authority, smacked of Popery. The two wings of the Church denounced each other as 'Puritans' or 'Papists' and James came to side with the Arminians. Not only did they not oppose his foreign policy, but many upheld royal authority in extravagant terms, denouncing criticism of the government as seditious or even treasonable (as Bishop Neile of Lincoln had done in the 1614 Parliament). Meanwhile, Puritan criticism of James' foreign policy reinforced his suspicion that they were subversive and anti-monarchical. His antipathy now embraced not only the aggressively nonconformist few but all those critical of ceremonies or his foreign policy. Puritans, he said, wanted parity, not purity.[21]

A similar, if less clear-cut, polarization developed in politics. The Commons feared that James, in relying on his prerogatives to raise money and silence criticism, was moving towards a more authoritarian form of government. Their fears led them to extend the scope of their activities, for example seeking to find out who was responsible for the patents. Sometimes, excitement, anger or fear led MPs into rash words. In general they wished to preserve the existing order against change and looked to the past, often the distant past, for guidance on how to do so. Few saw any way out of their problems except for the King to choose better advisers and follow better policies : they remained pathetically convinced that evil advisers were leading astray a well-intentioned King. This was not totally naïve : James revoked many patents in 1621, saying his good nature had been abused. Only a few hardy spirits argued for sweeping changes. James Whitelocke stated in 1610 that sovereignty lay with the King in Parliament, so that any of the King's powers could be curbed or removed by Act of Parliament. He found no supporters. MPs and lawyers continued to argue that precedent and the common law determined what the King could or could not do, but in practice both proved imprecise guides and such arguments subsided into pious hopes that the King would use his powers responsibly.[22]

One cannot tell how typical Whitelocke's views were. Few openly advocated political change, but this is not surprising, as the press was censored and James forbade discussion of public affairs. It seems likely, however, that few moved from criticism of the misdeeds of James' government to proposals to change the political order. A more serious challenge to the existing balance between the King's powers and the subject's rights came from within the court. Arminian divines defended royal power outspokenly : they depended on it for protection against Puritans and Parliament. James, never tolerant of criticism, had come to see any challenge to his view of his powers as a threat to monarchy. Where once he had blamed such criticism on a malevolent few, infected with 'popularity', he came to see the bulk of his subjects as 'ill-natured' : he would govern for the common weal, but not according to the common will.[23]

His views were shared by Prince Charles, who wrote in 1621 that James should make an example of 'seditious fellows' who made trouble in Parliament.[24] This was the first Parliament in which Charles played a part. Still shy, he was now physically more robust and developing opinions of his own. At first Buckingham had treated him disdainfully and James had taken the favourite's side against his son. Soon, however, Buckingham began to treat him more considerately. Charles, timid and lonely, responded warmly. Buckingham filled the void left by Henry's death, becoming an adored surrogate elder brother, a stronger personality to look up to and to lean upon. King, prince and favourite came to form a close-knit group: to James, the two were his 'dear boys' and, curiously, Charles came, through Buckingham, to occupy a major place in his father's affections.

Charles' role in politics was as an auxiliary to Buckingham, whose interests now grew to embrace foreign affairs. Early in 1623 it seemed that agreement on the Spanish match was in sight, as the Spaniards appeared ready to press the Emperor to restore the Palatinate. Charles, encouraged by reports of the Infanta's beauty, believed that he was madly in love with her. He started to learn Spanish and talked of going to Spain to seek his bride. He persuaded Buckingham that in this way they could force the Spaniards' hand and they talked James into letting them go. They set off, in false beards and hoods, under the names of Thomas and John Smith, across France and into Spain. It was a hare-brained escapade. Apart from the normal risks of sickness, broken limbs and brigands, it placed an extraordinarily valuable hostage in the Spaniards' hands, a fact of which James became painfully aware. Buckingham, for his part, feared that James' affection for him might wane in his absence, but he need not have worried. While the two young men discovered how dilatory and devious Spaniards could be, James became frantic with worry. The Spanish demanded freedom of worship for the Infanta and the repeal of the laws against Catholics, continually increasing their demands on the assumption that Charles would agree rather than lose his bride. Charles seemed inclined to do so, despite Buckingham's warnings not to make promises that he could not keep and James' plaintive pleas for his 'dear boys' to return home. Charles was most reluctant to do so: only when the Spaniards made it clear that they would do nothing about the Palatinate would he agree. Once he had left Spain, he began to see how dangerous the concessions were that he had been asked to make and to resent the way the Spaniards had treated him.[25]

Buckingham and Charles returned to England in the unaccustomed role of popular heroes. After all the fears that they would sell out to Spain, they had (after all) resisted the Papists' wiles. The night they arrived in London there were 108 bonfires between St Paul's and London Bridge. Their popularity increased when it became clear that Buckingham was now very hostile to Spain. Not only did he resent having been misled, but he believed only the threat of war could make Spain press for the restitution of the Palatinate.

James, however, still hoped the Spaniards could be brought to this without war, which would exacerbate his financial problems and perhaps put him at the mercy of the 'popular' element in Parliament.

At last, he succumbed to the pressure of his son and favourite. He summoned Parliament and opened negotiations for a French marriage, to cement an Anglo-French alliance against Spain. The Parliament showed clearly the interplay between court and parliamentary politics. Buckingham and Charles' demand for war was opposed not only by James but also by a number of councillors, notably Cranfield (now Earl of Middlesex and Lord Treasurer). Middlesex argued that James could not afford war, but Charles and Buckingham had little understanding of money: huge though his income was, Buckingham spent far more than he received and was several times bailed out by the King. Similarly, he saw no need to relate government expenditure to income, proceeding on the blithe assumption that money would be found somewhere. His zeal for a Spanish war made some diplomatic sense, but it was foolish to ignore the gritty practicalities of paying for it.

James invited the Commons to discuss foreign policy, but many MPs were more interested in domestic affairs. When they did talk of war, they had in mind a war against Spanish trade and especially the fleets bringing bullion from the Americas. This, they believed, would paralyse the Habsburg war-effort and bring about the restoration of the Palatinate; it would also be cheap and perhaps even profitable. Many saw such a war as an anti-Catholic crusade and called for stricter enforcement of the laws against Catholics at home. James and Buckingham, however, realized that only military intervention in Germany could recover the Palatinate and for that England would need the help of Catholic France. As James' timid soul recoiled at the dangers inherent in such a war and in a French alliance, Buckingham was faced with the problem of persuading James and the Commons to support a war which, for different reasons, neither wanted. In so doing, he gave many hostages to fortune. He persuaded James to accept less money than he needed and broke Middlesex' opposition by having him impeached on charges of corruption. As James presciently remarked, in encouraging the impeachment Charles and Buckingham were making a rod for their own backs and would live to have their bellyful of Parliaments.

Buckingham, meanwhile, pressed on with preparations for a war different from the one MPs had in mind and with negotiations for a French alliance, to be cemented by Charles' marrying Louis' sister, Henrietta Maria. The terms of the marriage treaty (agreed late in 1624) included a secret promise to halt the persecution of Catholics in England, even though Charles had solemnly assured the Lords that he would never agree to such a demand. In Buckingham's eyes, such details did not matter : the vital point was to secure France's co-operation. He was sure that the war would be a dazzling success and would win Parliament's enthusiastic support, but it was not to be. The expedition to Germany was to be commanded by an experienced mercenary captain, Count Ernst von Mansfeld. The gaols and poorhouses were scoured for the most expendable members of society and Mansfeld began to discipline and train them. When the time came for them to leave for Germany, however, Louis XIII refused to allow them free passage through France. As James thought it unwise to land them in the Spanish Netherlands, they had to travel via the Dutch Republic, where they melted away due to famine, disease and desertion.

While Mansfeld's expedition failed humiliatingly, the negotiations with France left James with nothing to show while he had conceded a promise not to persecute Catholics which he had every reason to conceal. Buckingham had been hopelessly outmanoeuvred : desperate for his alliance, he accepted less and less favourable terms. His conduct in 1624 — in Parliament, in the French negotiations, in promoting Mansfeld's expedition — did little to inspire confidence in his abilities. There was every reason to expect that awkward questions would be asked when Parliament next met. James was well aware of this. He was a cautious man and cautious men make fewer errors than impulsive gamblers like Buckingham, forever seeking a spectacular success to offset past failures. James, however, no longer had the energy or willpower to rein in his favourite or his son, so was left with the great consolation of prophets of doom — the certainty of being right. The Spaniards saw that he still hankered after an understanding and played on his unease, alleging that Buckingham planned to exile him to a country estate, while he and Charles took over the government. James' faith in Buckingham was badly shaken, but then the Duke fell gravely ill and James' concern for his recovery overcame all his suspicions. He might doubt the wisdom of Buckingham's policies, but his love for 'my sweet child and wife' was as strong as ever.[26]

In March 1625 James fell ill. Buckingham rushed to his bedside, giving him medicines which he had found effective (which later led to talk of poison). On the 27th James died, his feeble body twisted by a stroke and racked with dysentery. His high hopes of 1603 lay in tatters and he viewed the future, as old men often do, with gloomy foreboding. He believed that the forces of 'popularity' and Puritanism threatened the monarchy and that Charles and Buckingham's recent conduct had played into the trouble-makers' hands. Such a view was unduly pessimistic. Criticism of his government was inspired mainly by a fear of change, not a desire for change. Where James saw himself as a just king, using the crown's traditional powers in a traditional way, many of his subjects thought they detected an ominous movement towards a government like that of France. There was thus, on the part of both king and subjects, a considerable measure of mistrust and misunderstanding. James had a poor sense of public relations. He theorized and pontificated too much; his court created an impression of excess and extravagance; he did not offer an image of regal authority; he was insufficiently gracious to his people.

Government, however, is never purely a matter of public relations and presentation: content and policies are also important. When James became king the royal finances needed serious restructuring. He had to either take Parliament into his confidence and raise far more in subsidies, or rely more on prerogative sources (notably impositions), which would make co-operation with Parliament much more difficult. Experience was to show that the former was the more effective option, but it is doubtful whether in James' reign the Commons were willing or able to take on a major role in revenue-raising; even if they had, to do so would have required a greater trust in James than most MPs possessed. James was driven to adopt the second option — and to use many dubious forms of patronage.

James was thus faced with a financial problem to which there were no easy answers and which raised serious issues of principle. He was also faced with a Church whose divisions were becoming wider. How well did he deal with these difficulties? To say that he had homosexual inclinations and favourites is no answer. Henry IV was anything but homosexual, yet his passions led him into errors (like the promise to marry Henriette) potentially more damaging than any of James'. Moreover, James intended his favourites to share the burden of government, for which Buckingham seemed well equipped, until power went to his head. James' failures owed more to his not adapting to the demands of English kingship. As a public figure he failed to inspire respect, as a private man he could not resist importunity. England's polity was more complex than Scotland's and depended on consent and co-operation, which could not be taken for granted but had to be earned. The king needed to heed his subjects' wishes and to show that he had done so; it was, in short, a system based on give and take, on a large scale.

Whereas James successfully balanced factions and individuals in Scotland (and, for a while, in the English church), he had neither the energy nor the inclination for the highly detailed horse-trading which English government required. There was, moreover, one major difference of principle. Most Englishmen accepted that the king had wide discretionary powers, to be used in the best interests of the nation. James assumed that the way he used these powers was a matter for his judgement and conscience alone. He was an experienced king; he was also very vain and susceptible to flattery, with an exaggerated impression of both his intellectual prowess and his integrity. He saw criticism of his use of these powers as an attack on the powers themselves. He responded with forthright assertions of prerogative, using language which increased his subjects' anxieties. He converted disputes about specific, concrete issues into more general arguments about the nature of royal power. By changing political issues into constitutional ones, he helped to raise fears that he intended to introduce absolutism, whereas in fact he did not.

For all his arrogance and bombast, James was a timid man, increasingly concerned with survival in an alien and (he thought) hostile land. Often when he offended Parliament, he would later explain his words away, just as, after raging unjustly at a servant, he knelt and asked his pardon. He was weak rather than malevolent, petulant rather than cruel. Even Weldon, after all his harsh words, concluded that 'he loved good laws and had many made in his time.... He was such a king, I wish this kingdom have never any worse, on the condition, not any better, for he lived in peace, died in peace and left all his kingdoms in a peaceable condition.'[27] How well his son would cope with this pacific legacy remained to be seen.

\* \* \*

With Henry IV's death, the Dauphin became Louis XIII. Not yet nine, he found his change of status too much to grasp: when people shouted 'Long live the King!' he did not seem to understand that they meant him. As he was not of age, somebody had to act as regent. Of his three closest male relatives, Condé had fled abroad to save his wife from Henry's attentions, Soissons had stomped off to the country after a row about what his wife should wear at Marie de Médici's coronation and the Prince de Conti was deaf and mentally defective. None could stake an immediate claim to the regency, but the Queen Mother could. Within three hours of Henry's murder the Paris Parlement issued a decree appointing her regent. This, it was claimed, was what Henry had intended: the fact that he had wished her to be advised by a regency council was quietly ignored. Next day she and the King came to the Parlement to register formally the declaration of her regency. Squabbles over precedence marred the dignity of the proceedings. Four bishops refused to move from seats to which they had no right, some members of the Parlement objected to the presence of women and there were attempts to prevent Marie from leaving. Her speech was punctuated by sobs and tears and when Louis stammered a few sentences nobody could hear him because the councillors were talking among themselves.

In the days when kings ruled as well as reigned, minorities posed problems. With no adult king to impose his will, the great men (and women) of the kingdom struggled for control of the government and for the power and wealth which that would bring. Dissident nobles and peasants felt free to rebel, claiming that they were defying, not the king, but those who exercised power in his name. This had been very apparent in the minority of Edward VI — as luck would have it, the last English king to succeed while under age. The Bourbons were less fortunate. Both Louis XIII and Louis XIV succeeded as children and the disorders of their minorities interrupted the consolidation of royal power. Marie's authority as regent was soon challenged by princes of the blood and others of the high nobility. Condé proved most troublesome. Third in the line of succession, after Louis and his brother Gaston, his ambitions had been sharpened when the Spaniards put him forward as a rival to Henry IV: if the annulment of Henry's first marriage was regarded as invalid, then both his sons would be illegitimate. Condé strongly resisted any suggestion that the boy-king should marry — royal children often married at an early age — for if Louis were to have a son, Condé's claim to the throne would be weakened. The prince even talked, in his cups, of taking the throne himself.

Even when he did not press his own claims, Condé expected a major role in government: he was male and French, whereas Marie was neither. He and the other magnates had vast estates and formidable castles and could raise large bodies of armed men. Many governors of royal fortresses were their clients. Henry had excluded them from the highest levels of government, but now they pressed forward to demand places, pensions and power. Marie, timid by nature, lacked confidence in her military resources, so avoided confrontations, bought them off and played for time. Between 1610 and 1614 the crown paid out over ten million livres to the great nobility, including nearly four million to Condé. As a policy it was neither cheap nor dignified, but the country was at peace and the crown could afford it: not until 1614 did it need to raid Sully's emergency fund. Serious fighting was avoided and the regent kept a precarious grip on the government.

Although Marie was eager to wield power, she had little experience of government, Henry having kept her out of public affairs. She sensibly relied on the team built up by Henry, except for Sully. She had never liked him. He found money for Henry's mistresses but refused her money for her expensive little pleasures. He was rude and irascible and opposed her conciliating the magnates. He was Protestant and anti-Spanish; she was a devout, even bigoted Catholic, eager for a rapprochement with Spain. Out of step with the Queen and other ministers, Sully resigned in 1611. The remaining ministers were old — they were known as the greybeards — cautious and conciliatory. The nobles were bought off, the Huguenots' military privileges were renewed. In Guyenne, the *élus* were suppressed and the local estates restored. Henry's war in Germany was aborted, thus saving money and salving the Queen's conscience: she had never approved of joining with Protestants against fellow-Catholics. She hoped to bring the two great Catholic powers together by a dual marriage: Louis was to marry the Infanta Anne (the sister of Maria, whom Charles so wanted to marry), his sister Elizabeth would marry the heir to the Spanish throne, the future Philip IV. Henry had considered such an arrangement, but had abandoned it in the crisis of 1609–10. Terms were agreed in 1612 and the marriages took place in 1615.

During the regency the crown trod water and tried to avoid trouble.

Government was carried on competently ; there was no civil war, no invasion, no bankruptcy. The regime's essentially defensive approach was seen clearly in the Estates General of 1614. The French crown had long ago given up hope of turning the Estates into a means of obtaining consent : it was too divided and its demands were too unrealistic. It was called during the religious wars mainly as a propitiatory gesture. It met in 1614 as part of yet another fragile agreement between Marie and the princes. Condé hoped it would demand that he be installed at the head of the government, but his high opinion of himself was not matched by his political acumen or his application. Few of his supporters were elected, but the nature of the Estates, with deputies bringing grievances from their localities, put the regent on the defensive. She was helped by the usual friction between the orders. The president of the nobility compared the relationship of nobles and third estate to that of master and servant and called for an end to venality of office : the third estate responded by calling for a reduction in pensions to the nobility, plus a cut of one quarter in the *taille*. To a government short of money and dependent on noble goodwill, such demands seemed irrelevant and unhelpful ; it responded with promises it did not intend to keep and rebutted the Parlement's claim that it had the right to ensure that the Estates' demands were met.[28]

The Estates showed that the critics of the regency were irremediably divided among themselves : neither the nobility nor the Parlement could offer a viable alternative government. What was desperately needed was an effective king, to impose his authority and serve as a focus for loyalty. Louis was declared of age before the Estates met, but he was only thirteen and asked his mother to continue to direct the government. He was not an imposing figure. Thin and shy, he preferred the company of animals and birds to that of people. Like James, he loved hunting and would ride all night in pursuit of a stag. Like James, he disliked court life, preferring the company of a few chosen companions. Like James, he was highly emotional, craving affection. He was in many ways lonely and isolated.

His father's death affected him deeply : he never felt the same affection for his mother, who still beat him in public at the age of fifteen. Indeed, like James, he had little time for women. Henry was always brutally frank in sexual matters and Louis was taught the facts of life at a very early age. If the intention was to awaken an interest in girls, it failed dismally : as a boy,

Louis showed dislike, even fear, of the opposite sex. He married Anne of Austria, the Infanta, when they were both fourteen. His first attempt to consummate the marriage was an embarrassing disaster: it was four years before he could bring himself to try again, having been told repeatedly that it was his duty to sire a dauphin and secure the succession. This time, all went well. For three years the couple enjoyed an affectionate relationship, which ended in a bitter row when she miscarried in 1622. Thereafter, Louis remained cool towards her and she was caught up in Spanish conspiracies against him. They ceased to sleep together and it was sheer chance (see p.126) that led to Louis' spending the night with her when Louis XIV was conceived.

Despite his unsatisfactory marriage, Louis took no mistresses; although he had platonic friendships with women, he preferred male company and had several male favourites. Homosexual by inclination, he was often possessive and jealous, but it is uncertain whether his emotion was translated into physical action.[29] He was a pious Catholic, with a strong sense of sin and of duty. He was not ideally equipped to be king. Not unintelligent, he relied mainly on dogged determination to get to grips with a problem. From childhood he suffered from intestinal disorders, perhaps partly nervous in origin, which triggered ferocious rages. His frenetic hunting imposed a further strain on his frail health, but, like his father, he disliked sitting still. He loved soldiering and during his campaigns developed an extensive knowledge of his kingdom and people. He was not keen on reading or studying, nor was he a good listener. He was happiest when using his hands: he drew well, was a passable gunsmith, basketmaker and wheelwright and an excellent cook. After a long hunt he would cook omelettes for his companions at a wayside inn. He would have made a competent craftsman and would have been happier as a private person than as king, but a formidable sense of duty drove him to overcome his limitations. The effort affected his nerves (he had nightmares) and his health. He was as severe with others as with himself: he had none of his father's clemency and expected to be obeyed. Well aware of his deficiencies, he never overestimated his capacity to govern, as James did. Always careful to take advice, he sought, and at last found, a minister with the qualities he lacked.

When he came of age, Marie denied him an effective role in government, partly because she liked to exercise power, partly because of the influence of

Concino Concini and his wife, Leonora Galigai. Leonora's mother, a washerwoman, had been Marie's wetnurse; the two were brought up together, and shared an interest in the occult. Leonora was no beauty, but intelligent and ambitious; her husband had won Henry's favour by playing cards with him and concealing his amours. A double hernia made the rumours that he was Marie's lover implausible, but the couple were not on good terms, although they co-operated in seeking profit and power. Their house, next to the Louvre, was linked by a bridge to Marie's apartments and they used the access this gave to exercise great influence on the distribution of patronage. Concini was made a peer and a marshal of France, despite his lack of military experience. Although he was bitterly unpopular, with Marie's favour he was impregnable, unless Louis chose to assert himself. For this reason Marie and Concini tried to ensure that those around the King were political nonentities, but they failed. Albert de Luynes, an impoverished Provençal gentleman, was Louis' falconer and arranged his hunting trips. Calm, amiable and more than twenty years Louis' senior, he was a mature, almost father figure in whom he could confide. He seemed harmless, so Marie and Concini raised no objection when he moved into the Louvre with lodgings above the King's.

After the Estates General, Concini (now the Maréchal d'Ancre) acted almost as if he were king. He chaired council meetings, received ambassadors and issued orders to all and sundry. He travelled with an escort of two hundred gentlemen, hired mercenaries and fortified Amiens, of which he was governor, as a refuge in case of trouble. He declared that the King was childish and needed a good thrashing. Louis complained that he could not obtain thirty livres, but this mother could find 450,000 for Ancre, who responded that if Louis wanted money he should come to him. Ancre's refusal to take Louis seriously was a mistake. He was not an imposing figure — Condé refused to stand when he entered the room — but such contemptuous treatment made him burn for revenge. With a little group of confidants he plotted Ancre's downfall. Early in 1617 Louis proposed that the Concinis should return to Italy. Leonora was prepared to go: she was very rich and the sacking of their Paris house had shown how unpopular they were. Ancre, however, was furious. The previous year he had had Condé arrested and dismissed the 'greybeards' and he now thought himself invincible. He was planning to purge his remaining enemies from office and talked of confining Louis to the Tuileries; he may even have considered making Gaston king in his place.

Faced with Ancre's defiance, Louis resolved to have him arrested and tried for treason and was persuaded that he should be killed if he resisted arrest. On 24 April 1617, as Ancre stepped onto the bridge between his house and the Louvre, the door slammed behind him. The captain of the king's guard seized his arm. When he called to his escort, trapped behind the locked door, he was hit by three bullets and died at once. When his friends tried to bury him at night, the Parisians dug up the corpse, hung it on a gibbet, then burned it and cast the ashes to the winds. Louis was exultant: 'At this moment, I am King!' His mother was distraught: she realized her days of power were over. All she could hope for, she said, was a crown in heaven. When asked how Leonora was to be told, she shrieked: 'I have other things to think about.... If you can't say it to her, then sing it! ... I have enough to do thinking about myself.' Leonora expressed no surprise: her husband had brought it on himself, she said. The Parlement of Paris condemned her to death for treason and witchcraft and the Concinis' vast wealth was forfeited to the crown: Louis granted it to Luynes.[30]

The Queen Mother could not be disposed of so summarily. Louis told her coldly that he would continue to treat her as his mother, although she had not treated him as a son. He forbade his brother and sisters to visit her and blocked off all but one of the entrances to her lodgings, so that she could receive no unauthorized visitors. Marie had a boundless capacity for self-pity and a talent for emotional blackmail: she expressed horror that a boy of sixteen could treat his mother in this way. Louis gladly accepted her offer to leave Paris for Blois. Their parting was frosty, the Parisians showing clearly their dislike of the Queen and their enthusiasm for the King. His mother had used his popularity in her clashes with the nobles; now that he was his own master, Louis found it exhilarating, saying again and again that he was King at last.

The euphoria soon passed as he found that ruling was neither as easy nor as enjoyable as he had expected. He recalled the 'greybeards' to his council and attended its meetings assiduously, listened carefully and accepted the view of the majority. Among such venerable men, he was hesitant about giving his opinion and took time to make up his mind. He found it difficult to keep order and some meetings degenerated into slanging matches, but as

Luynes grew in self-confidence he came to impose his will on the proceedings, on the King's behalf. Despite his good intentions, Louis was too young and inexperienced to meet the demands of kingship, but he was learning. He received ambassadors on his own and impressed them with his courtesy, but he was too shy and immature to act as a focus for either the ceremonial or the social life of the court. He presided at ceremonies when he had to, but felt alien in a court given over to pleasure and vice, preferring to flee to the stables or the hunt with his beloved Luynes.

Luynes was no Concini: he was neither ruthless nor cunning, nor did he have Buckingham's ability. Like Louis, he was timid and pious; unlike Louis, he lacked physical courage and determination. His efforts to remain on good terms with everyone ensured that no-one, except the King, liked him. He heaped up riches and honours and provided for a tribe of needy relations. He had no clear political aims, but as the man in favour he was courted by a wide variety of interests and built an extensive clientele. Although he lacked the necessary experience, he was appointed to the top military and legal posts, constable of France and keeper of the seals: Condé, not renowned for his wit, remarked that he would be a good constable in peacetime and a good keeper in wartime. Eventually, his amiable nature was corrupted by power. He talked grandly of making war and peace and referred to the Queen as 'that woman'. When he died, of fever, in 1621 Louis' feelings were mixed. He mourned for his friend but admitted that 'he lacked something': Louis usually expressed himself simply and directly. He also ordered a strict investigation into Luynes' property, to see if he had stolen from the crown.

While Louis struggled to learn the art of government, his mother schemed (with Spain and the Pope) to regain power. Early in 1619 she eased her ample frame out of an upper window of the château of Blois and descended two rope ladders to freedom. As troops gathered round her and several provinces erupted in arms, Luynes wished to negotiate, but Louis was determined to fight: 'I place great hope in the innocence of my arms', he declared: 'My conscience does not reproach me for any lack of piety towards the Queen Mother, nor of justice towards my people, nor of generosity towards the great nobles. So, let us go!'[31] His resolution took his mother's followers by surprise and they quickly came to terms in the Treaty of Angers (10 August 1620). Then, instead of bringing his army back to

1 ABOVE The Place Royale (now the Place des Vosges) in Paris marked a new departure in urban design which was much imitated elsewhere, not least in Covent Garden in London.

2 LEFT James I by Mytens (1621). James was always timorous by nature and, as he disliked sitting still, he hated having his portrait painted. In his later years he also became prone to gloom and depression.

3 LEFT The Earl of Dorset was a leading proponent of 'new counsels' in the 1620s (see pp. 104–5). His costly and elaborate clothes were typical of the early Stuart court, where courtiers sought to outdo one another in conspicuous consumption.

4 OPPOSITE Rubens' sketch of Buckingham captures his striking good looks and intelligence better than more posed and formal portraits.

5 ABOVE In this triple portrait Champaigne gives some indication of Cardinal Richelieu's austere and formidable intellect.

6 OPPOSITE Appropriately painted in armour (by Juste d'Egmont), Louis XIII always preferred the straightforwardness of the camp and the battlefield to the intrigue and artificiality of the Court.

7 LEFT Honthorst's portrait of Charles I was painted in 1628, the year of the Petition of Right and Buckingham's murder. It shows a face less serene, more authoritarian than the later Van Dyck portraits (see jacket illustration).

8 BELOW Started for Anne of Denmark and completed for Henrietta Maria, Inigo Jones' Queen's House at Greenwich, then just outside London, marked a startling departure from traditional English styles of architecture.

9 OPPOSITE The Banqueting House in Whitehall, London, was designed not for banquets but for state occasions and for masques. The ceiling includes Rubens' painting of the apotheosis of James I, but it was also from here that Charles I walked to his execution.

10 ABOVE LEFT  Hollar's satire depicts a composite predator, made up of some of the commodities upon which Charles I granted monopolies.

11 ABOVE RIGHT  Van Dyck's portrait of Strafford in armour shows him as a military figure, a hard man, who never showed scruples about using force to achieve his ends.

Paris, Louis turned south, towards the little Pyrenean province of Béarn, to begin a nine years war against the Huguenots.

After the Edict of Nantes the Huguenots, threatened by a revived and aggressive Catholicism, depended on the military guarantees which accompanied the Edict. These guarantees were strictly temporary, but Marie, lacking the confidence to take on the Huguenots, renewed them in 1611 and 1615. For their part, the Huguenots resisted the blandishments of princely trouble-makers and stressed their loyalty to the crown, begging it to preserve the Edict: as a small minority in a largely hostile nation, they relied heavily on royal protection. Their natural leaders dwindled away. Some Protestant nobles became Catholics, so that Protestant worship ceased in their fiefs; others put their loyalty to the crown before their loyalty to their religion.

The Huguenots' strength in fortified towns like La Rochelle and Montauban and in the hills of the Cévennes made their subjugation a slow process, but that strength was defensive, with townsmen and peasants fighting for survival. Without noble leadership, the Huguenots could no longer take the offensive against the crown. This did not prevent Catholic militants from denouncing their privileges as an affront to royal authority. La Rochelle, especially, with its massive fortifications, seemed a virtual city republic, the epitome of the Protestant 'state within a state'. Moreover, attempts to chip away at their immunities provoked the Huguenots into actions which seemed to confirm the claim that they were politically subversive. The regency repeatedly meddled in the affairs of Huguenot towns and of their triennial assemblies and in 1617 Louis ordered the re-establishment of Catholic worship in Béarn: the hereditary principality of Henry IV was not technically part of France, so was not covered by the Edict. Alarmed by such challenges, the Huguenots began to call assemblies, without the King's permission, to provide for their defence, which only served to reinforce Louis' belief that they were republicans. While some of the Catholic clergy saw the war against the Huguenots as a crusade, Louis insisted that he was punishing rebels: those who submitted were well treated and the religious guarantees of the Edict were not challenged.[32]

Louis' expedition to Béarn was his first taste of real soldiering and he loved it. He met with little resistance and Catholic worship duly resumed, but the risings which now broke out in the Huguenot heartlands of the south and southwest posed far more serious military problems. Besieging well-fortified towns took time. Louis had to call off the siege of Montauban in 1621 and his puny fleet was defeated by that of La Rochelle. By 1622 it was clear that to crush the Huguenots would put a great strain on the fragile royal finances. Moreover, events outside France were taking an ominous turn. Imperial successes in Bohemia and Germany revived the old fears of Habsburg encirclement, not least because the Palatinate was close to France's eastern frontier. Attention focused on the Valtelline.

One of Spain's major problems was to maintain lines of communication between her Italian lands (notably Milan) and the Netherlands. The route through Savoy and Franche Comté passed dangerously close to France and the Dukes of Savoy were unreliable allies. The other route ran through the Valtelline and passed to the east of Switzerland and into southern Germany. Control of the Valtelline was contested between the Catholics of the valley (with support from Milan) and the Protestants of the Swiss canton of the Grisons, who were encouraged by France to revolt, in order to hamper the movement of Spanish troops and supplies : this became more urgent with the renewal, in 1621, of the long war between Spain and the Dutch in the Low Countries. By 1622, therefore, many at Louis' court argued that his first priority was not a war of attrition against the Huguenots, but to check the ominous growth of Habsburg power. Bellicose nobles cried : 'Sire, to the Valtelline !'

Then, in the autumn of 1622, Austrian forces occupied the Valtelline and the King hastily brought the Huguenot war to an end with the treaty of Montpellier. This gave the Huguenots a breathing space, but they were forbidden to hold political assemblies and their military power was greatly reduced : only La Rochelle and Montauban were to keep all their fortifications. The treaty put the Huguenots more than ever on the defensive and left them still less able to offer a serious threat to the crown. The truce in the war with the Huguenots was not followed at once by a foreign war. The crown could not yet afford it and the royal council was divided. The leading figures were the Brûlarts, father and son, Chancellor Sillery and Secretary of State Puisieux. Sillery, the last of the 'greybeards', was nearly eighty and neither he nor his son could offer positive leadership. Louis, on campaign, was greatly irritated by their indecision : 'My God, how annoying these people are ! While I think to spend my time agreeably, they come to torment me and for the most part have nothing important to say.'[33] Another important member of the council was Marie, restored in 1622. Louis was determined to allow her no real power, but she used her position to voice the views of her almoner, Cardinal Richelieu. He had had a first taste of power during the brief ascendancy of Ancre, but his career had suffered a severe setback with the Italian's fall. Now, as he sought to rehabilitate himself, his formidable intellect proved as much a handicap as an asset, for it made the King wary of admitting him to the council.

The years 1622–3 were difficult for Louis. His brief period of marital happiness ended when his wife fell while frolicking with her ladies and miscarried. Furious that his hopes of an heir had been ruined by feminine silliness, Louis ordered the ladies to leave the court, at which his wife was deeply offended. Meanwhile, he faced seemingly intractable problems at home and abroad, on which his ministers gave no clear guidance. He took refuge in hunting and pondered what to do next. At last, early in 1624 he dismissed the Brûlarts : they had, he said, embezzled money and kept him in ignorance. He would now take responsibility for the government and see all dispatches himself. The burden proved too great. There were too many complex details to grasp, too many awkward decisions to make. At last, on 29 April 1624, he bowed to his mother's pressure and summoned Cardinal Richelieu to his council.

# 4
# Decisions

Having persuaded Louis to call Richelieu to the council, Marie expected to wield again the power of which she had been deprived by Ancre's murder. It was not to be. Her son felt little affection for her or respect for her abilities, but she had shown that if excluded from power she could serve as a focus for disaffection. He sought, therefore, to involve her in government while denying her any real influence over policy. Richelieu, for his part, showed an unctuous deference to his benefactress. Even more than Louis, he realized what a dangerous enemy she could be and that her views had to be taken seriously. From 1624 to 1630, therefore, France was ruled by an incongruous trio: Marie, fat, stubborn and not very intelligent, but proud and vindictive; Louis, frail, nervous and lacking in confidence, but determined to do his duty; and the cardinal.

When he became a councillor, Richelieu was in his thirty-ninth year. A member of an old, but not very wealthy, noble family, poor health had ruled out the military career he had sought, so he was installed in what was, in effect, the family bishopric of Luçon, in Poitou. He proved a conscientious bishop and a serious student of theology, but his abilities and ambition could not find fulfilment in a backwoods diocese. During the regency he became Marie's almoner and gave the closing speech for the clergy at the Estates General. A few months in high office ended abruptly with Ancre's fall and it took seven years of patient manoeuvring to regain his place on the council, which he retained for the rest of his life, but not without difficulty, given the ferocious struggles for power at court. Richelieu was intolerant of rivals and implacable towards enemies. He heaped up great riches and used his access to royal patronage to build a large clientele, installing his followers in high office and securing distinguished husbands for his nieces. In this he had much in common with Luynes or Buckingham, but, unlike them, he did not owe his rise to his master's personal favour. Luynes' abilities were mediocre and Buckingham showed his only after achieving a position where he could use them. Richelieu, however, was at first disliked and distrusted by his king; if Louis later expressed real affection for him, he saw him primarily as an exceptional servant of the crown.

For Richelieu *was* exceptional. It was noted that 'there is something in this man which rises above normal humankind'.[1] He combined wide experience with the perception to apply it. The memoranda in which he set out the advantages and disadvantages of any course of action were models of logic and lucidity. His grasp of detail was prodigious, his psychological insight and political acumen were acute. By seeking full information, whether in diplomacy or in court politics, he was able to anticipate and overcome difficulties. His watchfulness and care were signs of an anxious, highly-strung temperament. He lived on his nerves, was quick to foresee problems and in moments of stress he would burst into tears. Like his master's, his health was poor: he suffered from bladder and kidney complaints and piles, exacerbated (like Louis' ailments) by nervous strain. One reason for this was that he was never entirely sure of the King's favour.

The King was moody and mercurial, depending on his state of health: he could be gloomy, lethargic or irritable. Richelieu's enemies at court tried to play on the King's moods; they claimed that the cardinal's creatures monopolized royal patronage, denounced his greed and criticized his policies. Most telling was the allegation that Richelieu acted as if he were King, reducing Louis to a figurehead. In fact, Richelieu knew well Louis' fierce pride in being King and never presumed to dictate to him. Although his advice was often forthright, he presented Louis with reasoned arguments, leaving him to make up his own mind. His memoranda, like those of a modern civil servant to his minister, might be slanted in a certain direction, but they set out the possible options and presupposed that the King had the capacity to make the final decision himself.

Richelieu's relationship with Louis was seldom smooth. Richelieu was suspicious and anxious, Louis was moody, but only in 1642 was there anything like a breach between them. Richelieu carefully placed reliable men in offices close to the King, who put the cardinal's point of view and reported on attempts to undermine him. In fact, Richelieu generally under-estimated the King's attachment to him and his own indispensability. Whereas contemporaries accused the crafty cardinal of usurping power, Louis delegated it deliberately, knowing Richelieu possessed a grasp of detail, a breadth of vision and a capacity for work which he (and other possible ministers) could not match. He knew, too, that Richelieu would use the power vested in him in the best interests of the crown and told him so, with his usual directness:

Everything (thanks be to God) has succeeded well since you have been involved in my affairs. I have confidence in you and have truly never before found anyone who served me as I wish to be served, as you do.... I beg you, do not fear calumnies. No-one can be free of them at my court.... You may be sure that I shall protect you against all and sundry and never abandon you.[2]

There is here none of the cloying sentimentality of James' letters to Buckingham, nor the easy familiarity between Buckingham and Charles: Louis would never have addressed the cardinal by his first name.[3] Richelieu was the King's greatest servant, but a servant none the less: he was not, like Buckingham, addressed as a 'prince'. At times Louis found his dependence on a subject irksome: Richelieu wrote that he wished to be 'governed', yet bore it with impatience. Richelieu was careful, therefore, to maintain a certain deference and distance in their relationship. They had much in common, not least their ill health. Neither had much time for women; Richelieu wrote: 'These are strange animals. One sometimes thinks them incapable of doing much harm, because they can certainly do no good; but I protest on my conscience there is nothing so capable of ruining a State.'[4]

Indeed, many of the cardinal's most intransigent enemies were women (not least Louis' Queen), but the most dangerous were men. Gaston was lively, frivolous and wilful, and totally lacked his brother's sense of duty, or any hint of loyalty or consistency, repeatedly betraying those who involved him in conspiracies. 'I complain that you pay so little heed to the promises which you have made', wrote Louis, 'I complain of your remaining away from me so often. I complain of the disorders and debaucheries of your life.'[5] So long as Louis had no heir, Gaston was the focus of a series of 'reversionary interests', easily drawn into intrigues, casually abandoning his co-conspirators, always protected by his rank from punishment. Louis tried to buy his loyalty, with offices, lands and money, for himself and his favourites, but he never mended his ways and remained a constant source of uncertainty and disruption. There was no danger that Gaston would win Louis over, but others threatened Richelieu because of their influence with the King. The cardinal always feared a new male favourite, like Luynes, but only at the end of the reign did this fear become a reality. Others tried to undermine Richelieu by playing on Louis' piety and his qualms about allying with Protestants against the Habsburgs. Usually his hatred of Spain proved stronger than his reservations, but at moments of crisis he could be seriously worried. One such crisis was to come in 1630.

Despite his deferential air, Richelieu had firm ideas about the way Louis should govern. He told Louis in 1629 that he was too suspicious, jealous and quick-tempered and too ready to let those close to him discuss matters of state. If he could not satisfy the exorbitant demands of Gaston and the magnates, he should at least be outwardly gracious to them. Above all he should work harder and make firm decisions only after the most careful consideration.[6] Richelieu was very aware of the need to control access to the King: 'All cabals take their origin and form in the court', so Louis should send nobles back to their offices in the provinces and the bishops to their dioceses.

Later he appreciated the impracticality of trying to send the rich and powerful away from court, the main locus of power, patronage and the 'beau monde'; the main priority was to bring greater order and decorum to court life. The king should dine with nobles, not with guards and servants, and he should be served by gentlemen. This would bring the nobles closer and provide opportunities for advancement around his person 'where luck and a certain familiarity can bring a fortune in an instant'. He should behave like a king, with his court providing an impressive setting of opulence and grandeur. As it was the court was dirty — the dining areas were often not cleaned after meals — and the furniture in the royal bedchamber was shabby. People wandered the court almost at will: Louis should imitate the court of Charles I, where access was tightly regulated.[7] By the 1630s, Richelieu appreciated that the court could help bring the magnates under the King's eye, instead of making trouble in the provinces; they could also be tied to him by household offices. The court and the royal patronage needed careful management, however, and the King had to serve as a focus for ceremonies and to impose his personality on those around him: not a role which appealed to the timid, stuttering Louis XIII, but one that would be filled superbly by his son.

When Richelieu joined the council, he was not yet Louis' leading minister.

It took some years to oust his enemies and to bring in his friends and protégés, men like Michel de Marillac, as keeper of the seals, and the Marquis d'Effiat, as finance minister. He had dangerous enemies at court. In 1626 a plot to assassinate Richelieu and to put Gaston in Louis' place gave the cardinal some anxious moments, but resulted in his greatly strengthening his position. Most of those involved in the conspiracy suffered nothing worse than imprisonment or exile: only one minor figure, the Marquis de Chalais, was executed, by a stand-in executioner who took twenty-one blows to decapitate him. This would suggest that, as in the 1610s, those nearest in blood to the King could conspire against him (and his ministers) with virtual impunity, but there was one major difference: the conspirators no longer had armies in the provinces. The days of armed noble revolt were not over, but they were numbered. Noble conspiracy, like noble social life, was coming to be concentrated in the court.

Soon after Richelieu became a councillor, Effiat wrote gloomily that France was 'an old state which has suffered all the excesses of a young reign'. The nobles saw their excessive pensions as a normal part of their income. Sovereign courts behaved as if they were indeed sovereign, judges who had bought their offices cared only for money. The crown was robbed while the people were oppressed by tax-collectors and soldiers. Foreigners regarded France with contempt. Expenditure was roughly double the royal revenue, but to reduce it might provoke the nobles to revolt, a theme taken up by Richelieu in 1625. He argued that the magnates would take advantage of any disturbance, but would not risk starting a rebellion themselves. Their power to do harm had to be restricted by suppressing private castles and their aggression should be curbed by a firm prohibition on duelling; if that were done, they might in time be made useful to the state. As for the Huguenots, though they seemed weak, if supported by some foreign power they could pose a serious threat: 'So long as the Huguenots have a foothold in France, the king will never be master at home, nor will he be able to undertake any glorious action abroad.'[8] His words proved prophetic: a Huguenot revolt was soon to force the French to end their intervention in the Valtelline.

The priorities of government in 1624–5 were thus financial reconstruction and to curb or suppress the disruptive forces within France. Only if this were done could Louis contemplate an effective foreign policy. For Richelieu, foreign affairs, the true métier of kings, always took precedence. As Imperial armies swept all before them in Germany and the Spanish gained ground against the Dutch, France was faced with an upsurge of Habsburg power. There was a real prospect that, having defeated their enemies, the Habsburgs would then attack a France paralysed by financial weakness and internal divisions. As yet Richelieu could merely harass Spain's supply lines, as in the Valtelline, while struggling to reorganize the finances and to prepare to meet the Habsburg challenge. In 1625 he produced a wide-ranging reform pro-gramme, based on tighter control of royal patronage and expenditure and the redemption of debts. He called for an end to the slapdash accounting methods and hidden payments of the regency, which had opened the way to frauds of all kinds.

Apart from carefully checking the claims of royal creditors, he made two specific proposals for reducing the King's debts. First, the repurchase of venal offices: officials' salaries were, in effect, interest payments on the money used to buy their places. Buying them back would reduce the King's expenditure and free taxpayers of the multifarious additional exactions to which the officials subjected them. Second, he proposed to redeem the royal *domaine*. The crown had sold off many of its lands and its lucrative feudal and judicial rights, but, because such sales were technically illegal, it always reserved the right to repurchase them. In France, as in England, many still believed that the king should subsist from his own resources, or 'live of his own', even though he had collected the *taille* for nearly two centuries. If the crown could buy back alienated lands and domanial rights, it would reduce the burden on the poor, partly because it would need less from taxation, partly because many who purchased such rights exploited them ruthlessly.[9]

These reforms might strengthen the crown's financial position and relieve the taxpayer, but they would harm the interests of many powerful people. Nobles would lose their pensions, officials and purchasers of domanial rights their opportunities for profit; crown creditors might find debts written off and interest reduced. As in England, France's fiscal system served a dual purpose: to bring in revenue and to provide rewards for members of the ruling élite. With France's administration swollen by venality and royal taxes collected, at a profit, by private individuals, far more people made far more money out of the royal finances in France than in England. In England, with the exception of wardship, there were few opportunities for members of the ruling élite to profit from the collection of the King's revenue. Subsidies were collected by unpaid commissioners appointed by Parliament, with money straggling in as and when taxpayers paid up. In France, by contrast, receivers of the *taille*, who gathered sums brought in by local collectors, advanced the money due to the King in monthly instalments. At first, they had to borrow from others or advance their own money, for which they were reimbursed. Once the money started to flow in, however, the receivers often lent it for short periods at interest before forwarding it to the treasury. The fact that they made fifteen monthly payments for each year's *taille* made accounting very complex.

Royal finance ministers faced two basic problems: getting hold of a substantial part of a limited national stock of gold and silver (the use of paper money was in its infancy) and making the cash come in fast enough. Moving money around posed serious logistical problems: one million livres amounted to about nine tons of silver coin. To keep the bullion flowing into the royal treasury, the crown looked to private enterprise. Financiers contracted to collect the *taille* (and its arrears), to farm the indirect taxes and to sell new offices. Most contractors were royal officials, for whom such contracts were part of the profits of office. From the King's point of view, such arrangements ensured a substantial advance, regular payments and the prospect of further loans from the contractors. Tax farming was also used in England, mainly for the customs, and the King sought loans from customs farmers and other London merchants; in France, the whole royal revenue and credit system depended on officials and tax farmers, rarely on bankers or merchants. To meet the crown's needs, both English customs farmers and French revenue officials had to borrow from others. In France, these investors in the revenue often preferred to keep their identities secret: the greatest families in the land would not like it to be known that they invested in anything as sordid as revenue contracts. As for the financiers, so often denounced as jumped-up lackeys, most came from those official and noble milieux where so many had capital to invest.[10]

This combination of widespread venality and massive investment by the rich and powerful meant that drastic reform of the fiscal system was impossible: too many vested interests would be affected. Thus the chamber of justice of 1625 proceeded hesitantly: it raised over ten million livres in fines, but often accepted a payment for dropping proceedings and was careful not to squeeze the financiers too hard, for fear of ruining the crown's credit.[11] A similar hesitancy was apparent in the programme put before the Assembly of Notables of 1626–7. Aware of its weakness, the crown sought some form of consent to its proposals. The members of the Assembly were nominated by the crown from among the élite groups in society: ten bishops, ten nobles and leading members of the sovereign courts, which would have to register and enforce any legislation that emerged.

Richelieu and his colleagues gave the Assembly a frank account of the crown's financial problems and made numerous proposals. Not all were financial: they included admitting some nobles to the council (to accustom them to administration) and using special tribunals to punish the misdeeds of the powerful. The financial proposals made no mention of venality, but included a call to buy back the *domaine*, to reduce pensions and to control expenditure more rigorously. It was suggested that each province should be responsible for maintaining part of the army: at present, Richelieu noted, soldiers were often left unpaid, which had a dire effect on discipline. The provinces would have a vested interest in ensuring that soldiers were promptly paid and so would have no need to prey upon civilians. The money, he suggested, would be handled by royal officials under the supervision of local representatives.[12]

These proposals were intended not only to resuscitate the royal finances, but also to relieve the people from the crushing burden of taxation and the oppressions of soldiers and overmighty subjects. The Assembly responded with the usual ritual denunciations of financiers and maladministration and called for a cut in pensions and secret expenditure. It welcomed the proposals to redeem the *domaine* and to build more ships, but did little to provide money for either. It agreed to decentralize payment of the army — provided two-thirds of the money came from the royal treasury. As in the Estates General, the orders pursued their own interests and feuds. The nobles demanded one third of the places on the council and restrictions on venality. The officials claimed that the sovereign courts should have the power to register the contracts for tax farms, amend royal edicts and control municipal elections.[13] With its hopes of structural reform thwarted, the crown was thrown back on a general tightening up of administration and accounting.

Retrenchment and reduction of borrowing produced a balanced budget and a modest surplus, but to sustain even this limited achievement it was vital that France should remain at peace.

Thus Richelieu's first attempts at reform bore little fruit. Some proposals were naïve and impractical: he was never a financial expert, but a specialist in diplomacy who (like Buckingham) expected money to be found from somewhere. He later abandoned the idea of decentralizing the payment of the army, having become convinced that most towns and provinces were not competent to manage their own affairs. It was naïve to expect the Assembly to agree to raise the vast sums needed to repurchase the *domaine* within six years, while many influential people found domanial rights a profitable investment. Richelieu did not dare to raise the question of venality and while he asked the Assembly to consider how to stop undue claims to exemption from the *taille*, he did not expect that much could be done.[14]

While the crown could get away with offending particular groups and could claw back money from individuals, it did not dare to take on the whole of the privileged orders, upon whose co-operation the government depended. No regime could subsist without the consent, overt or tacit, of the 'political nation', those whose support really mattered. These might include nobles and officials, as in France, or peers and gentlemen, as in England (plus, in each case, some lawyers, churchmen and urban plutocrats). The consent might be expressed through formal representative institutions, or it might not. Either way, if the King violated accepted norms of behaviour, if his conduct seemed tyrannical or seriously threatened his subjects' material interests, he would provoke discontent and even open resistance. One could argue, therefore, that radical financial reform was politically impossible in France in the late 1620s, a consideration to be borne in mind when considering the great debate about the priorities of policy: war abroad or reform at home?[15]

In Richelieu's eyes, Spain's insatiable ambition posed a constant threat to France, so it was vital to check the growth of Spanish power, even if that meant allying with Protestant states. The militant Catholics at court (*dévots*) argued that the first priority was to crush Protestantism at home and so restore unity of religion. They claimed that to join with heretics was morally wrong and that a major foreign war would impose an intolerable fiscal burden on the people. Richelieu thought such arguments simplistic. Not all the Habsburgs' enemies were Protestants: Italian states (like Venice) and German Catholic princes became alarmed at the growth of Imperial power. He agreed, however, that Louis could never be free to intervene abroad while the Huguenots retained their military power. This became clear in 1625, when a revolt by the leading Huguenot nobles, Rohan and Soubise, placed in jeopardy the government's plans for military intervention in the Valtelline. Richelieu quickly negotiated a treaty with the rebels, on much the same terms as those agreed at Montpellier. To the *dévots*, such a pusillanimous peace cast doubts on the sincerity of Richelieu's Catholicism, but he hesitated to mount the all-out war against heresy which they demanded.

The decision was taken out of his hands by Buckingham. Piqued that Charles' French marriage had not led to a close alliance, and fearful that France would join with Spain against England, he mounted an expedition to La Rochelle. This, he hoped, would spark off a Huguenot revolt and bring about the fall of Richelieu, whom Buckingham blamed for Louis' coolness towards England. If Buckingham's reading of French politics was defective, his generalship was little better. Having landed on the Ile de Ré, he failed either to take the citadel of La Rochelle or to safeguard his retreat and withdrew with heavy losses. Blockaded by sea and by land by Louis, La Rochelle at last surrendered and on 29 October 1628 Louis entered in triumph. Its walls were razed, its privileges were abolished and a Catholic bishop was installed. The most formidable Huguenot stronghold and the greatest of France's 'city republics' had fallen. Meanwhile, Condé (who had long since been reconciled with the King) ravaged the Huguenot towns of the south with fire and sword.

Early in 1629 Louis himself entered Languedoc. The small town of Privas was sacked for refusing to surrender: the message was clear — submit or expect a similar fate. As the cornfields blazed around the major Protestant centres, Louis spelt out his demands in the Grace of Alais (now spelt Alès). Towns which surrendered would be left in peace, those which did not would receive a royal garrison and their environs would be laid waste. This was not a treaty — the Huguenots were in no position to make stipulations — but a favour to a defeated enemy. Towns rushed to surrender; their fortifications were razed. Rohan, the last great Huguenot warlord, was given a command in Italy. The Huguenots were still to enjoy the religious privileges granted in the Edict of Nantes, but, having lost their military power, they were to be totally dependent on the King's goodwill.[16]

Louis' first intervention in Italy, in the Valtelline, achieved little, but he was soon given another opportunity closer to home. Late in 1627 the Duke of Mantua died. His duchy was of limited strategic importance, but he also ruled Montferrat, between Milan (ruled by Spain) and the independent Duchy of Savoy; Montferrat straddled Alpine passes vital to Spain's communications. As the next heir was French, the Duc de Nevers, Louis supported his claim, while Spain put forward a rival claimant and besieged the chief town, Casale. During 1628 Louis was preoccupied with La Rochelle, but in December, after a heated debate, the council agreed that he should march to relieve Casale and then finish off Huguenot resistance in Languedoc. Persuaded by the Spanish ambassador that any intervention in Italy must lead to a full-scale war with Spain, the *dévots* bitterly opposed this decision. Marie was furious that Richelieu's views had prevailed: 'I am reduced to nothing,' she complained, 'Monsieur le Cardinal is all-powerful.'[17]

Despite the *dévots'* gloomy prognostications, the campaign of 1629 went according to plan. Casale was relieved, the Huguenots were defeated and Louis returned to Paris safe and sound. After another lengthy debate, the council resolved to resume the war in Italy in the spring and on 29 March 1630 Richelieu's army captured the vital fortress of Pinerolo, near Turin. As Richelieu pointed out, Pinerolo could serve as a secure base beyond the mountains which would give France access to the Po valley and enable Louis to become the 'arbiter and master' of Italy. Properly fortified, it would be impregnable, but to keep it would require a long war and a massive financial commitment. 'If the king resolves upon war', he wrote, 'we must give over all hope of ease, of retrenchment and of reform within the kingdom. If, on the other hand, he wants peace, we must abandon any thought of Italy for the future.'[18]

The capture of Pinerolo thus brought to a head the conflict between the proponents of the two policies, war abroad and reform at home. So far the war effort had been limited and defensive, in the sense that Louis was protecting the inheritance of a French subject. Louis had probably decided to continue the war even before he read Richelieu's memorandum, but in the following months Richelieu's opponents did their utmost to change the King's mind. They were led by Marie and by Marillac, Richelieu's erstwhile ally, whose devout Catholicism led him to denounce the cardinal's policies. War, argued Marillac, forced the crown to use immoral and unpopular fiscal methods, which could lead to revolts which could prove very dangerous if the King was out of the country.[19] Richelieu agreed that war brought 'inconveniences', 'being one of the scourges by which God is pleased to afflict mankind'. This did not mean that Louis should make peace on shameful terms. 'The people's aversion to war is not a very considerable argument for such a peace, seeing ... that they are as incapable of appreciating what is useful to a state as they are aware and ready to complain of evils, which must be suffered in order to avoid greater ones.'[20]

Marillac's talk of 'the misery of the people' may have made little impression on Richelieu, who later compared them to mules, used to burdens, who could be spoiled by too much ease.[21] The King had more sympathy for his subjects and such arguments troubled his conscience; Richelieu's opponents also played on his unease at fighting fellow Catholics. While the war went well, Louis' commitment was unlikely to waver, but after his troops had secured most of Savoy things began to go wrong. Louis fell ill and had to return to Lyons. Richelieu's enemies blamed him for endangering the King's life, by leading him into inhospitable climes. An Austrian army, marching from Milan, overran Mantua and the French agreed to a truce in Savoy. Could it be that Marillac was right, that Richelieu's war policy was too ambitious? Was God punishing the French for their aggression, presumption and impiety? Such conjectures were given added credence when Louis fell desperately ill on 22 September. The sacrament was exposed and he was sure he would die. So was Marillac, who drew up a list of ministers who were to take power after Richelieu's fall. Then, on the 30th, an abcess in Louis' intestine burst and he began to recover. By 19 October he was well enough to leave Lyons for Paris.

Throughout his illness, those close to him had stressed that it was God's punishment for his war policy. Weak and vulnerable as he was, such arguments made a great impression. When his mother demanded that he choose between Richelieu and herself, he said he would do so when he returned to Paris; he may also have promised his confessor to dismiss the cardinal if he survived. Well aware of the machinations against him, Richelieu followed the King to Paris with a heart filled with foreboding. On 10 November Marie at last made her feelings towards him clear: he was an ungrateful wretch; he and his family were to have nothing more to do with her affairs. Next day the cardinal came, at Louis' command, to take his leave of the Queen Mother at the Luxembourg Palace. Marie did not want to see him and had the doors locked, but Richelieu managed to enter through the chapel. He found Louis ashen and silent, while his mother, red-faced, screamed that he preferred a mere menial to his mother. Richelieu threw himself on his knees, kissed the hem of her dress and burst into tears. As he had lost her protection, he sobbed, he could only ask the King's permission to resign. She replied that if the cardinal did not go, she would. Louis told Richelieu to withdraw and, moments later, left the palace.

Marie exulted, convinced that she had won. Well-wishers flocked to the Luxembourg and her cronies reallocated the offices of Richelieu's supporters. As for the cardinal, his nerve was shattered and he thought only of flight, but Louis had no intention of abandoning him. He had been upset by his mother's histrionics — he was said to be so angry that his buttons popped — but they could not change his mind. He left for his hunting lodge at Versailles, where his ministers never came, sent to Richelieu to follow him and summoned Marillac to a small village near the château. Marillac understood: he burned his papers and was at mass when Louis' emissary arrived to demand his seals of office; he was subsequently imprisoned. Richelieu, overwrought, was reluctantly persuaded to go to the King. He again offered to quit, but Louis would not hear of it: loyalty to the State came before his personal feelings, he said, although if Richelieu had not shown proper respect for his mother, he would have dismissed him.

That night he sent to tell his mother of his decision to retain Richelieu. At the Luxembourg, joy turned to despair. Those who had come to pay their court mumbled their excuses and left. As one bystander remarked: 'This is the day of dupes.'[22] Marie's hopes of controlling the government had gone. She refused to attend the council if Richelieu was present and demanded that Marillac be released. When Louis tried to isolate her from evil influences, she complained loudly that she was a prisoner and fled to the Spanish Netherlands. She never returned to France, remaining a focus for plots against her son. In 1637 her court numbered some six hundred persons and when she died she left eight million livres, which showed how efficiently she had plundered the crown's revenues. As for Louis, he had made his choice: 'Stay with me', he told Richelieu, 'and I shall protect you against your enemies.'[23]

After the Day of Dupes, it was clear that war would take priority over reform. Historians have tended to see this decision as inevitable and right: national survival had to come first. It is easy to be mesmerized by Richelieu's genius and to see everything through his eyes, not least because his papers provide most of the surviving evidence, but he was not infallible. He probably underestimated the difficulty of conquering Savoy; he certainly underestimated the cost.[24] His attitude to questions of money was always somewhat cavalier and by 1630 he was showing little interest in domestic affairs. He argued that the King had to choose between the interests of France and 'a shameful peace' — in effect, there was no choice. Against this, Marillac argued that Richelieu's policy was militarily over-ambitious and that the cost, in human suffering at home, was too high. But did Marillac have an alternative to offer, other than careful financial management? It is possible.

In 1629 the King announced the establishment of *élus* in Languedoc, Burgundy and Provence, all of which had provincial estates far more formidable than the petty assemblies which Henry IV had suppressed in Guyenne. The motives behind this move are uncertain. Claims that the estates imposed an excessive burden on the people had little foundation: they collected taxes more cheaply and efficiently than *élus*. There are three more plausible possibilities. First, by suppressing the estates the King would be able to increase taxes without having to bargain with recalcitrant assemblies: it was widely believed that the provinces with estates were grossly undertaxed. Second, the offices of *élus* were to be sold — for around four million livres in Languedoc. Their creation might, therefore, be just another fiscal device or *affaire extraordinaire*, a way of raising ready cash at the cost of increasing future expenditure. A third possibility is that the motive was not fiscal but political: to break the tradition of local self-government and to bring all France under effective royal control.[25]

It is uncertain who was the moving spirit behind the introduction of *élus*. It could have been Marillac, who had a passion for uniformity and order; it could have been Effiat, desperate for money; some claimed it was Richelieu. As Marillac's papers, which may have contained the answer, do not survive,

one must consider the situation in 1629–30. The war against the Huguenots
had been expensive : the siege of La Rochelle cost forty million livres, not far
short of an average year's revenue. These were years of bad harvests and
soaring food prices. Peasants spent all they had on avoiding starvation, so
the yield of the *taille* fell. Ministers thus faced the problem of raising more
money without provoking the revolts of which Marillac warned. To introduce *élus* into three independently minded frontier provinces was bound to
be contentious, but the crown pressed ahead because (I think) the financial
rewards for doing so were very large : either the offices would be sold, or
the provinces would pay heavily to have the *élus* withdrawn. In January 1630
Marillac wrote that Louis had rejected an offer from Burgundy of 1,800,000
livres, saying that 'the uniformity which the King desires to establish in his
kingdom' would not allow him to accept it. This suggests that Marillac, and
perhaps Louis, saw this as a move towards greater centralization ; it could
also be that they hoped the province would offer more. In the event, there
were revolts in all three provinces and, after Marillac's fall, all three secured
the withdrawal of the *élus*, at a price.[26]

It is possible, then, that the introduction of *élus* meant different things to
different ministers, but it is improbable that Marillac's fall prevented a wide-
ranging programme of centralization. The obstacles to effective royal power
were too intractable to be swept away. With determination the crown might
have suppressed the provincial estates, but that would not have solved its
financial problems. As Louis XIV was to show, the king could extend his
control only by coming to terms with existing institutions and vested
interests, not by trying to overthrow them. Ironically, although Marillac's
fall seemed to mark a retreat from centralization, the following decades saw
an extension of central control into the provinces. This control was far from
complete and was the product not of the centralizing policies ascribed to
Marillac but of the crown's attempts to wrestle with the practical problem
of raising men and money for war. The war which Marillac saw as a
distraction from reform led, slowly and painfully, to the strengthening of the
French monarchy.

\*    \*    \*

When Charles I entered London as King in March 1625 it was raining. It
was noted that the weather :

was suitable to the condition wherein he find the kingdom, which is cloudy; for he is left engaged in a war with a potent prince, the people by long desuetude unapt for arms, the fleet royal in quarter repair, himself without a queen, his sister without a country, the crown pitifully laden with debts....[27]

To this might have been added ominous signs of mistrust between ruler and ruled. Some subjects feared for their liberty and religion, while Charles saw 'popularity' and Puritanism as threatening the monarchy. It was necessary to re-establish a working partnership between king and people; how well fitted for this task was the new monarch?

Charles I was not a strong or confident character. He disliked difficult decisions and preferred to be presented with straightforward choices. He saw everything in terms of black and white, good and evil: he who was not with him was against him. He found communication difficult: he was shy, stammered and did not think quickly. Fearful of being worsted in an argument, he would either delay his answer, to gain time to collect his thoughts, or fall back on his authority and demand to be obeyed. He inherited James' high sense of kingly authority without his quick mind and facility in debate. Nor did he have Louis XIII's dogged sense of duty. While prepared to devote some time to administration, he often became bogged down in trivia and usually referred matters to the appropriate minister or body, and endorsed their decisions. Faced with difficult problems, he vacillated. When he asserted himself, he did so not as a strong king, confident of his abilities and of his subjects' respect, but as a weak man, invoking his authority to compensate for his own insufficiency. He was, therefore, ill-equipped to operate a political system based on trust, dialogue and co-operation.

His father had been bombastic, vain and hasty, but his basic shrewdness and canny caution (or cowardice) led him to avoid lasting confrontations. Charles, less able and less subtle, was uninterested in, and unable to understand, viewpoints which differed from his own. Increasingly convinced that his legitimate authority was under attack, he came to depend on his prerogatives, as he understood them. By insisting on taking responsibility for his servants' actions, he made his own powers and actions the focus of controversy. Infuriated by Parliament's refusal to pay for a war which, in his eyes, it had demanded, he decided to provide for the war without Parliament, if he had to. Convinced of the purity of his own motives, he saw criticism as malicious or seditious. The more vehement the criticism became, the more heavily Charles rested on his prerogatives.

If ever a king was fitted by character to provoke confrontation, it was Charles I. He combined an uncritical faith in his own righteousness with a habit of behaving in ways which others saw as dishonest. His dismissal of Lord Justice Crew for refusing to declare that a forced loan was legal was widely seen as an example of political pressure on the judges; to Charles, convinced that the forced loan was legal, Crew's conduct showed that the infection of 'popularity' had affected even the judiciary. Charles had a great respect for the law, but never understood that its letter could differ from its spirit: something could be technically legal but still appear unjust. It seemed doubly unjust if he put pressure on the judges or if they chose, where the King's discretion was concerned, to give him the benefit of the doubt.[28]

The first years of his reign saw an escalation of mutual suspicion: Charles extended his authority, his subjects protested, so Charles extended his authority further; his distrust widened, as he came to see opposition as the work, not just of a few troublemakers, but of the greater part of the nation, a view confirmed by the general rejoicing at Buckingham's death. As he came to believe that the onus was on his people to show their loyalty, so the circle of those he thought 'reliable' narrowed. As the divisions in the Church became more bitter, so the Arminians', and the King's, definition of 'Puritan' widened and he came to equate Puritanism with political opposition: only the Arminians — and the Catholics — could be trusted. The King's hardening of attitude provoked a similar hardening among his critics. Fearful of Popery and absolutism, their complaints became more strident and their demands more extreme. A few questioned the very basis of the constitution. Many more hoped that Charles would see the light if only he were better advised and then things could be as they were before.

Charles did not set out to create 'absolute monarchy' in England. When a paper was found urging him to set up a standing army, financed by arbitrary taxation, he was horrified: such a system, he said, was fitter for Turkey than a Christian country. He believed in the existing law and constitution — as he understood them. He said he would always comply with the judges' opinion, when they did not speak in riddles.[29] His prerogatives were, he believed, given him by the law to act in emergencies, suppress sedition and defend the realm. In the late 1620s he believed England was threatened with Spanish or French invasion; he was perplexed and angered by his subjects' indifference to this threat and their complaints about the measures he took to protect them; many saw in the King's soldiers a more immediate danger than Spaniards who never materialized. The eventual outcome of this growth of distrust was that Charles turned his back on the tradition of government by consent, as epitomized by Parliament. In England, as in France, the later 1620s was a time of decision. In France the commitment to war meant a retreat from reform at home. In England, the strains of war helped bring about a political breakdown, while the end of war allowed Charles to dispense with Parliament — perhaps permanently.

For much of this period Charles' government was dominated by Buckingham: no matter how disastrous the Duke's policies might appear Charles' faith in him never wavered. No longer a mere royal plaything, he was now a figure of European stature, addressed by petitioners as 'most illustrious and renowned prince', while Charles treated him as an equal or even a superior. When Buckingham entered a playhouse, the play was restarted, even though Charles had been there from the beginning.[30] Some suspected that Buckingham's sway over the King was sustained by magic; in fact, Charles was simply very fond of his George, not in an overtly homo-sexual sense, but as a shy person often admires a stronger personality. Unlike his father, Charles was not capable of grasping the subtleties and intricacies of diplomacy or administration, but Buckingham was. He was sometimes reckless and slapdash, but he was intelligent and decisive and worked hard: sometimes his nerves and health collapsed under the strain. Charles followed admiringly in his wake, endorsing his decisions and backing them with his authority. His disillusionment with Parliament paralleled, and in some ways anticipated, that of his favourite. As MPs became more critical of Buckingham, the Duke laid greater stress on his followers' loyalty to himself. Where once his patronage had embraced a wide range of viewpoints, it became restricted to his wholehearted supporters, many of them Arminians and Catholics. Like the King, he became more suspicious and demanding as time went on.

When considering the attitude of Charles' subjects, it is pertinent to ask what proportion of them took an active interest in public affairs. Active participation in local government, above the parish level, and membership of

Parliament were confined to a small, wealthy, leisured élite, but interest in politics was more widespread. In France, Richelieu used the press in an effort to win public support for his foreign policy. In England, the government tried to censor the press, but handwritten newsletters circulated widely. Ministers, aware of this public interest, sometimes 'leaked' details of council meetings : it was reported that Charles said he 'did abominate' the name of Parliament. As the government raised money and men for the war, its impact on the localities became heavier and more intrusive. Complaints multiplied and the growing volume of complaint and of political information came to be reflected in Parliament. Candidates became more sensitive to the wishes of the electorate and the conduct of MPs was influenced by the need to justify themselves to their constituents.[31]

MPs were not, however, simply mouthpieces of the people. Most held local offices, granted by the King, upon which their standing and power partly depended. To enhance their position, locally or nationally, they needed the favour of the King, or a powerful councillor or courtier. Most MPs were thus in an ambivalent position, both governors and governed, servants of the crown and representatives of the people. Often, it was possible to reconcile the two roles, to serve both crown and locality, but in the 1590s and 1620s the crown's demands were so deeply resented in the localities that they had to choose between the two. Most took up their constituents' grievances, not just because they feared for their seats, but because they shared the same sense of anxiety and outrage.[32]

Given the nature of the Commons, it was most unlikely that MPs were trying (as Charles feared) to seize power from him. Few wanted power at a national level and those who did sought it in the king's service. They wanted, not a change in the constitutional balance of power, but changes of men and measures. This was a conservative age. Agricultural societies are usually dominated by tradition. English law, with its stress on precedent, led men to seek guidance in the past (although they might misinterpret what they found). Few had any conception of the possibility of progress. Little ever changed, man remained at the mercy of his environment. Preachers explained disease and harvest failure as God's punishments for human wickedness. Mankind was hopelessly flawed, life was a painful pilgrimage, perfection and happiness could be found only in the next world. Such a pessimistic view of human potential made it difficult to develop confidence in the possibility of human progress. History was seen in cyclical terms, with the same situations recurring. In so far as a pattern of development could be seen, it was provided by the prophecies of the Bible. History showed God's purposes being fulfilled over the centuries: many believed that His plan was nearing completion. While such a view could stimulate a call for moral and spiritual reform, to make all ready for the Second Coming, it was not conducive to secular, human progress: change was to be brought about by God, not by man.

Charles' fears that MPs were seeking change were thus largely unfounded: but not entirely. The Commons extended their investigative role, revived impeachment and criticized the King's ministers more bluntly than their predecessors had done. They refused to grant Charles tonnage and poundage at his accession, though such a grant had become virtually automatic by the sixteenth century (see p. 33). They criticized some of the judges' rulings, implying that they, not the judges, should interpret the law. They sent a sheriff of London to the Tower for 'unsatisfactory' answers to their questions. Yet if the Commons behaved in many respects more aggressively than their Tudor forebears, their aggression owed less to a desire for change than to anger and anxiety, provoked by the measures used to sustain the war and by the rise of Arminianism.

Charles began his reign convinced that Parliament had called for the war and so was morally obliged to support it. This was not really true. The Commons had been persuaded to endorse a war against Spain, but assumed that this would be a cheap maritime war and wanted success: Parliaments never liked paying for failure. Buckingham hoped that a striking victory would sweep MPs off their feet, in a fervour of patriotism and admiration. Instead, MPs heard first of Mansfeld's army wasting away in Holland and then of the Cadiz fiasco of 1625. Raiding a Spanish port had a respectable pedigree — Drake had done it — but this raid was a disaster: the soldiers discovered the main Spanish naval winestore and soon were too drunk to fight anyone, except perhaps each other. On the way home they suffered the usual privations of seafaring life: bad food, rotten beer and disease. Worse was to follow, in Buckingham's expedition to Ré in 1627. Although he behaved with great courage, he made serious errors and it was a sorry army that staggered ashore, half-naked, sick and starving. The expedition was seen as 'the greatest and shamefullest overthrow the English have received since we lost Normandy'.[33] Unabashed, Buckingham blamed his failure on the lack of supplies from home and was preparing another expedition when he was killed in 1628.

Thus to Charles' claim that the Commons should support the war, they could reply that it was not their war and that it was being grossly mismanaged. Foreign issues, however, took second place to domestic ones: as one MP said: 'I more fear the violation of public rights at home than a foreign enemy.'[34] In 1625 most MPs did not want Parliament to meet, as plague raged in London. The Commons granted tonnage and poundage for one year only, pending the resolution of the thorny question of impositions, and irritated Charles by criticizing his foreign policy and stressing the need for 'grave counsellors'. When a new Parliament met in 1626, the confrontation became open. Buckingham was impeached and Charles and his ministers threatened to do without Parliament. Charles told the Earl of Totnes, interrogated by the Commons, 'it is not you they aim at, but it is me upon whom they make inquisition'.[35] He told the Commons:

Now ... that I am so far engaged that you think there is no retreat, now you begin to set the dice and make your own game; ... it is not a Parliamentary way, nor is it a way to deal with a king.... Remember that Parliaments are altogether in my power for their calling, sitting or dissolution; therefore, as I find the fruits of them good or evil, they are to continue, or not to be.

The threat was made even more explicit by Secretary Carleton, who urged MPs not to bring Charles 'out of love with Parliaments' by 'trenching upon his prerogatives', for that would force him into 'new counsels'.

In all Christian kingdoms, you know that Parliaments were in use anciently ... until the monarchs began to know their own strength and, seeing the turbulent spirits of their Parliaments, at length they ... began to stand upon their prerogatives and at last overthrew the Parliaments throughout Christendom, except here only with us.

He begged them to consider the misery of the subjects of absolute rulers, taxed beyond endurance until they were mere skin and bone.[36]

Such threats did not cow the Commons. Some claimed that Charles was not fully aware of the charges against Buckingham, or that he was mesmerized by the Duke, but Charles insisted on taking responsibility for Buckingham's policies and brought his impeachment to an end by dissolving Parliament. Soon afterwards, he asked a French cleric, the Bishop of Mende, how the French kings had rid themselves of Parliaments. The bishop replied that they had done it when they had plenty of money, which was not the case at present.[37] A circular was sent to the JPs of each county to assemble the people and tell them that Parliament would have granted four subsidies, but for the disorderly conduct of a few members. His 'loving subjects' were then to be asked to give Charles a similar amount. In many counties the request was met with cries of 'a Parliament, a Parliament!'. Little money came in and the council debated what to do next.[38]

Although Charles was disillusioned with Parliaments, he was not confident or forceful enough to impose his will on the council, which was deeply divided. Some said that he must rely on his prerogative. The Earl of Dorset claimed that his subjects had forced him to use violent methods: 'War must be maintained with the property of the subject, all being bound to contribute, when it is just, and if in the last Parliament the people had agreed to the promised contributions, they would have paid much less than the King will eventually compel them to disburse.' He added that as there were no fortresses in England, there was no danger of rebellion.[39] Here were 'new counsels' of the sort threatened by Carleton; indeed, official documents often talked of 'necessity' and of the people's duty to provide for the nation's defence.[40] To such secular arguments were added those of the Arminian clergy, who declared that disobedience to the royal will was an affront to God and that subjects were obliged to give their property to assist the government.[41]

Such views did not go unchallenged in the council. Some argued that the people were loyal, that 'new counsels' would be dangerous and ineffective and that co-operation with Parliament was both the proper and the easiest way to raise money. Sir Thomas Edmondes said that he had 'learnt by what has passed at this board that it is dangerous to put any of these things in practice, without either the consent of a Parliament or the hope of gaining the conformity and submission of the people thereunto'.[42] From the summer of 1626 until the spring of 1628, proponents of the rival viewpoints were locked in combat. When Charles demanded a forced loan, there were arguments about how best to extract money from recalcitrant lenders. The hardliners urged that refusers should be imprisoned, have troops billeted on them or even be pressed for foreign service; the moderates relied on persuasion. Much of what was raised went to repay money already advanced by the localities for the war and some councillors promised that there would be no more forced loans. Even so, many refused to lend, arguing that only Parliament could grant money.[43]

In purely financial terms the forced loan was a success, but not one that could easily be repeated. Meanwhile, the Ré expedition exacerbated the crown's financial plight. Buckingham raged at the lack of ready cash, but few felt impelled to bestir themselves or to secure the best possible value for money. 'What should I trouble myself to husband his majesty's money?' asked Viscount Wimbledon. 'More men prosper with spending and getting the King's money than saving it ... and he is the wisest that getteth his part.'[44] The privy council struggled manfully under an impossible workload, while the King did little but complain. When Buckingham blamed the Ré débâcle on lack of supplies from England, Charles alone believed him: he may have felt guilty at having diverted some £15,000 to buy the Duke of Mantua's collection of paintings. Throughout the winter of 1627–8 a struggle raged within the council about calling Parliament. There was talk of a debasement, of another forced loan, of an excise. Charles repeatedly changed his mind as to when (or whether) Parliament should meet and whether to demand a payment from the counties first. His indecision made it clear that he was neither enthusiastic nor optimistic about calling it and it was rumoured that if it did not vote money at once he would dissolve it.[45]

MPs came up to London with more on their minds than forced loans and rumours of excises. Many were concerned at the King's open support for Arminianism. William Laud, an Arminian and a leading hardliner on the council, was made Bishop of Bath and Wells; Neile was promoted first to Durham, then to Winchester. Abbot, meanwhile, was disgraced for refusing to license a sermon which argued that the subject's property should be at the King's disposal. Another divine declared that MPs were 'wedded overmuch to the love of epidemical and popular errors'. While Charles favoured those whom more evangelical Protestants regarded as 'Papists', he tried to silence any challenge to their views by a declaration against 'controversial' preaching. Meanwhile, he seemed ominously friendly towards Catholics, allowing them to compound for the fines to which they were liable for absence from church. Buckingham was believed to be strongly influenced by the Catholics around him, including his wife and mother. For the first time since Elizabeth's reign, leading Catholics began to participate in county government, while Charles' French Queen flaunted her Catholicism. Clearly, Arminianism and Popery were thriving and in high favour at court.[46]

Still more ominous was the activity of the military. There had already been complaints from the areas where soldiers had been billeted before the Cadiz and Ré expeditions, but these reached a crescendo in the winter of 1627–8. The soldiers who returned from Ré were unpaid and unruly. Respectable householders had no wish to receive them in their homes and JPs doubted if they could legally be made to do so. As the soldiers had no money to pay for their keep in inns, their officers became impatient. One threatened to cut off the head of a denizen of Amersham who refused to have a soldier billeted on him; a local JP had the officer arrested, but he was rescued by a gang of soldiers. In some places, friction between soldiers and civilians was exacerbated by the fact that some soldiers were Catholics or Irish: at Witham this gave rise to a major riot. Behind the complaints of indiscipline lay the deeper question of why the soldiers were being kept on foot. The answer was simple: the King had no money to pay them off; but many feared he planned to create a standing army. The council had discussed the possibility of setting up such a force and had sent to Germany to raise a thousand horse.

In February 1628 the King held a great muster of troops and militia on Hounslow Heath, which many saw as an implied threat to the Parliament. Anxiety and alarums continued when Parliament met. When the Lord Mayor and aldermen of London refused a loan, Buckingham threatened to billet soldiers on the City; the Lord Mayor replied that to do so would lead to bloodshed. Although Charles countermanded the order to raise soldiers in Germany, and assured the Commons that he had never intended to bring them to England, MPs remained anxious. After Parliament had been prorogued, it was reported that Charles had ordered that all the arms and powder in the City should be taken to the Tower, that the same was to happen in the counties and that strange 'engines and fireworks' were being prepared at Tower Wharf. Small wonder that some said Charles was preparing to make war on his people.[47]

Throughout the lifetime of the 1628 Parliament, there were fears that Charles might resort to force; his own conduct gave credence to these fears and he may have harboured such intentions. MPs feared that they would be murdered in their beds, their homes ransacked and burned and their wives and daughters raped by soldiers, many of them Papists or foreigners. Their only hope was that Charles could be deflected from the path into which he was being led by evil advisers. When it seemed that Charles might be reclaimed, they were jubilant. When their hopes were dashed, they were distraught: in one extraordinary debate the whole of the Commons were in floods of tears. Although many debates dealt with grievances of the usual kind, the seriousness of the apparent threat to the fundamentals of the constitution shifted MPs' attention from the particular to the general. They began to wrestle with such questions as the nature of the law and of the constitution. Some argued that if the King could not be trusted to rule according to law, then the law (especially Acts of Parliament) should be used to limit his powers. Faced with a king with an unusually elastic view of his prerogatives, some began to see a need to change the constitution in order to preserve it. Such arguments reinforced Charles' belief that they aimed to destroy the hereditary powers of the monarchy.[48]

Charles' opening speech to the new Parliament, on 17 March 1628, showed a mixture of wariness and hostility. He urged the Commons to provide money to meet the common danger, or else he would use other means. This was not a threat, 'for he scorned to threaten any but his equals'.[49] The Commons showed more restraint and tactical sense than in the previous Parliament; there was no direct attack on Buckingham and they agreed in principle to vote five subsidies, but delayed completing the bill. Charles sent a message, stressing his forbearance in letting them debate matters such as billeting and urging them to rely on him to ensure that the laws were observed: yet again, he focused attention on the question of his own trust-worthiness. Later he sent to ask 'whether they would rest on his royal word and promise', while one of the secretaries of state reminded them that the King had a sword in his hand for the good of his subjects.[50]

Faced with Charles' determination to force a confrontation, the Commons sidestepped, adjourning their debate on grievances, but the issues could not be evaded indefinitely. Could the King raise loans or taxes without consent? Could soldiers be billeted in private houses? Could martial law be used to punish soldiers or sailors (as mutiny and desertion were not offences under common law)? Could the King commit people to prison without showing cause, as he had done to some who refused to pay the forced loan? On all these questions, the King had a plausible case. There were precedents for forced loans and for raising money, through the militia rates or ship money, to defend the realm. Some provision had to be made for lodging and disciplining troops in wartime. The monarch had often committed without showing cause where state security was involved. There had been few complaints when Catholic plotters had been sent to the Tower, but now the same power was invoked against men charged only with political non-co-operation. Powers which aroused little controversy when used with restraint and discrimination had become contentious, because Charles had extended their use to a point where they seemed to threaten liberty and property. It was all very well for Charles to urge the Commons to trust him; he seemed eminently untrustworthy.[51]

In seeking satisfaction on these issues, the Commons wished to avoid new legislation, which would imply that they were changing the law and so, perhaps, undermining the foundations of monarchy. They decided on a Petition of Right, which in theory restated existing law, yet, once it received the royal assent, was said to have the same force as statute. To Charles, however, to take away the council's power of commitment would 'dissolve the very frame and foundation of our monarchy'; the judges assured him that, even if he accepted the Petition, the council would still be able to commit without showing cause. Charles tried to fob the Commons off with an ambiguous answer, but the Commons stood firm and won the support of the Lords. On 7 June, after a long debate in council, Charles gave his consent to the Petition. That night there were more bonfires in London than had been seen since Charles and Buckingham's return from Spain, five years before.[52]

When he accepted the Petition, Charles said that he knew that the Commons could not, and did not mean to, hurt his prerogative. He had done his best to satisfy them: 'if the Parliament have not a happy conclusion, the sin is yours; I am free from it'. The Commons were far from satisfied. Already some had denounced Buckingham and the House had begun to draw up a remonstrance setting out their grievances. This talked of a 'Popish plot' against religion and liberties and linked the tolerance shown to Papists, the favouring of Arminianism, the stationing of Catholic troops in Kent and the hiring of soldiers in Germany. Charles expected that he would hear no more of this remonstrance after he had assented to the Petition, so was angry when the Commons persisted with it and added a statement that the main source of the 'present evils and dangers' was the excessive power of Buckingham; they called on Charles to dismiss him. Outside Parliament, hatred of the Duke reached new heights. Dr Lambe, who advised him on matters astrological, was so badly beaten up that he died; the crowd shouted that it would like to do the same to Buckingham. When the Commons presented the remonstrance, Charles remarked that they understood public affairs even less than he thought; as for their grievances, 'he would consider of them as they should deserve'.[53]

By now, with the subsidy bill completed, Charles can have seen little reason to prolong the session. The Commons' conduct (especially towards Buckingham) had served only to reinforce his aversion to Parliament. He made a point of promoting those Arminian divines whom MPs had singled out for condemnation and ordered that all copies of the remonstrance should be destroyed. Then he and Buckingham resumed their plans for a second expedition to Ré. Meanwhile, public anxiety persisted. Parliament's proceedings had been reported more widely than ever before and the remonstrance circulated in manuscript, further increasing hatred of Buckingham. Wild rumours circulated, occasionally mixed with fact: Buckingham was alleged to be bringing in a foreign army, to put London to fire and sword. While Buckingham treated these canards with haughty disdain, Charles' attitude was more than ever one of embattled defiance. Following Lambe's murder it is possible that, as rumour had it, the council considered whether to disarm the citizens of London. Meanwhile, Buckingham went to Portsmouth and prepared to embark for France. On 23 August he was stabbed as he breakfasted by John Felton, a disgruntled army officer. Like Ravaillac, Felton refused to escape, confident in the rightness of what he had done. Cheated of promotion, he had come to see Buckingham as the source of all the ills of the kingdom, just as the remonstrance said. In striking him down, he had freed England of a tyrant: his conscience was clear. Unlike Ravaillac, Felton became a national hero. Londoners drank his health, while Buckingham was buried furtively at night, for fear that his corpse might be treated as Ancre's had been.

Charles was at prayers when he heard of the murder. He showed no emotion, but in the privacy of his bedchamber he wept uncontrolledly and would not come out for two days. He called Buckingham his martyr, paid his debts and took care of his family and his followers. He wanted to have Felton tortured, to make him reveal his accomplices, but the judges said that that would be illegal. Felton was hanged at Tyburn and his corpse was suspended in chains at Portsmouth. For Charles, however, those really responsible for the murder were malicious rumour-mongers and the MPs who drew up the remonstrance. The attacks on Buckingham had, to him, been aimed at himself, for Buckingham's policies were his policies.

The Duke's death left a void that was never wholly filled. On a personal level, he soon lavished on his wife the affection monopolized by Buckingham. His marriage to Henrietta Maria had failed to usher in the expected Anglo-French alliance and relations between the two crowns had gone from bad to worse. The Queen saw the English as an inferior race and herself as a missionary, come to spread Catholicism in a heretical land. Surrounded by a bloated French entourage and a plethora of priests, her attitude provoked quarrels with her husband and aroused his subjects' dislike. She refused to be crowned by a Protestant archbishop and went to Tyburn, where many Catholics had been executed, on what was seen as a pilgrimage. While Henrietta was frivolous and difficult, Charles was inclined to be petulant; Buckingham's insistence on installing his kinswomen as ladies-in-waiting added to the friction. Even after Charles sent his wife's French servants packing, their relationship did not improve. Henrietta had a filthy temper and saw the Buckingham womenfolk as spies, watching her every move; it did not help that Charles was on such bad terms with France. Buckingham's attempts to provide Charles with a mistress failed and made matters worse. His death left Charles free to love another and removed the main obstacle to his loving his wife. With Buckingham dead, peace between England and France soon followed and Henrietta began to return his affection. Her English improved and they became a devoted couple. Later she was to exercise a political influence which was almost unremittingly disastrous; for now she showed little interest in politics — when Buckingham died, she was only eighteen — and devoted herself to pleasure, religion and her husband.

If the Queen filled the emotional vacuum left by Buckingham's death, no one person fulfilled his political role. Charles threw himself into government, but soon lost interest; the burden devolved on others, notably Lord Treasurer Weston, whose message was simple: Charles could not afford to continue the war. Peace was soon made and the armies were disbanded, which cooled the political temperature. The ending of the wars removed a central contradiction from Charles' position. From at least mid 1626 he had wanted to be rid of Parliaments, but his commitment to Buckingham and his wars made him desperate for money. Non-parliamentary expedients, like the forced loan, were not very successful, so Charles remained susceptible to the argument that, if he kept trying, Parliament might help to solve his financial problems. Conversely, it would be difficult to do without Parliament while war imposed such a strain on his finances.[54] After Felton's claim that the remonstrance justified his killing Buckingham, and as the end of the war effort reduced the pressure on his finances, it might seem surprising that Charles agreed to recall the Parliament which he had prorogued in June. Whatever his own feelings, however, he was seldom sufficiently confident in his own judgement to act without the support of his councillors, many of whom felt that, with Buckingham gone, Parliament would be more amenable. They also hoped that Parliament would confirm his right to collect tonnage and poundage: since its legality had been questioned in the last session, some merchants had refused to pay.[55]

Charles' opening speech to the new session was unusually conciliatory, but the Commons' response was not. MPs attacked Arminianism furiously, claiming that Parliament, not the bishops, should define the Church's doctrine. Even the vexed issue of tonnage and poundage took second place to religion. Charles ordered an adjournment, to allow MPs to cool off, but when he tried to renew the adjournment on 3 March 1629, the Commons refused to rise. While the Speaker was held down in his chair, Sir John Eliot denounced Weston as a Papist: he was, indeed, ambivalent in religion. He pressed the House to resolve that anyone who promoted Arminianism or Popery, or who collected or paid tonnage and poundage, was 'a capital enemy to the kingdom or commonwealth'. There was a great shout of 'Ay!', the doors were thrown open, and MPs rushed out of the chamber, sweeping aside Black Rod as they went. These disorderly scenes made up Charles' mind. The open defiance of his command to adjourn and the force used against the Speaker made it clear that he could expect nothing from Parliament and discredited the Commons in the eyes of the public. On 10 March he dissolved Parliament, giving his reasons in a declaration which was circulated nationwide. He accused the Commons of usurping investigative powers and of seeking to dictate to the judges. They had pretended to aim at Buckingham, but their true objective was 'to cast our affairs into a desperate condition, to abate the powers of our crown and to bring our government into obloquy, that in the end all things may be overwhelmed with anarchy and confusion'. 'Their drift was . . . to erect an universal over-swaying power to themselves, which belongs only to us and not to them.'[56]

This declaration expressed views which Charles had held since at least 1626 and contained a measure of truth. The Commons *had* extended their claims and activities, but not for the reason he gave, for they were motivated more by fear than by ambition. They wished not to strip the King of his powers but to defend themselves against what they saw as dangerous extensions of his prerogatives. Some of Charles' councillors claimed that a new Parliament would be more amenable, but Weston, scared by the attacks on him, was against it and Charles would not hear of it. He also rejected proposals for radical innovations, such as raising direct taxation without Parliament's consent.[57] Freed of the financial burden of war, he was content to use legal methods — or at least methods the judges would endorse.

In both England and France the later 1620s saw a move away from the tradition of government by consent, towards greater reliance on the royal prerogative. The choices facing the English monarchy were less clear-cut than those facing Louis XIII, not least because there was no Richelieu to set down the alternatives so lucidly. In France the debate took place not so much within the King's council as within his circle. The options were basically simple : war abroad or reform at home. Each had positive advantages : on the one hand, military glory, a revival of French influence in Italy and a check to Habsburg power ; on the other, financial stability, the relief of the people, administrative rationalization and religious unity.

In England, the circle of debate was wider, embracing to some extent Parliament and public opinion, but the choices were more limited : the King could muddle through with Parliament, trying to extract inadequate grants of money in return for insincere concessions, or he could muddle through without Parliament, by stretching his existing 'legal' revenues. The two more radical options were not seriously considered. It was not in Charles' nature to take the Commons into his confidence, to explain his needs and to take account of their wishes in framing his policies. Even if he had been willing to do this, it is uncertain whether MPs would have responded. They would have had to take a more active part in decision-making and to assume financial responsibility for the measures they advised, grasping the nettle of underassessment of the subsidy and rationalizing the crown's ramshackle fiscal machinery.[58] A later House of Commons did indeed take such measures — but only under the exceptional stimulus of civil war.

The second radical option was to impose new direct taxes, on land and other forms of property, by royal fiat. In a mainly agricultural economy, with a large measure of local self-sufficiency, trade was limited and so was the possible yield of taxes on trade. Although the English believed that French kings could tax their people at will, there were grave political and psychological obstacles to their imposing new taxes on property. Most politically important people were exempt from the *taille*, so that the burden fell most heavily on the peasantry ; the monarchy failed to mount a serious challenge to such exemptions until it was too late. Many believed that new direct taxation would be illegal and immoral. As the fount of justice the King should normally respect the established laws, which allowed him to create new indirect taxes, offices for sale and other *affaires extraordinaires*, but not new property taxes : even after nearly two centuries, the *taille* was not, in theory, permanent. If even the French king felt unable to introduce new direct taxes, it is not surprising that Charles, while talking of a king's right to demand such taxes in an emergency, did not try to collect them.

If, as Dorset said, Charles' subjects were more docile than Louis', his means of coercion were far weaker. If Charles and Buckingham seriously considered creating a standing army, which is doubtful, Charles made no effort to retain his troops once peace had been made. Moreover, he too believed strongly in the law, as interpreted by his judges. He rebutted indignantly the suggestion that he could tax at will (except, perhaps, in an emergency). He dispensed with Parliaments because he believed that they threatened his lawful prerogatives, not because he wished to extend his powers : if MPs' motives were fundamentally defensive, so were his. Charles was thus faced with a choice between two half-baked alternatives, and reached his decision haltingly, as befitted a man of limited intelligence and self-confidence. There was no big showdown, no Day of Dupes. Charles' decision to rule without Parliament was delayed partly by Buckingham's wars, partly by his own irresolution. In the end the decision was made for him, by Felton and by the Commons' outrageous conduct in 1629. The consequences of that decision remained to be seen.

# 5
# Civil War

After the traumas of his first years as king, Charles I entered a period of calm and contentment, both politically and personally. He called no Parliaments and lavished his affection on his wife, who gave birth to a son, Charles, in 1630 and later to five more children. With three sons the dynasty was secure and this burgeoning family completed the couple's marital happiness. Charles was a devoted and faithful husband and his wife, despite her effervescence and frivolity, was equally devoted to him. This model couple presided over a model court. James I's had been extravagant, chaotic and often debauched. Charles' household was if anything larger and more costly, but he sought to impose upon it order and decency. The court was still to provide an opulent setting for monarchy, but the opulence was to be restrained and dignified. Charles was obsessed with the need for regularity and style. He laid down who was to be admitted into which part of the court and how they should dress. Only peers, councillors and gentlemen of the bedchamber were to be allowed into the privy chamber; no boots or spurs were to be worn in the King's presence. His day was ruled by the clock, with set times for meals, business and recreation. His meals were served in public, with great ceremony; this meant that his food was usually cold, but created a sense of dignity which Richelieu advised Louis XIII to emulate.[1]

Charles' love of order, decorum and his wife was reflected in his court's cultural life, notably the masques, in which both King and Queen took part. Those of James' reign had been staged by the distinguished, but not always happy, partnership of Ben Jonson and Inigo Jones. When Jonson decided he could no longer work with Jones, it marked a victory for Jones' special effects over Jonson's complex allegories. The ideas expressed in masques became more predictable and more remote from reality: Charles was the epitome of idealized kingship, brave and virtuous, Henrietta the embodiment of beauty. Their love, pure and platonic, enabled them to overcome all obstacles and, with divine help, to bring order out of chaos: in an instant, rough crags were transformed into a scene of pastoral tranquillity. Court drama, too, became polished, mannered and artificial, losing the roughness and originality of that of James' reign.

The King's tastes in art and architecture showed a similar concern for order and refinement. In 1600 England had been something of a cultural backwater, unaware of developments on the Continent. Under James, a few Englishmen developed a taste for the recently rediscovered classical art and sculpture. Jones travelled in Italy and there learned of the work of the Roman architect Vitruvius, whose stress on arithmetical proportion had been taken up by Palladio. Their influence was seen in Jones' designs for the Queen's House at Greenwich and the Banqueting House at Whitehall, both very different from anything built in England before. The latter, completed in 1622, was intended for state occasions and for masques and Jones later designed a chapel for Henrietta at Somerset House, whose features included a 'machine ... to exhibit the holy sacrament', brilliantly lit. A similarly baroque exuberance could be seen in Rubens' painting of the apotheosis of James I, on the ceiling of the Banqueting House. Charles drew well and was a discerning buyer of paintings, so impressing Rubens with his knowledge that the painter gave him a rare self-portrait. The painter who best captured the spirit of Charles and his court, however, was not Rubens but Van Dyck, whose portraits stressed the qualities of dignity and serenity. Instead of surrounding his figures with the allegorical trappings of power, he usually set them in a sylvan landscape. Rarely dressed for battle, they suggested an inner power derived from virtue and wisdom and a calm confidence that these qualities would triumph over adversity. One character in a masque of 1640 told the king:

> All that are harsh, all that are rude,
> Are by your harmony subdued;
> Yet so into obedience wrought
> As if not forced to it, but taught.[2]

The court was thus an oasis of order and propriety, where the King could dictate standards of taste and behaviour. It is possible to exaggerate the originality of Caroline court culture: much dated back to the previous reign and continental styles were often blended with English traditions. Although the cultural style of the court was rarefied and exclusive, not least because of Charles' efforts to limit access, it was imitated by magnates like the Earl of Pembroke, for whom Jones designed the magnificent 'double cube' room at Wilton.[3] Nevertheless, the style of Charles' court was in many ways novel and tended to isolate Charles from his subjects. There were reasons other than cultural insularity for disliking the Catholic religious imagery in many of the paintings which Charles bought. It was also, perhaps, symbolic that the Banqueting House, where so many masques were staged, was built on the site of the 'preaching place', constructed under Henry VIII. Although many Protestants, and even Puritans, were hostile to neither foreign art nor the theatre, they would not find it easy to participate in or to appreciate what was in many ways an esoteric court culture. Jonson's allegories had often been so complex that he had had to publish explanations for the uninitiated. If the imagery of Charles' masques was less subtle, they were no less artificial and even further removed from everyday life.

Within his court, Charles lived in an ordered and harmonious world, far removed from the uncouthness and sedition which reigned outside. He showed no wish to meet his people : when he travelled around the country, the common herd were kept away. Shy and conscious of his stammer, he avoided having to produce the everyday pleasantries which are the necessary small change of monarchy. By cutting himself off in this way, he seriously impaired his capacity to govern and in some respects deluded himself. Many of his courtiers failed to live up to his high standards. The day he published new rules regulating access to the court, two of his body servants quarrelled and spat in each other's faces ; a sermon extolling virginity prompted the comment that it was not appropriate to the court.[4] Like Louis XIII, Charles was a virtuous King presiding over a less than virtuous court, but unlike Louis he tried to maintain a veneer of propriety. He always assumed that if he laid down rules, they would be obeyed, and remained wilfully unconcerned about his subjects' reaction to his government. Time was to show the perils of such an attitude.

Although in 1631 Charles said that the very name of Parliament was an affront to his authority, he may not have intended to dispense with it permanently. Given time and experience of his wise and benevolent government, he hoped his people would see that their fears and suspicions had been groundless. This might take ten or fifteen years, but then — and only then — he would call Parliament again.[5] Meanwhile, he sought to bring to his government the same order and regularity which he sought to impose on his court. His ideal was of a wise and just king, assisted by conscientious councillors, ruling paternalistically over a docile and grateful people, while the gentry lived on their estates, dispensing hospitality and justice to the peasantry. He was conscious that he would have to answer to God for his conduct, believed firmly in the rule of law and set high standards of personal behaviour.

Unfortunately his ideal bore as little resemblance to reality as his masques. It was not enough to have benign intentions : they had to be translated into action, using an inadequate administration staffed by men greedy for power and profit, and who made much of their income from payments from members of the public. A few, like Laud, did approximate to the King's ideals, but Laud was often a lone voice who, while denouncing financial corruption, was sometimes used by financial projectors : 'a confident, senseless and for the most part a naughty people'.[6] Laud's main ally in his calls for impartial, vigorous and 'thorough' government, Sir Thomas Wentworth, could give him only limited support, as he spent most of the 1630s away from London. Wentworth's own conduct, moreover, was not free from ambiguity. His rough methods achieved some temporary success in Ireland, where his intolerance of others' corruption did not prevent him from accumulating a considerable fortune.

To impose higher standards on the government required far more determination and effort than Charles was capable of. Much of the time he spent on business was spent endorsing the recommendations of others, rather than pursuing a firm line of his own. He was interested in his court, the navy and foreign policy, but often found problems too difficult for him and made no decision. He disliked paperwork ('I have not the patience to read them all') and showed a princely disdain for the grubby business of raising money, though he expected it to be there when he wanted to spend it.[7] The flaws in his vision of monarchy went deeper than his indecision, however. In both England and France, the greatest obstacle to reform was the crown's fiscal weakness. Without Parliament, Charles had to make the most of a ragbag of revenues, which often depended on archaic feudal rights or the royal prerogative. He was bombarded with projects, devised by financiers and pressed upon him by greedy courtiers. 'Projects of all kinds, many ridiculous, many scandalous, all very grievous, were set on foot', wrote the Earl of Clarendon, 'the envy and reproach of which came to the King, the profit to other men, insomuch as, of £200,000 drawn from the subject by these ways in a year, scarce £1500 came to the King's use.' The King received less money from fines for encroaching on the royal forest than was paid by the Earl of Salisbury alone, while the Earl of Holland made over £10,000 a year from royal grants.[8]

New projects and fiscal devices increased the complexity of Charles' finances, making reform more difficult. He was never sure of his priorities. Torn between trying to stamp out the sale of office, as corrupt and inefficient, and building it up into a major source of revenue (as in France), he did neither. Proposals for administrative reform were dropped after a 'gift' from those whose interests were threatened.[9] Financial need and vested interest thus offered major obstacles to Charles' hopes of reform, but they were not the most fundamental. Charles had a high sense of his own integrity, yet his government fined men thousands of pounds for allegedly contravening antiquated laws. He stretched and twisted traditional powers of the crown, which were supposed to be used for the well-being of the realm, in order to raise money. His government expressed sympathy for the poor and down-trodden and punished landowners who enclosed land illegally, but he began to enclose Richmond Park (for hunting) before he had bought out all who owned land there and used Star Chamber to crush opposition to his fen drainage schemes. Thus although his faith in his own rectitude never wavered, many of his subjects had good reason not to share it. He never broke the letter of the law, as interpreted by his judges, but his law officers stretched his powers to a point where the letter of the law was far removed from its spirit. 'If it does not altogether violate the laws of the realm', wrote the Venetian ambassador of ship money, '. . . it is certainly repugnant to usage and to the forms hitherto observed.'[10]

The money-raising devices of the 1630s were so varied as to defy brief analysis. The King sold a group of merchants a licence to infringe the East India Company's trading monopoly, then withdrew the licence after a payment from the Company. The City of London was fined £70,000 by Star Chamber for alleged mismanagement of its Irish lands. When it was discovered that the royal forests had once been far more extensive than they now were, landowners (great and small) were fined for encroaching upon them. Monopolies had been declared illegal in 1624, but the Act had left a loophole, designed to protect craft guilds, excepting corporations whose task was to maintain standards of workmanship. Charles granted a monopoly on soap to a company consisting mainly of cronies of Weston, which undertook in return to pay the King a substantial annual rent. In order to comply with the Monopolies Act, the company had to show that its product was superior to that of existing soap-makers, so held public tests, before an audience of peeresses and laundresses, to show that monopoly soap washed whiter. Consumers, however, proved commendably resistant to such promotional techniques, complaining that the company's soap was more expensive and blistered the hands; as some members of the company were Catholics, there were fears that the soap might do even worse things to the soul.

The devices mentioned so far affected particular products or groups. Many, like the forest fines, could be used only once and proved far less profitable (for the King) than their promoters had claimed. There was one, however, which might solve the crown's problems permanently. The crown had often required coastal areas to provide ships or money for their own defence against pirates or invasion. Charles extended this ship money to cover the whole country and demanded it every year. In theory, it was (like the militia rate) a local rate for local defence; one could argue that inland areas, too, should pay to defend the realm against invasion: the money was indeed spent on the navy. In practice, ship money was a regular tax on land. Moreover, instead of taxpayers being charged a proportion of their declared net income, allowing opportunities for inventive under-assessment, each county was given a quota, apportioned between its communities and inhabitants. Thus, whereas subsidy yields had fallen lower and lower, that of ship money was predictable; it came in virtually in full and comparatively quickly. Charles was already collecting tonnage and poundage, and impositions, without consent. If ship money became permanent, he would have an English version of the *taille*, but which (unlike the *taille*) allowed of no exemptions and accurately tapped the nation's wealth, so could be made to yield far more than the £200,000 a year that Charles demanded.

At first ship money was collected with little difficulty; rating disputes were settled and few refused to pay. Not until 1637 was one of them, John Hampden, reputedly the richest commoner in England, brought to trial. His counsel did not deny that the King could raise money for defence in an emergency, but questioned whether the alleged danger was so pressing that the King did not have time to call Parliament — especially as people were allowed up to seven months to pay. Against this it was argued that the King's use of his discretion was a matter above subjects' understanding : to question his judgement was 'a presumption above the presumption of the law'. One judge declared that if the King could levy 20 shillings in this way, there was nothing to stop him levying £20, or £20,000, but the majority of his colleagues found against Hampden. While the trial aroused considerable public interest, ship money continued to be paid.

Hampden's was one of a number of cases in which the courts had been used to test the extent of the prerogative. Normally, the English expected the courts to protect liberty and property, but now, when faced with cases of apparently arbitrary taxation and imprisonment, the judges always found in favour of the King. Not only did their jobs depend on his goodwill, but they were reluctant to question his judgement or his honesty. They were content to establish whether the King possessed a certain prerogative, but preferred not to ask whether he was using it for its proper purpose. Moreover, when Charles took Hampden to court, he knew he would win because he had already consulted the judges in Exchequer Chamber about the legal justifiability of extending ship money. Such prior consultation avoided embarrassment in the courts and put the judges under pressure to endorse the King's measures. It raised the possibility that the judges might usurp Parliament's legislative and, in cases relating to money, financial role, as had happened in Ireland under James. The English government in Dublin sought to extend its authority by undermining that of the Gaelic chiefs. Much of the chiefs' power derived from the Gaelic system of law and land tenure, so these were replaced by the English system. No elected Parliament would have agreed to such radical changes, so they were implemented by the Irish judges (all Englishmen, trained in the common law) meeting in the court of Castle Chamber. In a few years, their rulings paved the way for the Anglicization of Ireland's laws and government.[11]

It is unlikely that Charles planned a systematic transformation of English law to provide the basis for an 'absolute' monarchy. He consulted the judges on an ad hoc basis to test the legality of the proposals, mainly fiscal, which were put before them. He sought not to extend his powers but, in his view, to confirm the legality of those he already had. There were numerous references to his 'absolute' power, but the word was used in varying senses and contexts. Sometimes it indicated that the King had no superior on earth (least of all the Pope). It could refer to his emergency powers or could imply that he could do whatever he pleased : it was remarked that 'a king in his absolute and unlimited power is able to do more than a good king will do'.[12]

Despite the high-flown rhetoric of some divines, however, and the claims that in an emergency his powers were virtually boundless, Charles and his advisers did not claim that he could tax and imprison at will. Ship money was not a tax but an emergency rate. There were no political executions in the 1630s and offenders were punished only after a trial, although in Star Chamber the scales were weighted against them. Charles lacked the imagination or the determination to create a new form of monarchy, yet many of his subjects believed that he intended to do so. They may have been wrong about his motives, but his actions seemed to tend that way. His aloof and high-handed manner and poor sense of public relations did nothing to remove such misconceptions. Moreover, fears of radical change in the State were reinforced by fears of retrograde change in the Church, as Laud embarked on a 'counter-reformation' within the Church of England.

Laud became Archbishop of Canterbury only in 1633, but was already the dominant influence on Charles' ecclesiastical policy. The greatest historian of the reign, Gardiner, remarked : 'In our time [Laud] would have been in his place as the dean of a cathedral in need of restoration.'[13] Such a view understates Laud's spiritual preoccupations — his Puritan enemies later found, from his private diaries, that he shared many of their anxieties — but captures the image he conveyed. An energetic man — he ruptured himself swinging books in his study, for exercise — with no wife or family, he devoted his energies to bringing the Church up to his standards. At St John's College, Oxford, he refitted the chapel in a more elegant style and he sought to bring a similar decency of worship and 'the beauty of holiness' to the parishes of England. He ordered that the Prayer-Book services be used in full, that communion tables be moved to the east end of the church and railed off and that people behave with due reverence during divine service. He encouraged the clergy to stand up for their property rights against the laity and dealt severely with moral offenders and with those who criticized his demands.

Laud's measures had the full support of the King. An instinctive High Churchman, Charles found the seemliness and sumptuousness of Laudian services aesthetically pleasing and appreciated the Laudians' magnification of royal power. His backing for Laud linked the secular and ecclesiastical aspects of the Personal Rule, so that the unpopularity of one rubbed off on the other. While Charles' ministers were accused of promoting absolutism, Laud was said to favour the related evil of Popery. In a way, this was unfair. He consistently urged severity against Catholics as well as against Puritans, adulterers and political dissidents; he firmly refused the Pope's offer of a cardinal's hat. In a less literal sense, however, the charges were plausible. Whereas James' Church had been broad, Charles' episcopate was dominated by Laudians. Although Laud tried to avoid theological controversy, his liturgical preferences had doctrinal implications. In emphasizing the importance of communion and railing off the altar, he suggested that something mysterious happened to the bread and wine and that the priest who consecrated them was not as other men, a view reinforced by his distinctive vestments. To many this seemed a step towards Catholicism in which the priest, through the sacraments, controlled access to salvation, a vital intermediary between man and God.

Laud and the Puritans had much in common. Both saw a need to combat drunkenness, violence and promiscuity, although the Puritans saw this as a task for godly magistrates, not for Laud's Church courts, which also prosecuted Puritans for nonconformity. Neither was satisfied with the state of Sunday worship: Puritans bemoaned the mindless mumbling of Prayer-Book formulae, with far too little preaching of the Word; to Laud, services were often scruffy and disorderly. He wanted churches to be clean and in good repair, with pews of uniform size, in orderly rows and the congregation well behaved. His attitude might seem fussy and superficial, but he had a point. Churches were often squalid and dilapidated. Those attending services sometimes played cards, stuck pins in each other, slept or fought. One man's bitch gave birth in the pew beside him; the misbehaviour of dogs was one reason for railing off the altar. There were parishes where babies were baptized in a bucket or communion wine was served in an ale flagon.[14]

For decades Puritans had denounced those who preferred to dance, drink, play games or even work on the sabbath, rather than listen to long sermons. As one complained: 'People hear much, learn little and practise less. Which cannot be imputed to the want of good preaching, but rather to the want of good hearing.'[15] Puritanism was the creed of an élite minority : God had marked out only a fortunate few for salvation. Most people fell far short of the Puritans' high standards, but that did not mean that they derived no spiritual benefit or understanding from attending church ; many clerics pitched their teaching at a level people could understand. Laud, however, like the Puritans, was not tolerant of human imperfection. In seeking to impose on poor villagers the standards appropriate to an Oxford college, he caused confusion and annoyance. Chopping pews down to size offended those who saw a large pew as a mark of status. Many resented the introduction of new ceremonies or the growing assertiveness of the clergy. By provoking resentment among those who had little quarrel with the Church and its worship, Laud gave the militant Puritans the chance to promote their long-cherished plans for radical reform. They denounced Laudianism as disguised Popery and claimed that this deadly infection could be removed only by getting rid of both bishops and the Prayer Book.

In early 1637, however, the militants' time had not yet come. Laud's critics were silenced by Star Chamber, some losing their ears. England seemed to be enjoying the peace and order which Charles craved. The judges would punish those refusing to pay ship money. There were hints of possible opposition to Charles and Laud's new Scottish Prayer Book, but Charles had gone to unusual lengths to consult the Scottish bishops and anticipated no trouble. The Personal Rule seemed set to last. As one contemporary wrote :

All business goes undisturbedly on ... for I think that great tax of the ship money is so well digested ... I suppose [it] will become perpetual ; for indeed if men would consider the great levies of monies in foreign parts for the service of the State, these impositions would appear but little burdens, but time can season and form minds to comply with public necessities.[16]

✳   ✳   ✳

If England seemed calm in the mid 1630s, France did not. Aristocratic conspiracy and popular revolts abounded, but the partnership of Louis and Richelieu continued to function. The cardinal was more secure after the Day of Dupes, but did not take his master's favour for granted, packing the councils with his men and installing his creatures as secretaries of state. He watched closely those whom the King favoured, trying to oust those he distrusted and to advance others in their stead. His anxieties were not groundless: with his rudeness, arrogance and commitment to the war, he had made many enemies among the nobility and clergy. Some of the King's favourites were pro-Spanish and the last, Effiat's son, the Marquis de Cinq-Mars, threatened both Richelieu's power and his life.

For Louis, government was a matter of duty rather than pleasure. As France moved towards open war with Spain, his conscience was troubled, partly by having to fight another Catholic power, but more by the suffering war would inflict upon his subjects. 'Victories and defeats alike', he told the Venetian ambassador, 'end only in the destruction of the people and the desolation of the country.'[17] He worried far more than Richelieu about the human cost of the war, but by the later 1630s both would gladly have brought it to an end, if only they could have obtained acceptable terms. Depressed and often in pain, Louis let slip bitter remarks about Richelieu, complaining almost childishly of his dominance in the government. Richelieu's enemies were eager to take these complaints at face value and sought to capitalize on them. In 1637 Caussin, Louis' confessor, urged him to recall his mother and make peace with Spain. Caussin was banished to Normandy, but he had only said openly what others insinuated.

Louis' personal life brought him only limited consolation from the burdens of kingship. His affection for his wife had cooled: he slept with her only because it was his duty to beget an heir. After four miscarriages Anne gave birth to a son, Louis, in 1638. After twenty years' wait, the arrival of a dauphin was greeted with wild rejoicing; many, Louis included, saw it as a mark of God's especial favour and ascribed it to Louis' placing the kingdom under the protection of the Virgin Mary. A few days later, a daughter was born to the Queen of Spain, offering the prospect of an eventual reconciliation between the two kingdoms. The birth of Louis the 'God-given', soon followed by a second son, Philippe, changed the Queen's position. For years Louis had treated her with suspicion, resenting the gallantries of various gentlemen, not least Buckingham, whose conduct towards her on a visit to the French court created more than a whiff of scandal. Louis had even talked of having the marriage annulled, on grounds of sterility.

Anne, for her part, disliked hunting and resented following her morose, irritable husband around the countryside. Bored and frustrated, upset by Louis' hostility to Spain, she was drawn into dangerous intrigues and in 1637 Richelieu obtained proof that she had been in correspondence with the Spanish and English courts. Although Louis was not inclined to forgive her. Richelieu persuaded him to do so, after she had signed a full confession. Her position was transformed by her pregnancy and the birth of the Dauphin. Louis became more attentive and affectionate. Richelieu, too, hastened to seek her goodwill: if Louis died before his son came of age, she would be regent. The Queen's becoming a mother gave her a commitment to the Bourbon dynasty and to France which she had hitherto lacked. She became involved in public affairs and her opinions were heeded.

The Queen could not, however, meet all Louis' emotional needs. He continued to show a fear and dislike of women and of female sexuality. He strongly disapproved of low-cut dresses, once spitting a mouthful of wine into a woman's décolleté. The hedonism and promiscuity of many courtiers repelled him and attempts to provide him with a mistress failed lamentably. When he formed close friendships with two young women, it was their innocence and purity that attracted him. He wore Mlle de Hautefort's colours as her 'knight and servant', but talked to her of nothing more carnal than hunting (and kept a full record of their conversations). Mlle de la Fayette became so disgusted with the intrigues and malice of the court that she yielded to her confessor's pressure and entered a convent; the confessor acted at the behest of Richelieu, who feared that her sympathy for Spain might influence the King. Louis did not stand in her way, but visited her regularly. After one visit, he was caught in a torrential rainstorm and took refuge in the Louvre. No room had been prepared for him, so he slept with the Queen. That night, Louis XIV was conceived.

Despite his fondness for Mlles de Hautefort and de la Fayette, Louis' closest friendships were with men. The male favourites who followed Luynes were closely watched by Richelieu, who ousted any who showed political ambitions. The most durable was the Duc de St Simon, whose favour depended on such skills as blowing a hunting horn without dribbling and showing Louis how to leap from one horse to another without touching the ground. Louis may have talked to St Simon of politics but he was primarily an agreeable companion. Louis was often tetchy, especially when ill, and the two had many flaming rows, followed by emotional reconciliations. Louis was especially offended by St Simon's suggestion that the King should make Mlle de Hautefort his mistress. When the Duke eventually left the court, he made way for the far more dangerous Cinq-Mars, who brought Louis more heart-searching and sorrow.[18]

After the Day of Dupes, there could be little doubt that war with Spain would come, but France needed time to gather sufficient resources. The weakening of the anti-Habsburg forces in Germany forced Louis' hand and he declared war in 1635; France was not really ready, but it was vital to prevent the Habsburgs from imposing peace on their terms. Richelieu probably underestimated the difficulties France would face. He hoped that France's entering the war would bring the Spaniards to a speedy peace and did not appreciate how exhausting siege warfare could be or how much war cost. His attitude to money was somewhat cavalier: 'I am so willing to confess my ignorance of affairs of finance', he wrote to finance minister Bullion, '... that the only advice I can give you is to use those methods which you find most useful to the King's service and to assure you that I shall support you in every way I can.'[19] Armies could not, however, be raised, moved or kept together without money and at times, as in the Valtelline in 1637, France was defeated simply because the money ran out.

In its efforts to mobilize more men and money than ever before, the crown extended its authority in the provinces and resorted to rough and novel methods. The needs of war did not allow for the use of regular procedures, full consultation or the respecting of legal rights. French constitutional ideas were essentially ambiguous. On the one hand, writers stressed the King's absolute authority to legislate and tax at will, limited only by his obligation to observe the fundamental laws, notably those governing the succession and stating that the King must be a Catholic. On the other, it was argued that he should respect France's customs and traditions. He should seek the sovereign courts' endorsement of new legislation, which allowed them to remonstrate against it and delay its implementation. He should respect the privileges of provinces, towns, courts and other groups. In seeking to persuade the King of his obligations, some put forward a quasi-contractual view of monarchy. These ambiguities were set out in speeches by the Archbishop of Narbonne in 1651 and 1653. Kings, he said, were 'the masters of the universe', whom the people must obey and provide with the money they needed for their government. The King, however, was to be frugal in using his subjects' property and the relationship between them involved reciprocal obligations : the people were to expose their lives and property in the King's service, but he was obliged to render justice and to protect their property. This was a basic maxim of Christianity and from it the Archbishop deduced that provinces should be ruled according to their ancient customs and that the King should respect the conditions upon which they were joined to the crown of France.[20] This view was shared even by some of the King's representatives : one intendant talked of 'a sort of contract' between King and people.

Most royal spokesmen, however, stressed royal authority more than customary privileges, arguing that particular interests should be subordinated to those of the whole realm, or of the State. When comparing the King's power with that of a father of a family, as many did, one could either stress the moral responsibilities of parenthood or argue that children were less able than their father to judge what was in their best interests : 'Children kept to their duty by a good father are no less free than others left to their own sinful devices.'[21] Increasingly it was argued that subjects could be happy only in subjection. Their obligation to the State was older than any privilege, for it was part of the natural order of things. If the King condescended to ask the consent of provincial estates for taxation, they should show themselves worthy of such condescension.[22]

The increased demands of war heightened the tension between the State's needs and local and corporate privileges. Against the argument that the King was, like any Christian, obliged to keep the promises of his predecessors (for in law the King never died), royal spokesmen argued that affairs of state could not be subjected to the laws of personal morality. Taken to its logical conclusion, the invocation of 'reason of state', as in Marillac's plea that 'necessity is above the laws', could have been used to justify the King's overriding all customs and moral constraints. In practice, this rarely happened. Louis XIII accepted that he was obliged, wherever possible, to rule according to law. If he sometimes had to override existing law, he regretted it and tried to keep it to a minimum. Moreover, his kingdom was large and diverse, under only limited central control. If the Huguenots no longer had a 'state within a state', many nobles wielded great political and military power ; one or two, like the Princes of Monaco, were sovereigns in their own right. Although the crown had a large army, it found it difficult to cope with large peasant insurrections against taxation.

Finally, the extension of venality led to the creation of quasi-independent bodies of officials, who had a duty to serve the king but expected him to proceed in a regular, legal manner and to respect their material and professional interests. Attempts to override custom and privilege or to increase taxation provoked non-cooperation and even open revolt. Louis and Richelieu therefore resorted to authoritarian methods only intermittently, when absolutely necessary. They used devices which affected only particular groups, rather than the whole spectrum of officials, or all the nobility. Richelieu stressed the dangers of alienating the people in wartime: 'The consent of the people at a time like this is worth more than all the force which one might use on another occasion.'[23]

In both France and England the crown, in the 1630s, invoked its emergency powers in its search for money. Both Kings expressed respect for the law; neither claimed to override it at will. French ministers talked of 'reason of state', English lawyers argued that the prerogative was a part of the common law, but both Kings claimed a wide discretion to do what was necessary for the common good in an emergency. Both recognized that there were limits to their competence. Charles never claimed that he could make laws or taxes on his own authority. Louis claimed wide legislative powers, limited only by the fundamental laws of the realm, but he never tried to introduce a new direct tax, to supplement or replace the *taille*. Both Kings were driven to use morally dubious and fiscally inefficient devices, such as monopolies or sales of office. Apart from legal scruples, there were political obstacles to a further extension of the King's emergency powers.

In France, there were limits to the burden which peasants would bear without revolting and to the amount the crown could squeeze out of its officials without seriously disrupting tax collection and law enforcement; the crown never dared to tackle exemptions from the *taille*. In England, the king could not press JPs and militia officers too hard, or he would meet with obstruction and resignations from office. The collection of money, especially ship money, depended on taxpayers' willingness to pay. For much of the 1630s ship money yields ran at over ninety per cent, but once people stopped paying, in 1639–40, there was little Charles could do: he had no army to put pressure on taxpayers.[24]

While there were similarities between the extensions of royal authority, there were also major differences. First, Louis was fighting a major war and Charles, whatever he pretended, was not. When Charles had to prepare for a real war, the insufficiency of his authority and his need for his people's goodwill became glaringly apparent. Secondly, Louis' authority was — and was accepted by his subjects as being — much more extensive. However much the sovereign courts challenged particular edicts, they never denied the King's power to legislate. However often officials denounced new offices which threatened their interests, they did not deny that the King could create such offices. Charles could harass his critics in Star Chamber, but Louis dealt more arbitrarily with those who annoyed him: executions for political offences were frequent and many were imprisoned or exiled without trial. Louis had a much more powerful state apparatus, albeit one that was not easy to control, and a large army. The extensions of royal power in the 1630s differed in degree, not in kind. French kings were more powerful than English kings partly because they needed to be, as they faced greater problems, partly because that need was accepted by their subjects.

While Louis' 'absolute' power was acknowledged in theory, its use gave rise to many complaints. The biggest problem was to increase the crown's revenue without provoking so much resistance that the costs of forcible collection exceeded the yield. The King could either impose more taxes or borrow, by persuading his wealthy subjects to invest in offices, loans or tax farms. Often taxes and borrowing went together: new offices of tax-collectors were created and sold, but there could come a point where such methods proved counter-productive. Offices were subdivided, so that up to four men carried out the functions in rotation. Established officials resented such inroads upon their profits and often bought the new offices themselves, or paid the King to revoke them. As the market became glutted, new offices could be sold only by endowing them with exorbitant fees and sweeping tax exemptions, both of which further increased the burden on the ordinary taxpayer, while the crown was saddled with an ever-growing salary bill. The taxpayers' ability to pay, undermined by war and famine, was further and further reduced. As tax collection slowed down, loans were negotiated on ever more ruinous terms, with interest rates averaging 24 per cent in the 1630s. To conceal this fact, the royal accounts were doctored, which created opportunities for frauds and fiddles of all kinds, for it was hard to tell who had loaned what and on what terms.

Effective financial planning was impossible. To keep the precious loans coming in, ministers staggered from one fiscal expedient to another. The financiers were rapacious and sometimes crooked, but the interest rates they charged reflected the risks of lending to a government whose credit was so shaky: the King might go bankrupt or set up a chamber of justice. They also had to consider the interests of those who invested in their contracts, who were profiting mightily from the crown's fiscal devices, although they might not admit this publicly. The fiscal systems of France and England provided a rich source of patronage for members of the ruling élite, but in the 1630s in both countries those upset by the crown's fiscal methods were more numerous and powerful than those who gained from them.[25]

In order to maintain the flow of taxes, on which its credit depended, and to discipline and supply its armies, the crown increasingly used intendants. Venal officials were often dilatory, sometimes corrupt and usually liked doing things according to well-established routines. Jurisdictions often overlapped; financial officials showed favouritism in assessing taxes; endless appeals to the council disrupted the working of government and wasted time. With the coming of war, it was vital for the crown to galvanize and supervise its officials. It needed agents who were not local men, who put local interests first, and were not members of established bodies of officials; it needed agents whose loyalty was only to the crown and whose power was derived entirely from the king. It found them in the intendants.

Commissioners had for many years been sent into the provinces to perform specific tasks. Some had been called intendants, but only from the 1630s did they become permanent and their functions become standardized. Starting with a supervisory role, they were granted increasingly wide financial, judicial and military powers. They punished rebellion and military indiscipline and intervened in tax assessment and collection, trying to eradicate anomalies and unfairness and taking over the collection of the *taille* in 1642. They reduced existing officials to a subordinate role and curtailed their profits and fiddles, which led to their being denounced for violating established methods. They responded by invoking 'reason of state': suppressing rebellion and winning the war took priority over the interests of individuals.

The intendants performed two vital functions : they supplied and organized the armies and maintained the flow of taxes on which royal credit (and the war effort) depended. Their increased responsibilities further alienated royal officials already displeased by the crown's fiscal methods and the pro-liferation of new offices.[26] Faced with what seemed a concerted attack on their authority and livelihood, the bodies of officers, usually bitter rivals, began to work together. Sovereign courts refused to register fiscal edicts until their arguments against them had been answered. This delayed the implementation of the edicts, and thus the flow of money ; Louis tried to override their resistance and declared in 1641 that they had no right of remonstration on matters of state, thus raising an additional source of contention, the competence of the sovereign courts. Traditionally, their power to delay registration pending an answer to their remonstrations gave them a semi-legislative role. The judges' legal expertise and the fact that they would apply the laws they registered meant that the King usually took their arguments seriously : he was, after all, expected to rule according to established law. The sovereign courts could thus persuade the King to amend legislation, or refuse to register or fail to enforce it : they could not shape legislation, as the English Parliament could. Louis' attempts to override the judges' objections, and his resorting to authority rather than consultation, were natural results of the pressures of war. They raised major constitutional issues and provoked some judges to make novel claims, which found their fullest expression during the Fronde.[27]

While the officials' dissatisfaction grew, aristocratic intrigue continued, often centred on the feckless Gaston. In 1632 he marched into Burgundy with a motley following and declared that he had come to free his brother from the tyranny of Richelieu. He found little support until he joined up with the Duc de Montmorency, governor of Languedoc, who came from one of the greatest families of France. Their army was defeated at Castelnaudary and Montmorency was convicted of treason, but most assumed that his rank and long service would earn him a reprieve. Louis was bom-barded with pleas for clemency, but he was adamant. While he wept at Montmorency's fate, the needs of the State came before his personal feelings.[28]

When Montmorency was executed in the courtyard of the town hall at Toulouse, it showed Louis' determination to establish his authority over the nobility. Neither he nor Richelieu wished to destroy its wealth and power. Richelieu, himself a noble, saw the nobility as a principal sinew of the State, but wished its members to live up to the obligations of their rank. They should not tyrannize over the poor, or throw their lives away in duels, but should serve the State. If they could not afford to buy offices of justice or finance, they should be guaranteed a proportion of military and court offices and their sons should receive preference in the allocation of places in the church.[29]

Richelieu thus hoped to create a service nobility, curbing the nobles' inclinations towards destructive violence and channelling their aggression into service in the royal armies. Some of his hopes were realized. Many noble fortifications were demolished, but others survived, as did many small private armies. Moreover, he could not have crushed the great nobility, even if he had wished to do so. Their great estates brought great power. Lesser men sought their favour and protection. Their wealth and influence at court enabled them to build extensive clienteles. Such power could not be broken, but it might perhaps be controlled. Richelieu himself built up a massive clientele, installing his followers in high office, securing provincial and town governorships for himself and his kinsmen and establishing alliances, through marriage, with France's greatest families.

Through a careful distribution of rewards, he tried to win the loyalty of the great nobility. He did not always succeed — many of them hated him — but they gradually became less disruptive. They spent more time at court, perhaps because there were richer pickings there as the revenue and administration grew, perhaps because they were attracted by Parisian society. Of the highest rank of the peerage, dukes and peers, only two families did not live in Paris. Although Louis was hardly the one to give a lead, a distinctive 'court society' was emerging, aristocratic and metropolitan, displaying a high level of conspicuous consumption and of restraint and politeness. Often this politeness was little more than a veneer, but even before Louis XIV established his system of court etiquette the nobility was in the process of taming itself.[30]

In England the nobles' military power had been curbed by the end of the sixteenth century. A long period without major foreign wars made military skills redundant: William III was disgusted that the English nobility talked only of farming and horses and knew nothing of war. Only with the growth of a standing army, mainly after 1689, could the sons of the nobility once more follow a military career.[31] France, however, was often at war; as her armies grew, there were many opportunities for young noblemen to make their mark. Most of those who became dukes and peers were military men (or their sons); many also held posts at court. Military service was thus an accepted route to wealth and rank, but the nobility did not immediately become obedient and responsible subjects. Backwoods squireens skulked in their castles, preying like brigands on the peasantry. The greatest nobles continued to behave like independent princes (which some of them were), changing allegiance as it suited them. Some provincial governors showed a cavalier disregard for the King's commands, but the days of such behaviour were numbered. Montmorency's execution showed that Louis would not tolerate rebellion, even from the greatest in the land, his brother excepted.

With the magnates spending more time at court, their local influence was weakened and the King and his ministers had more opportunities to influence them; it also raised the stakes and the ferocity of court intrigue. The increase in the rewards at the King's disposal made co-operation more profitable; investment in revenue contracts gave nobles a vested interest in the royal government and in orderly tax collection. Provincial governors often helped intendants to bring financial and judicial officials to heel and spent more time in Paris, where they acted as brokers between the crown and provincial interests. Not the least important aspect of centralization in France was the way in which, as in Tudor England, the nobility, and its political influence, became concentrated in the capital and at court.[32]

The growing intrusiveness of central government caused widespread resentment in the localities. Finance officials disliked the growing power of the intendants, officials of all kinds complained of the proliferation of new offices. Urban oligarchs had long lent money to their towns at high interest and travelled to Paris on 'corporation business' at the town's expense; now they found such perquisites of office threatened by the intendants' rigorous scrutiny of municipal accounts. Landowners found their tenants so overwhelmed by the crown's demands that they could no longer pay their rents, but the greatest sufferers were the poor. They bore the brunt of increases in taxation; they had to pay the fees and gratuities demanded by the swelling army of officials; they had to lodge unpaid and ill-disciplined soldiers; and, at times, they reacted violently.

The poor did not revolt against the King: they remained convinced that he was just and good, blaming only those who claimed to act in his name. Usually they attacked the farmers and contractors who collected indirect taxes 'with so much vexation and insolence that they irritated the people, who would willingly have tolerated the establishment of these duties if they had proceeded with greater moderation'.[33] Rioters and rebels concentrated their attack on the persons and property of the hated tax-collectors: many were lynched and their corpses mutilated and dragged through the streets. Often there was an air of carnival, with many rioters emboldened by drink. They saw their conduct as legitimated by custom and tradition, a view shared by many of the wealthy. Peasants were often protected by their seigneurs against soldiers and tax-collectors, while town governments and sovereign courts encouraged, and even joined, demonstrations against new fiscal measures.[34]

From the crown's point of view, the revolts impeded the war effort and had to be ended as quickly and cheaply as possible. When it lacked the power to suppress them, it conceded many of the rebels' demands, in the hope of getting taxes flowing again. To save face, it might execute one or two ringleaders, or punish local officials for failing to prevent the revolt. Then, a few months later, it would introduce new devices similar to those which had caused the trouble. The relative success of violent resistance to the crown encouraged others to resist and there were signs by 1642 that tax collection was grinding to a halt, which would destroy the crown's credit. Faced with the threat of a financiers' strike, the crown handed over the collection of the *taille* to the intendants and gave them draconian powers to deal with refusers.

Slowly, resistance to royal fiscal demands was broken. In Languedoc the estates came to see that voting money for the troops' subsistence was a lesser evil than voting nothing and leaving them to take what they wanted. Increasingly, they worked with the intendant to make the burden of soldiers as bearable as possible.[35] Only gradually, however, did the French become used to meeting the cost of war. The early years of the war saw the crown lurching from crisis to crisis. In 1636 Spanish forces advanced deep into France, taking Corbie, just east of Amiens; Imperial troops marched into Burgundy. In 1639, after a major revolt in Normandy, finance minister Bouthillier wrote: 'The financiers abandon us and the people will pay nothing.... We are now scraping the bottom of the barrel, lacking the means to choose between good and bad projects. And I fear that our foreign war will degenerate into a civil war.'[36] In fact, from 1640, although money remained desperately short, the tide of war began to turn and in May 1643 Condé crushed the Spaniards at Rocroi.

By then, both Louis and Richelieu were dead. In the last year of their lives, their partnership almost broke down, thanks to Cinq-Mars, whose political ambitions seriously threatened Richelieu. In many ways, King and favourite were polar opposites. Cinq-Mars was dashing, fond of women and high living, who found it hard to reconcile his love of night-life with the King's penchant for early rising. Louis, so often swept along by stronger personalities, adored him and hoped to bring him to change his ways. Richelieu, having used Cinq-Mars to counter the influence of Mlle de Hautefort, now found that the young man sought to exploit Louis' fitful resentment of the cardinal's tutelage. Convinced that Louis wanted to be free of Richelieu, Cinq-Mars agreed to a treaty whereby France would hand back all it had taken from Spain and would undertake not to ally with Protestant states; in return Spain would provide an army to overthrow Richelieu, whom Cinq-Mars hoped to have assassinated. Richelieu secured a copy of the treaty and Louis was persuaded to order the conspirators' arrest. On 28 June 1642, in a four-hour interview at Tarascon, Richelieu offered to resign; when Louis would not let him, he demanded more extensive powers than ever before. While Richelieu suspected that Louis may have known of Cinq-Mars' plans, Louis resented the imperious way in which Richelieu treated him : never had he made his indispensability so obvious.

Cinq-Mars was tried and executed : again Louis' sense of duty overcame his personal feelings. He returned to Paris deeply distressed, only to find that Richelieu's demands multiplied. He drafted letters for Louis to sign and insisted on the removal of household officers linked with the fallen favourite. He wanted a new contract, giving him wider powers, surrounding Louis with his creatures and committing the King to take no more favourites. No longer did he even go through the motions of consulting the King : he commanded him. Scarcely had Louis agreed to his demands than Richelieu fell ill : he died on 4 December, to widespread rejoicing; even Louis may have felt relieved. His new chief minister was Richelieu's Italian protégé, Jules Mazarin : Richelieu's foreign policy was to continue, but the style of government would change. Where Richelieu had become authoritarian and abrasive, Mazarin was supple and ingratiating, seeking to divide and neutralize his enemies, rather than crush them; Gaston and others exiled by Richelieu returned to court.

By the start of 1643 it was apparent that Louis' days were numbered. For the first time he was too ill to accompany his armies on campaign. He was weary of government: he wished only to see his son come of age and talked of retiring to Versailles with four Jesuits, to talk of his salvation. In his heart, however, he knew he would not live that long, so he tried to put his affairs in order. His will stipulated that his widow should rule with a council chosen by himself, which was to ensure that she continued his policies. As his maladies worsened, he bore the constant, excruciating pain with his usual fortitude. On 14 May, his feeble body finally succumbed. He asked to be buried without pomp, to avoid burdening his people further; he had brought them enough suffering, not through any lack of concern for their welfare, but because the needs of State left him no option. In his eyes, the war with Spain was a battle for national survival. He sacrificed his own health and happiness for his kingdom's good and expected others to do the same. Of mediocre abilities, he had the sense to appreciate Richelieu's genius and the humility to subordinate himself to one of superior talent, although he found it irksome and even humiliating to do so. It was typical of his misfortunes that he died a few days before the victory at Rocroi, which vindicated his war policy, but in general his legacy was a difficult one: overstretched finances, bitter internal divisions and, above all, a royal minority. With no adult king to impose his authority, those who had contained their resentments under Richelieu could emerge to seek their revenge.

* * *

Compared with France, England seemed in the 1630s to enjoy 'the greatest calm and the fullest measure of felicity that any people in any age for so long time together have been blessed with'.[37] There were no revolts and few riots, which may have owed something to the docility of the English: successive French ambassadors thought them less violent and volatile than continentals.[38] Riots were usually directed against property rather than persons. Many were in defence of traditional rights against greedy landlords, or entrepreneurs backed by the crown. Both used chicanery and strong-arm tactics and some called in Star Chamber to punish those who opposed them. Violence was rare : only two people were killed in a century of disturbances in the fens, as whole communities fought to defend their common rights against the drainers.

Resistance to the crown's fiscal methods was very limited : when asked for new taxes, or fined for breaking long-forgotten laws, most grumbled, but paid up. The fiscal burden on England was lighter than that on France : Louis drew a revenue six times as large as Charles' from four times as many people. Moreover, the French fiscal system was probably even more inefficient than the English, and certainly placed an even more disproportionate burden on the poor. The English were also now spared the depredations of soldiers, against which they had protested so loudly in 1626–8. The English system of poor relief and the crown's efforts to maintain the food supply together made revolts provoked by mere hunger less likely. Yet even if the condition of the English was less desperate than that of the French, they still showed greater restraint, or inertia. Perhaps decades of indoctrination about the subject's duty of obedience had had some effect. Perhaps the English had become used to resolving disputes and grievances by peaceful means, through the law courts and Parliament.[39]

For much of the 1630s, however, it seemed unlikely that Parliament would meet again. Only a foreign war could make Charles call one and he sedulously avoided war. Then, in 1637, came the crisis in Scotland. Charles believed that he understood the Scots and was taken aback when the introduction of his new Prayer Book caused a riot in Edinburgh. Undeterred, he insisted that the clergy should use the book, which many in their congregations denounced as Popish. At Brechin the people remained quiet, but only because the bishop brought a pair of loaded pistols into the pulpit. Charles saw the Prayer Book as bringing a much needed uniformity to the Scottish Church and treated the Scots' opposition as an affront to his authority.

In England he had silenced the few who dared to criticize his ecclesiastical policies, but resentment of being treated as a mere adjunct to England brought together, in the Covenant of 1638, the most powerful forces in Scotland : the aristocracy and the Presbyterian clergy. The latter had long resented James' reintroduction of episcopacy, which they regarded as unscriptural and Popish; now they saw a chance to return to a presbyterian system of Church government. The general assembly of the Scottish Church required all adult males to subscribe to the Covenant: any who refused were threatened or denounced as Papists. Realizing that only by force could he impose his will, Charles cobbled together an army, showing his fondness for legal antiquarianism by summoning to his standard all nobles who held land by feudal tenure. He also showed his poor judgement by appointing two generals who hated each other. Many soldiers deserted; a Catholic officer was lynched by his men. Faced with a highly motivated army, urged on by militant preachers, Charles' soldiers had little stomach for a fight and he was forced to negotiate.

While preparing for war, Charles summoned Wentworth from Ireland and created him Earl of Strafford. Unlike the shyster lawyers and pettifogging bureaucrats who dominated Charles' government, Stafford was a hard man, who saw things in simple, not to say brutal, terms. The Scots, he said, were rebels who must be made to bow to the King's authority. Such simplicity appealed to Charles' tidy and limited mind, but he lacked the courage to pursue Strafford's arguments to their logical conclusion. He sought financial help from the French, Dutch, Spaniards and Genoese, even the Pope. He toyed with the idea of debasing the coinage and forcing the City to lend money. While Strafford's authoritarianism appealed to one side of his character, his legalism led him to agree with most of his other advisers that he should stay within the letter of the law. He could not accept that, if his subjects refused to help him, he was 'loose and absolved from all rules of government' and could take whatever the State required.[40]

In the spring of 1640 even Strafford agreed that if Charles wished to continue the war he would have to call Parliament: he should at least give his people the chance to help him. Charles complied, but with little hope of success. He continued to seek aid from abroad and considered resorting to force if no money was granted. He insisted on a grant of twelve subsidies as the price of giving up ship money. The Commons were not averse to some such arrangement, but wished to discuss grievances first; when they urged him to come to terms with the Scots, Charles dismissed them. The conduct of the Short Parliament (it had lasted only three weeks) reinforced his dislike of Parliaments and his distrust of his subjects, a distrust strengthened when London apprentices demonstrated against Laud and the Queen. Strafford, having learned that some of the Commons' leaders had been in contact with the Scots, pressed Charles to act decisively, but that was not in his nature. Rather than impose arbitrary taxation, he again demanded ship money and revived the long-defunct device of coat and conduct money to pay for raising and clothing his army. By now, however, the taxpayers were no longer docile: they refused to pay either of these levies and local officials refused to collect them. The government, however, remained sublimely confident that ship money would be paid as the law was on the King's side, 'there having been a public judgment passed for the King'.[41]

It may seem odd that at one moment Charles regarded most of his subjects as disaffected and at another assumed that they would meekly obey whatever the judges declared the law to be. Charles, however, was always inconsistent. He oscillated between panic fears of sedition and naïve confidence that uniformity could be established by administrative fiat. With each new piece of news, he lurched from fatalistic pessimism to lunatic optimism, and back again. At times he believed that almost all his subjects, except the Catholics, sided with the Scots, at others he expected them to unite as one against the invaders. The events of 1639–40 showed that he was incapable of meeting the demands of kingship. He lacked the human and political understanding needed to operate the English system of government. He would neither trust his subjects, nor give them any good reason to trust him — and then complained bitterly of their mistrust. He combined an unswerving faith in his own rectitude with a habit of assuming that he had no need to adhere to any agreement he made. His inability to frame a coherent strategy and stick to it drove Strafford to distraction. His insistence on pursuing two mutually incompatible policies ensured that he got the worst of both worlds and created a well-founded impression of deviousness and duplicity.

Having failed to secure money from Parliament, Charles somehow raised an army, which was roundly defeated by the Scots at Newburn. They occupied Northumberland and Durham and began to negotiate, insisting that Charles pay £850 a day for their subsistence during the negotiations. Charles' advisers mostly believed that he had no choice but to end the war on the best terms he could get, but Charles would not sacrifice either Scottish episcopacy or his Prayer Book and expected Parliament to support him if

French ambassador, 'the town would have been engulfed in fire and blood within twenty-four hours.' His friends in Parliament assured him that they had commanded that the apprentices should not harm the Queen's priests, for whose safety he feared.[43]

Amid rumours of plans to impeach the Queen, Charles decided on a pre-emptive strike. He went to Westminster, with several hundred armed men, to arrest Pym, four other MPs, and one peer. He found that 'the birds are flown' and left with cries of 'Privilege of Parliament!' ringing in his ears. That day the newly-elected London common council set up a committee of safety, which took over the government of the City and appointed new commanders for the City militia; the Commons withdrew to the Guildhall, where they were guarded by thousands of armed citizens. Convinced that his wife and family were no longer safe in London, Charles took them, on 10 January, to Hampton Court; no beds had been prepared and they had to share one room. Next day the Commons returned to Westminster in triumph, escorted by the City militia carrying copies of the Protestation on their pikes.

Contemporaries wondered at these strange and dramatic events: how had it happened? At the heart of the problem lay the distorted views which Charles and his opponents, led by Pym, harboured of each other's intentions. Charles saw his enemies as ambitious men, cynically manipulating the ugly passions of the mob in order to seize power. They aimed to strip him of all authority and even to abolish the monarchy. The Scots were, said Strafford, 'a rod over the king, to force him to do anything the Puritan popular humour had a mind to'. Pym saw Charles as the tool, or victim, of a Popish plot in which courtiers, the Laudian clergy and the Papists joined to destroy religion and liberties and to establish Catholicism and absolutism. Pym believed that Charles was being driven by the Catholics, especially the Queen, to use armed force to overawe or expel Parliament, to renege on any concessions he made and to establish a truly absolute monarchy.[44]

Charles' and Pym's views of each other's intentions were flawed, but not implausible. Pym and his allies did want office, not just for its own sake, but in order to rebuild trust between King and people, by ensuring that Charles pursued acceptable policies. Pym and his patron, the Earl of Bedford, appreciated the need to overhaul the royal finances, so that government could be carried on without recourse to the expedients of the 1630s. In his efforts to persuade the King and Lords to accept his proposals, Pym appealed to public opinion, by publishing the Protestation, the Grand Remonstrance and the Commons' votes, traditionally regarded as confidential. Moreover, although one should perhaps view with scepticism the French ambassador's claim that the Commons' leaders directed the apprentices, Pym's allies (notably the MPs for London) organized demonstrations and petitions and were not too concerned if these carried a threat of violence. Lastly, if Pym's aims were conservative, he made novel demands. He tried to make Charles share with Parliament his control of the armed forces and his choice of ministers. The Commons resumed its investigative role and began to take on executive functions, partly to compensate for Charles' inadequacies — he made no provision for carrying on government when he went to Scotland late in 1641 — but the House also increasingly acted as if it were part of the government. It took steps to defend the realm, ordered the removal of some clergymen and the reinstatement of others, encouraged the destruction of images and altar-rails and effectively nullified the Church's independent authority.[45]

If there was thus some substance to Charles' conviction that Pym wished to strip him of his authority, there was more to Pym's belief that there was a 'Popish plot' and that Charles intended to resort to force. There were many Catholics and crypto-Catholics at court. Charles supported Laud's attempts to impose ceremonies reminiscent of Catholicism and to reassert the clergy's authority over laypeople, while showing little of the hostility to Popery so widespread among his subjects. He re-established informal links with the Papacy and found in successive papal envoys, notably the Scotsman George Con, an Italianate sophistication and appreciation of fine art far removed from the boorish insularity of most Englishmen. Con found that Charles sympathized with the Catholics' plight and sought to reinforce the antithesis in Charles' mind between the loyal Catholics and disloyal 'Puritans'. Catholics figured prominently in Charles' military preparations in 1639. Many became army officers and Charles hoped to use the Catholics of Ireland, South Wales and the Scottish Highlands against the Scots rebels. The Queen arranged a collection among English Catholics for the war effort and Charles sought money from foreign Catholic powers; one of the Irish rebel leaders claimed (falsely) that he had a commission from Charles to make war on Parliament.

Fear of a Popish plot merged into fears that Charles would use armed force against his subjects. Pym was convinced that Strafford had planned to bring over an 'Irish Popish army' to intimidate the English Parliament. During 1641 there were two 'army plots'. In the first, some officers planned to use the forces in the north against Parliament and to seize Portsmouth, which could serve as a landing-place for foreign troops. In the second, it was proposed to circulate a petition in the army, which some hoped would turn it against Parliament. There were also moves to raise troops in London, ostensibly for the Portuguese service, and to seize the Tower and rescue Strafford; later Lunsford's appointment provoked panic, as Londoners feared he might use the Tower's cannon to pound the City to rubble.

For much of 1641 Charles refused to disband the Irish army, which kept alive fears that he planned to bring it to England. When he went to Scotland, there was a plan to seize, and perhaps kill, his leading opponents there. He returned to London with a large armed escort and more armed men gravitated to Whitehall, whence they sallied out to pick fights with the citizens. Finally, there was the attempt on the five members. Charles may not have known of all these designs. Some reports may have been exaggerated and accompanied by wild rumours of French or Irish armies marching on London, or of Papists rising and cutting Protestants' throats. There was still much solid evidence and, as Pym said, 'The plots have been very near the King, all driven home to the court and the Popish party.' The Queen pressed her husband to find men and money from somewhere and rout his enemies: she boasted that she had ten thousand men ready to rise at three days' notice. Charles, however, while he was attracted by the idea of reasserting himself, lacked the nerve, or the resources, to do so effectively.[46]

Amid these rumours and anxieties, emotions ran high. It was fear, above all, which lay behind the hounding of Strafford. He alone had the resolution needed to use force against Parliament, so he had to be destroyed, like a wild beast: Laud, who was even more hated, was not tried until 1644. It was fear that brought respectable Londoners on to the streets and drove conservative MPs to endorse measures which normally they would have rejected. In time, however, a reaction set in against the Commons' leaders' extremism, which was to give Charles the support he needed to fight a civil war.

When the Long Parliament met, Charles had no choice but to make concessions. He agreed to a Triennial Act, whereby Parliament was to meet at least once every three years, for a minimum of fifty days : he was no longer to be free to call and dismiss Parliament at will. After the reform legislation of 1641, Charles' only revenues were from the crown lands, wardship and the customs (now given for a limited period), so he was dependent on additional grants from Parliament. With most of the obvious grievances and obnoxious advisers removed, it might have seemed possible to make a fresh start. Charles would have to call Parliament regularly and the Commons would have the financial power to stop him misusing his authority ; he would thus be forced to pursue policies acceptable to his people. Pym and Bedford proposed that Charles should rebuild trust by taking leading parliamentary figures into office, while they would overhaul the royal finances. Pym struggled to persuade the Commons to tackle this problem, but MPs wanted fewer taxes, not more. Even if Pym had succeeded, Charles was unlikely to place any trust in men he saw as hostile to monarchy, especially after Strafford's death. Although Charles made substantial concessions, he did so with bad grace — he said he disliked the Triennial Act so much that no-one could blame him if he did not observe it — and the army plots and other scares suggested that he could not be trusted. And yet, by the end of 1641, he had won substantial support in both Houses. Why?

One reason was the Commons' leaders' growing extremism and ruthlessness. Strafford's attainder seemed unjust to many and Pym came to rely on scare tactics and intimidation to push his measures through the Commons, restricting debate and denouncing his critics as 'Papists'. After the Irish rising, he called for more sweeping restrictions on the King's powers, notably his command of the armed forces and choice of ministers. Instead of defending the ancient constitution against the King, the leaders now sought to change it drastically : many found the argument that they had to change the constitution in order to preserve it unconvincing.

Meanwhile, there was a major campaign to abolish bishops. Complaints against Laudian innovations came in from hundreds of parishes. Many wished simply to return to the pure Protestantism and moderate episcopacy of James' reign, but others argued that only by removing episcopacy 'root and branch' could the Church be purified. Radical Puritans, long thwarted in their search for religious renewal, believed that Antichrist had fallen and that God would now bring a new godly order.[47] There was an explosion of religious debate and excitement, generating apocalyptic prophecies of change, but not everyone was swept along. Many conservative gentlemen were worried by the call to abolish bishops, not least because it was strongly supported by the Scots : they did not like foreigners telling them what to do. Whatever they felt about Laud, episcopacy was part of the ancient constitution. To abolish it would weaken authority and order, not only in the Church, but in the State and in society. 'If we make a parity in the Church', said one MP, 'we must come to a parity in the Commonwealth.'[48]

The Church and clergy helped to maintain social and moral discipline : the independent congregations which now emerged, many with lay preachers, were subject to no-one. Those who wanted a reversal of Laud's innovations without a total reconstruction of the Church, however, faced the problem that most existing bishops were Laudians and that Charles gave no lead to those seeking limited reform. Meanwhile the Commons' leaders changed the Church as they wished, pointedly refusing to condemn those who contemned the Prayer Book. They met little resistance, but time was to show the depth of popular attachment to the familiar services and even in 1641-2 there were signs of popular hostility to sectarian radicalism.[49]

While the Commons' leaders challenged established authority in Church and State, their appeals for popular support threatened the social order. The general elections of 1640, a flood of petitions to Parliament and the collapse of press censorship unleashed an unprecedentedly open political debate, riots in the provinces and demonstrations in London, which brought about Strafford's death and the bishops' withdrawal from the Lords.[50] The effect of these developments was traumatic. Most MPs wished to preserve the established order in Church, State and society. Until 1640 the main challenge to that order seemed to come from above, from the king, the bishops and the judges. Liberty and property, moderate Protestantism and lay control of the Church seemed to be threatened.

From 1640 it became clear that the existing order could also be menaced from below, by politicians apparently bent on destroying monarchy, by 'mechanic preachers' and by riotous apprentices. For those who wanted a responsible monarchy, a moderate Protestant church and gentry rule, the two threats were both disturbing, but more and more came to see that from below as the more dangerous. By 1642 the extremism of Charles' enemies had given Charles enough support to fight a civil war. For most, taking sides was a choice between evils ; many took refuge in neutrality. In the words of the Earl of Northumberland: 'The alteration of government is apprehended on both sides . . . neither king nor Parliament are without fears and jealousies, the one of having his authority and just rights invaded, the other of losing that liberty which freeborn subjects ought to enjoy and the laws of the land do allow us.'[51]

Charles described his opponents as 'traitors, most of them Brownists, Anabaptists and atheists, such as who desire to destroy both Church and State'. In fact, many who adhered to Parliament did so with great reservations. 'Let us not think we have nothing because we have not all we desire', pleaded one. The two Houses seemed unsure how much authority they possessed without the King: not until 1643 did they introduce compulsory taxation and they appointed new judges only in 1646.[52] Many found it difficult to justify resistance to the King, clinging to the fiction that Charles was the prisoner of evil advisers, or deranged, and so not answerable for his actions. Parliament, called into being by the King, took up arms by his authority against his person. Others invoked the law of nature and the right of self-preservation. Many tried to justify resistance while conceding that he possessed a measure of independent authority, two propositions which were logically incompatible with one another.[53]

Despite their caution and qualms of conscience, to win the war the Parliamentarians had to assume more and more sweeping powers and to look, realistically and constructively, at the problems of government finance. No longer could they take refuge in talk of royal waste and mismanagement: they needed to raise large sums, quickly. The monthly, or weekly, assessment, based (ironically) on ship money, fixed a quota for each county, which was then apportioned between its inhabitants. Parliament also introduced an excise, mainly on alcoholic drinks, which Charles had considered, but had never dared to introduce. Both taxes were burdensome and unpopular: the excise affected the poor more than the rich and excisemen could enter people's homes to check on their brewing. There was some violent resistance, but Parliament, unlike Charles in the 1630s, had an army, which suppressed it. In other ways, too, MPs had to use methods which they had earlier condemned.

In wartime, governments faced larger problems (raising men, money, horses, carts and provisions) and could not spare the time for the normal slow procedures of local government. Parliament and its agents rode roughshod over legal rights, arguing that individual interests should give way to that of the nation: in other words, they invoked reason of State. The property of Royalists and alleged 'delinquents' was confiscated, often on flimsy evidence, critics of Parliament were sent to the Tower. The war imposed a horrific burden, as armies of both sides demanded to be supported by the civilian population. Parliament's 'tyranny' came to seem worse than that of the 1630s and England found itself with a government more 'absolute' than any it had ever known.

The revulsion of feeling against Parliament did Charles little good. Royalist armies were often the most ruthless and predatory of all and distraught civilians sought salvation, not in Royalism, but in a return to peace and normality. The outcome of the war was decided by Parliament's superior resources, organization and performance on the battlefield. It defended the richest part of the kingdom, with London's trade and money market a priceless asset. The Royalists were spread around the periphery, embarrassed by Parliamentarian strongholds in the areas they controlled. The Scots' decision, in 1643, to enter the war increased the Royalists' problems, especially in the north. Parliament, which controlled the existing machinery of government, proved better able to develop a fiscal and administrative system, controlled by parliamentary committees, to support the war effort; their sense of commitment was symbolized by the creation of the New Model Army in 1645.[54] The Royalists relied more on improvisation and increasingly used naked force to extract money from their shrinking territorial base.

Rather surprisingly, Charles enjoyed war. The refined aesthete found camp life exhilarating and showed real courage on the battlefield, but his political weaknesses persisted. He still found it difficult to choose between different options and indulged in wildly unrealistic intrigues with foreign Catholics, notably the Irish. These were usually found out and gave credence to his enemies' claim that he was a tool of the Papists. At times he showed an alarming lethargy and fatalism: God would either punish him for betraying Strafford or forgive him and scatter his enemies; 'either I will be a glorious king or a patient martyr'. This submission to divine providence may have given him more in common with Oliver Cromwell (now emerging as one of Parliament's leading generals) than either of them realized, but it did not make for positive decision-making. When asked to negotiate after the crucial defeat at Naseby, Charles replied that God would not allow rebels to prosper.[55] Meanwhile, the close-knit royal family dispersed. In 1644 Henrietta left to complete her final pregnancy in France : Charles never saw her again. As the war ended in 1646, the Prince of Wales made his way to France, to be followed by James in 1648. As Mary was in the Dutch Republic with her husband, William II, Prince of Orange, only two of the younger children, Henry and Elizabeth, remained in Parliament's custody.

The many moderates in Parliament had agreed to the arbitrary methods needed to win the war because they were sure that, once defeated, Charles would have to agree to their demands. These centred on shared control of the armed forces and the King's choice of advisers, plus the establishment of a Presbyterian church (the price of Scottish aid). These demands were designed to prevent a recurrence of the abuses of the 1630s in Church and State, but Charles refused to agree to any of them, except on a temporary basis. He saw his defeat in the civil war as irrelevant : politically he was indispensable, as no settlement could be reached without him, and he hoped to play on the divisions among his enemies. He also believed it would be morally wrong to abandon any of the crown's powers : they were not his to give, but were held in trust for his successors ; nor would he abandon the Church. The constitutional and religious issues were inseparable : 'If the pulpits teach not obedience' he wrote 'the king will have but small comfort of the militia.' Presbyterianism taught that rebellion was lawful 'and that supreme power is in the people to whom kings ... ought to give account and be corrected when they do amiss'.[56]

Charles' attitude gravely embarrassed the majority in Parliament, who wanted a settlement based on limited, responsible monarchy, and who now faced two unpalatable alternatives. They could either reach a settlement on Charles' terms, which after the bloodshed of the civil war was unthinkable, or they could reach a settlement without the King and abolish the monarchy, which for most was equally unthinkable. Unwilling to think the unthinkable, they went on negotiating, hoping that Charles would, in the end, see reason. By 1648 it seemed that Parliament, faced with a populace desperate for a settlement and a restive army, was the more likely to weaken. Then Charles started a second civil war, by persuading the Scots to invade England on his behalf. Parliament's response was ambivalent — some were more afraid of the army than of the Scots — but the army's was not. To men who saw

God's hand in every event, the army's victory in the first civil war showed that God was with them: to challenge His verdict was tantamount to blasphemy. They resolved to bring 'Charles Stuart, that man of blood, to an account for the blood he has shed and the mischief he has done'.

The New Model was in no way typical of English, or even Parliamentarian, opinion. Always more radical in religion and politics than the other Parliamentary armies, it had learned at first hand in 1647 just how slippery a negotiator Charles could be: the second civil war completed its disenchantment. The majority of MPs, however, still wanted a settlement based on monarchy. They rejected the army's demand that they break off negotiations with the King so, on 6 December 1648, Colonel Pride brought a file of musketeers to the door of the Commons. He arrested forty-five MPs and kept out another ninety-six; many more stayed away in protest. Here was a far more drastic infringement of the liberties of Parliament than Charles' attempt on the five members, which brought to an end efforts to achieve a settlement broadly acceptable to the political nation. For more than eleven years England was to be ruled by the army, fronted by a variety of assemblies, all more or less unrepresentative of civilian opinion. Those who continued to sit in Parliament after the purge — nicknamed the Rump — made it clear that only a select few, marked out by godliness and political radicalism, were now to exercise political power.

Pride's Purge sealed Charles' fate. For years he had believed his enemies were bent on destroying monarchy: now his prophecy came true, thanks mainly to his own obduracy and penchant for confrontation. The Rump wasted little time in giving Charles the chance to play the role of martyr, for which he had long prepared. While it set up a 'high court of justice', Charles prepared for death, making notes on holy living and holy dying which were to form the basis of John Gauden's *Eikon Basilike*, a book which bequeathed to posterity an image which bore little resemblance to Charles' conduct as King. Brought to trial, Charles conducted his defence with dignity and articulacy: even his stammer disappeared. The judges had difficulty in countering his arguments and were reduced to ordering him to be silent. Witnesses swore to seeing Charles making war on his people; the soldiers, and some spectators, made hostile noises. On 27 January 1649 the judges resolved that Charles was a 'tyrant, traitor, murderer and public enemy to the good people of this nation'. Three days later he walked through the Banqueting House and took his place on a scaffold draped in black. Troops held back the crowds so that few heard his final words : that he died a member of the Church of England, that he was going from a corruptible to an uncorruptible crown and that 'a subject and a sovereign are clear different things'. The executioner struck his head from his body with a single blow.

*　　*　　*

As news of Charles' troubles of 1641-2 reached France, Richelieu remarked ruminatively that Strafford 'has been and is no more ; we are here at present and one day we shall no longer be'. He blamed Henrietta Maria. 'The nature of women' he wrote 'inclines them to follow their instincts rather than reason.' France's war with Spain, he added, ruled out any chance of sending help to Charles.[57] The deaths of Richelieu and Louis left France even less able to intervene across the Channel. Royal minorities were always difficult. Anne of Austria was proud, irascible and inexperienced in government, while Mazarin was an able diplomat, but knew little of France's internal affairs. Like Richelieu he was a shrewd politician, who created an extensive clientele. Like Richelieu, he lent to the crown on a vast scale : indeed, he accumulated the greatest personal fortune of the century. He was widely hated : many saw him as a greedy foreigner, plundering France for his own profit, flaunting his ill-gotten wealth and foisting his upstart nieces onto the cream of the nobility. Where Richelieu sought to crush opponents, Mazarin tried to buy off or neutralize them ; he was smooth and insinuating, a master tactician with little sense of strategy, who often ended up being too clever for his own good.[58]

The key to Mazarin's power lay not in his political skills but in his relationship with the Queen. Anne had not greatly enjoyed her marriage — Louis XIII was not easy to live with — and she had spent most of her time in the normal pastimes of a lady of wealth, leisure and limited abilities — the theatre, gambling and gossip. When Louis died she was in her early forties, a handsome woman still susceptible to masculine charm. Charm was something Mazarin had in abundance : exquisitely polite and deferential, he spoke excellent Spanish and seemed, as a foreigner, to be dissociated from the factions at court. Anne came to trust him implicitly and, almost certainly, became his wife; their partnership was based far more on affection than that of Louis and Richelieu and so was more secure. Mazarin was also to serve as a surrogate father to the young Louis XIV.

Louis' will provided that Anne should govern with a regency council, but she persuaded the Parlement to set the will aside, just as Marie had done in 1610. The new regime was very vulnerable. Anne lacked both ability and experience and Mazarin was unpopular, not least with Richelieu's many enemies, some of whom plotted to assassinate him. Unlike that of the 1610s, the regency was committed to carrying on a major war, using resources that were already overstretched. More new offices were sold, the intendants' fiscal powers were extended, troops were used to coerce taxpayers. More and more fiscal legislation was pushed through increasingly hostile sovereign courts; loans were contracted on ever more ruinous terms. In their desperate effort to sustain the crown's credit, ministers resorted to dangerous expedients. To provide security for yet more loans the *taille* was farmed to a syndicate of financiers and collected by the intendants. The crown seized the revenues of the towns, forcing municipal authorities to borrow to meet their needs. Revenues were pledged for years ahead as security. The crown had no immediate prospect of repaying its creditors and so was effectively bankrupt. Any serious interruption of tax collection would trigger a major crisis.[59]

That interruption came in May 1648, when the Paris Parlement called a meeting of the Parisian sovereign courts in the Chambre St Louis. For years the courts had delayed the registration and hindered the implementation of fiscal edicts; the crown had responded by relying more and more on intendants and armed force. The regular revenue officials were increasingly excluded from tax collection, and the profits that went with it; legal officials resented the frequent interference of the royal council. Officials of all kinds found their livelihood threatened by the creation of new offices and the 'raising' of their salaries, which were often not paid, in return for which they paid a further capital sum to the crown. Forced loans proliferated, the crown haggled over the renewal of the *paulette* and failed to pay the interest on its annuities. By early 1648, the officials, usually embroiled in disputes among themselves, were showing an unwonted solidarity. Charles I's fiscal devices mostly affected particular groups, but multiplied to a point where those groups formed almost a national opposition. Similarly, the regency's fiscal policies upset so many of the diverse groups in French society that, for once, they banded together and demanded that those policies should be reversed.[60]

At the news of the forthcoming meeting in the Chambre St Louis, hopes rose of a cut in taxation ; many taxpayers stopped paying, as the English had at the time of the Scots invasion. The meeting lasted three weeks and produced a broad programme of reform which would have seriously weakened the monarchy and reversed recent moves towards centralization, epitomized by the intendants. The Queen accepted the proposals, hoping to abandon them later; law courts applied them in deciding cases which came before them. The Paris Parlement was not satisfied : it called for reductions in taxation and stringent restrictions on the crown's fiscal powers. Convinced that the Parlement was being led astray by a few trouble-makers, Mazarin ordered the arrest of three of its leading members, including the popular Pierre Broussel. The Parisians reacted much as Londoners had reacted to the attempt on the five members : they took to the streets. When the government tried to deploy troops, barricades were erected across the narrow streets and the soldiers were met with a hail of stones and bullets. 'All the rabble at London when they were highest', commented an English observer, 'were not worthy to be named with this people, who will burn, kill and slay all who oppose them.' The Queen released Broussel, but it was two days before calm was restored.[61]

The days of the barricades showed that the crown could not impose its will on the Parlement and the Parisians. Henrietta Maria, with a sense of *déjà vu,* prophesied the end of the monarchy. On 22 October the regent issued a declaration promising various reforms, including the revocation of new offices and taxes, the withdrawal of most intendants, restrictions on royal powers of arbitrary imprisonment and a cut of one quarter in the *taille*. The parallels with Parliament's legislation of 1641 were clear : the crown would now be unable to introduce taxation unacceptable to the law courts or to deal arbitrarily with its critics. The courts would curb the King's actions to a point where he might become a mere figurehead. The Queen was in an impossible position. If she implemented the reforms she had promised she would not have the money to continue the war; if she did not she would provoke howls of protest. Amid continued reports of disobedience on the part of law courts and taxpayers, news came of the preparations for Charles' trial. On 5 January 1649 the royal family fled from Paris to St Germain-en-Laye and found (like the Stuarts at Hampton Court) that no preparations had been made for their arrival.

The conduct of the Parlement and Chambre St Louis convinced Mazarin that the contagion of rebellion had spread from England to France; their demands would, he believed, 'abolish the best part of the monarchy'. The crowds who had called for the release of Broussel reminded him of those who had called for Strafford's head: Mazarin tended to identify with Strafford and blamed Charles' troubles on his sacrificing his chief minister. The Queen thought that Charles' execution was 'a blow to make all kings tremble', a view shared by the English Royalists at her court. She and Mazarin believed they were fighting for the very existence of monarchy, a struggle in which no holds were barred: deceit, trickery and brute force were legitimate weapons in a fight for self-preservation.[62] Mazarin resembled Charles, not only in accusing his opponents of seeking to destroy the monarchy, but also in refusing to recognize that they might have genuine grievances.

Both Parlement and Parliament believed in monarchy, but expected the monarch to rule responsibly, in the best interests of the people. A leading member of the Parlement told the Queen: 'The greatest advantage a sovereign can possess on earth consists in reigning always by love over his subjects ... he cannot commit a graver mistake than to have himself obeyed continually through terror.' If the king behaved unjustly, his majesty was debased.[63] The Parlements argued that he should comply with the nation's laws and customs, as defined by the sovereign courts, and defended traditional individual and corporate interests against the proponents of 'reason of state'. They accepted that the king could override the law in an emergency, but argued that he should not invoke his 'absolute' power unless it was absolutely necessary.[64]

Both the sovereign courts and Parliament were faced with the problem of how to make the king use his powers within proper limits, if he refused to limit himself. Neither really developed an ideological justification for restraining the king, preferring to stress his obligation to restrain himself. The practical steps which they took reflected their different natures. Parliament was basically a legislative body, which did not claim a right to participate in government: indeed, the Triennial Act envisaged that the King would continue to direct the government and the further constraints they demanded — a share in control of the armed forces and the choice of ministers — were essentially negative, to prevent the King from misusing his authority. The sovereign courts had a permanent assured existence: they could secure amendments to, or delay the implementation of, royal edicts. The king could override their objections in a *lit de justice*, but it was uncertain whether an under-age king could do so, nor did this prevent the courts from interpreting and applying the laws as they saw fit. During the Fronde, they often remonstrated against edicts and decreed that, pending an answer from the crown, the edicts should not be observed. This virtual veto on legislation limited royal power as much as Parliament's demands would have limited that of Charles I.

However deferential their outward demeanour, both sovereign courts and Parliament sought changes which would have substantially reduced the king's power. In that sense, both Charles and Mazarin were right, but they failed utterly to appreciate the motives behind such demands. Some members of the Parlement and Parliament were ambitious, or narrowly selfish, but there was also a measure of principled outrage at the predatory, dishonest and heavy-handed conduct of both governments. Apart from protecting their property, or seeking office, many wished to restore to the monarchy the integrity and the respect for justice which it had lost. The methods used might be novel, but the basic aim was conservative and restorative: to ensure that the king fulfilled properly his responsibilities to his people.

Faced with the crown's intransigence, both Parlement and Parliament were driven to use methods which ran counter to their basic principles. A few members may actively have encouraged demonstrations and riots: both bodies made use of them, to put pressure on the crown and, in England, the Lords. To Charles and Mazarin, to countenance such demonstrations was irresponsible: the people were volatile and violent, a 'many-headed monster' which, once awakened, might overthrow government and order. Both Paris and London had a history of crowd violence: note the mutilation of Ancre's body and the lynching of Dr Lambe. While favourites like Ancre or Buckingham might be hated, the kings themselves were popular. Louis XIII was cheered whenever he visited Paris ; James I may have been less than gracious to his subjects, but they turned out in droves to watch him pass. Charles was cheered when he returned from Scotland late in 1641 and after the civil war Parliament refused to let him return to London for fear of demonstrations in his favour.

Most people blamed evil advisers, not the king, for the ills they suffered and few harboured any hostility to monarchy. If they rioted in London in 1641 or in Paris in 1648, it was mainly because they were afraid that the king would use violence against them : the most serious disturbances occurred amid rumours of the movement of royal troops. Both Parlement and Parliament were forced into a posture of rebellion by the ruler's leaving the capital and resorting to force : the Queen and Mazarin mounted a blockade of Paris early in 1649. It was not a position which most members relished. The councillors of the Parlement were royal officials, as were many MPs ; loyalty and obedience to the crown ran deep. They knew, however, that to submit meekly would lead not only to further fiscal abuses but also to swingeing vengeance. The Parlement showed its royalism by sending condolences to Henrietta Maria on Charles' death, and politely declined nobles' offers of military aid, but it had no intention of capitulating and the Queen had to come to terms with the Parlement in the Treaty of Rueil (March 1649). Parlement and Parliament resisted the King with great reluctance, but in the final analysis resistance was a lesser evil than submission.

If there were strong similarities between the conduct of Parliament in 1640–2 and that of the Parlement in 1648–9, the magnates' intervention in the Fronde added a complication that was absent in England. Some nobles felt that they had been unjustly excluded from high office, others wanted governorships or pensions. They rarely agreed among themselves. Condé, the greatest of all, a brilliant general who had inherited his father's hopes of the crown, was tetchy and capricious. Gaston, that perpetual focus of faction, kept dithering and changing his mind. Yet however unpredictable or even unstable the nobles might be, their military power created further problems for a government already wrestling with a virtual bankruptcy and the 'revolt of the judges'. The Parlement, the Parisians and the nobles had little in common, but they could agree in denouncing Mazarin and the crown's fiscal policies. They claimed that the cardinal kept the war against Spain going for his own gain and that he and other financiers made excessive profits; they called for his dismissal, peace with Spain, cuts in taxation and a rigorous inquiry into the financiers' misdeeds. Much of this programme was naïve. Spain would not make peace, except on terms humiliating to France. Tax cuts would leave the crown still less able to pay the officials' salaries, the interest on annuities or the pensions which the nobles craved. A chamber of justice would lead to a collapse of royal credit and bankruptcy, which would mean heavy losses not only for the hated financiers but also for the many important people who invested discreetly in the king's debts.[65]

Mazarin and the Queen were faced with demands which they could not meet, but were too weak to crush their opponents, so resorted to risky, short-term expedients. They promised concessions (as in the declaration of 22 October 1648) which they tried not to implement. They promised rewards which they could not afford (often the same one to more than one person), in order to win over individuals and foment divisions among the nobles. They tried force, but with little success: the treaty of Rueil left things much as they were. They imprisoned Condé and two other princes, which led to denunciations in the Parlement of arbitrary imprisonment; after a year, they were released. Forced to agree to cuts in the *taille*, they fell back on still more dubious expedients, further anticipation of the revenue and loans at still more ruinous interest. Each manoeuvre bought a little time, won over a noble or two or brought in a little money, but at the cost of creating more resentment and plunging further into the financial mire. With the crown unable to impose its authority, local rivalries raged unchecked and mercenary armies ravaged the countryside. In the spring of 1651, the Queen felt so isolated and vulnerable that she believed she had no choice but to release the three princes and send Mazarin into exile. France seemed ungovernable. Surely the days of effective monarchy were numbered.

# 6
# Rebuilding

Mazarin's enforced departure was a striking testimony to the crown's weakness. It also removed the only factor uniting the various elements in the Fronde. As noble armies inflicted upon the peasantry suffering worse than any seen in England and Condé intrigued with the Spaniards, the sovereign courts became alarmed. They wished to preserve the concessions they had gained, but they had no wish to see France slide into anarchy. Like some English MPs, they wondered whether the repercussions of opposing misgovernment might prove more damaging than the misgovernment itself. In England, defiance of the King was followed by the growth of religious radicalism and popular political action, by a destructive civil war and by the army's intervention in politics. France saw no radical political force comparable to the New Model (except, perhaps, at Bordeaux), but the nobles' violence and irresponsibility came to seem a greater threat to the officials' interests and sense of propriety than the crown's fiscal measures had been. So they came to terms, reluctantly, with the Queen and even with Mazarin (who returned to court late in 1652); but not immediately.

For two years after Mazarin left for Cologne, the Queen's government lurched from crisis to crisis. The King was declared of age in 1651, but at thirteen he was too young to assert himself effectively. Condé levied taxes, raised an army and marched towards Paris, where his allies seized control of the city government and imposed a reign of terror reminiscent of the days of the League. With the Parlement and the Parisians torn between hatred of Mazarin and hatred of Condé, resistance to the royal will slowly crumbled. On 22 October 1652 the King held a *lit de justice* in which he forbade the sovereign courts to meddle with 'affairs of state', but did nothing to undo the reforms of 1648. With his position in Paris increasingly untenable, Condé fled and entered the service of Spain.[1]

The Fronde's failure was due less to the monarchy's innate strength than to divisions among the Frondeurs and to luck: it was fortunate that Spain did not mount a major invasion. Had the nobles been united, they might have imposed their will on the Queen through a regency council, but long exclusion from state affairs had left them ignorant of government and their programme consisted mainly of a call for an Estates General, more jobs for nobles and the removal of Mazarin. Many, concerned only for themselves, were willing to obey even a regime headed by Mazarin, provided their material interests were respected. The sovereign courts, too, were willing to serve the crown, but expected it to treat them fairly. Both nobles and officials stood to gain substantially from the existing system — from offices, pensions and investment in the royal finances — provided the crown did not cheat them of their gains. Civil war disrupted agriculture and the collection of taxes, so would do them considerable harm if it lasted for more than a short time.[2]

In dealing with the Fronde, the Queen could exploit not only the divisions among the Frondeurs but also the people's loyalty to the King. Nobles and judges might argue that he was manipulated by others, but this fiction became hard to sustain when he came of age and declared his will in person. The crown could also rely on the support of many financiers: it owed them so much that they preferred to lend more, however weak it might seem, rather than risk losing everything in a royal bankruptcy; Mazarin's own credit, wealth and contacts helped to maintain confidence. When the crown finally triumphed, its victory was not unqualified. The royal debt was larger than ever and financiers expected to be rewarded for their loyalty. The disruption of civil war and the habits of disobedience which had developed would make a return to ordered government slow and difficult. Finally, the lessons of the Fronde had to be remembered: it was dangerous to provoke the officials and nobles too far by tampering with their material interests. The crown would have to shore up its finances and raise enough to continue the war with Spain, without using expedients which would unduly upset the officials and nobility. Its choice of fiscal methods would be more restricted than before.[3]

Gradually the old tax-collecting machinery was reactivated. Intendants were restored with the primary task of getting revenue flowing again. There was no attempt at the sort of radical reconstruction of the revenue system undertaken by Parliament: Mazarin was never much interested in administrative detail and to attack the vested interests involved would have been politically suicidal. The intendants sought to ensure that peasants paid their taxes and that nobles did not protect their villages against the taxman; troops were billeted on the most recalcitrant. The crown's methods were brutal, but it had little choice. It had borrowed heavily on the security of future revenues, so had to ensure that those revenues were collected: it still needed the financiers' loans for the war against Spain.[4]

Habits of disobedience were not confined to taxpayers. The sovereign courts had been shaken by the upheavals triggered off by their challenge to the crown, which now avoided gross assaults on their privileges and jurisdiction, but they had lost neither the capacity nor the will to oppose its edicts. The Paris Parlement still saw itself as representing the interests of the nation; the King had forbidden it to meddle in affairs of state, but had not taken away its power to do so. It still challenged royal edicts and obstructed their implementation; such opposition was less dramatic than the broad constitutional claims made in 1648, but was far harder to overcome. The courts had a more detailed knowledge of law, and better records, than the King's councillors, who found it difficult to monitor and to counter the manifold cases of obstruction and evasion. The only effective way to prevent such opposition was to avoid measures which would antagonize the judges, but the financial needs of war meant that such self-restraint was not yet possible; the crown continued to resort to bribery and to imprisoning recalcitrant individuals.[5]

The opposition of the provincial estates was less formidable. They were occasional institutions, often weakened by divisions between clergy, nobles and third estate, whereas the sovereign courts were tightly knit, permanent and administratively indispensable. The stubbornness of the most powerful, the estates of Languedoc, succeeded only in bringing more arbitrary taxation and the lodging of more troops in the province. Their future lay, not in political confrontations which they were destined to lose, but in extending their administrative role, notably in assessing and collecting taxes. In that way, they were to become as valuable to the crown as the sovereign courts and developed similar tactics of evasion and obstruction.[6]

In the difficult years after the Fronde, Louis XIV grew to manhood. Never very interested in reading and booklearning — he preferred to have documents read to him — he was physically very active, passionately fond of hunting and martial exercises. Unlike his father he had a very robust constitution which enabled him to survive a lifetime of gross overeating, sexual indulgence, violent exercise and the attentions of his doctors. He exuded a self-confidence which he did not always feel: the traumas of the Fronde left a deep psychological scar. He believed that there were, in both England and France, powerful forces hostile to monarchy, which had taken advantage of royal weakness — his minority, Charles' abandoning Strafford — to make a bid for power. After having to flee his capital, he never really trusted Paris: he saw it as a potential source of trouble which needed to be controlled, not as a symbol of his power and glory. The difficult experiences of his early teens left him suspicious and insecure. He hid his feelings and weighed his words carefully; he had a penchant for secrecy and the use of spies. Always quick to assert his authority, he would not tolerate defiance, dissent or even reasoned criticism, so drove opposition underground. Wary of possible betrayal, he placed his trust in a few carefully chosen ministers and balanced one against another. He rarely dismissed a minister and expected them to reciprocate the loyalty he showed them; he tolerated incompetence more readily than disloyalty.[7]

His views on the Fronde and the monarchy owed much to Mazarin. While many saw the cardinal as a duplicitous and rapacious adventurer, he gave Louis a far fuller training in kingship than his father had had. Louis XIII had learned the hard way that even those closest to him wanted to use him for their own ends; Louis XIV grew up within a secure and affectionate domestic environment. Whether or not Anne married Mazarin, he acted as a father, endlessly discussing with Anne the progress of the 'confidant', as they called him. Mazarin instilled into his charge his own views on government, so that Louis could become the ideal master whom the cardinal had never had. They read official documents together — by 1661 Louis had a wide knowledge of European affairs — and the young king participated in the business of the royal councils. In addition, Mazarin tried to mould Louis' character, stressing the responsibilities as well as the techniques of kingship.

Neither doubted that royal authority came from God, so that resistance to it was tantamount to blasphemy, or that policy and decision-making lay solely with the King: he should take advice, but the final responsibility was his alone. When Parliament forced Charles II to make war on the Dutch, Louis wrote: 'It is perverting the order of things to attribute decisions to the subjects and deference to the sovereign.' Popular assemblies were always led by the least sensible of their members. In France, he told his son, 'you will find no authority that is not honoured to derive its origin ... from you ... no corporation that does not see its principal greatness in the good of your service and its sole security in its humble submission.'[8] Yet the King's exceptional powers imposed exceptional obligations: 'The deference and respects that we receive from our subjects are not a free gift from them, but payment for the justice and protection that they expect to receive from us.' 'We must consider the good of our subjects far more than our own ... we are the head of a body and they are the members. It is only for their own advantage that we must give them laws and our power over them must only be used by us in order to work more effectively for their happiness.'[9]

Such sentiments were conventional, as were the images of a body politic, or of a king as father to his subjects. Similar views can be found in James I's writings; Charles I, too, believed that he should rule for his people's good. Yet Louis XIV went beyond both traditional views of the French constitution and those of the early Stuarts, both of which assumed that kings should always observe the laws and customs of the realm. James I and Charles I accepted this, although sometimes they interpreted the laws differently from most of their subjects. Louis XIV, in theory, did not. He did not share Charles' exaggerated respect for the judges: he respected their expertise, but thought they were often more concerned to thwart the king's will than to dispense justice to the people. 'The good of the people', not observance of the laws, should thus be the king's main aim: a subjective criterion which, like 'reason of state', put the general interest before the particular. Whereas 'reason of state', like Charles' emergency powers, was invoked only in times of difficulty, 'the good of the people' could be invoked at any time, in overriding particular laws and interests. Just as Louis stressed the concentration of authority in his own hands, so he claimed a supreme discretion in matters of justice; just as the people had no role in decision-making or legislation, so the judges had no autonomous role in justice. Indeed, kings (unlike their subjects) could not evade responsibility for the justice of their actions by remaining within the letter of the law.[10]

'The good of the people' was one of Louis' objectives; pursuit of his 'gloire' was another. This implied not only honour and reputation, but the duty to use to the full the powers and abilities which God had given him in the service of God, the State and himself. Kings should be both 'humble for ourselves and proud for the place that we occupy'.[11] In pursuit of his *gloire*, a king must maintain the dignity of monarchy: magnificence pleased the people. He should uphold the honour and promote the interests of his kingdom through success in war; he should maintain true religion, dispense justice and protect the weak. With so many obligations, kings had to work hard, for, as Mazarin stressed, a king could achieve far more than the greatest of ministers.[12] Louis believed that God had given him the abilities and the sense of duty he needed to carry out his responsibilities. The secrets of successful kingship were hard work and common-sense: he urged his son to take as his model Henry IV, a successful warrior, now seen as wise and benevolent. (He scarcely mentioned his father, or Richelieu.) God, he wrote, 'is infinitely jealous of His *gloire* ... if we fail ... perhaps He will let us fall into the dust from which He raised us'.[13]

While Louis was learning the art of kingship, he developed a rigorous self-control. The perils and humiliations of the Fronde taught him to hide his feelings: several times he had someone arrested after an apparently amicable conversation. His mother had punished him severely for rudeness and swearing, once sending him to his room for two days. Both she and Mazarin stressed the need for politeness and self-discipline: men were moved more by passion than by reason, so kings should set an example of self-restraint. Louis' became legendary: he almost never lost his temper in public, although he argued angrily with ministers or members of his family in private. When his self-control snapped, the effect on bystanders was awesome.[14]

In one respect, however, he proved unable to live up to his own standards. From his initiation by the one-eyed Mme de Beauvais, Louis showed an appetite for women reminiscent of Henry IV's. A dose of gonorrhoea in his late teens did little to cool his ardour. Chastity had never been much in fashion at court and the rewards for giving in to the King could be considerable: even Mme de Beauvais was granted a pension for life. Others seemed destined for still greater rewards, notably Marie Mancini, one of Mazarin's many nieces, with whom Louis fell madly in love in 1658. For kings, however, love and marriage were often different things. In 1659 Spain was at last ready to make peace and Louis' marriage to the Infanta Marie Thérèse was to consummate the reconciliation. Louis, deeply infatuated with Marie Mancini, hoped against hope that the marriage would somehow not come to pass, but Mazarin told him sternly: 'It is not a question of your desires ... your subjects' welfare and your kingdom are at stake.' He added ominously that Condé and others would be quick to profit from any opportunity which Louis gave them.[15] Louis bowed to the inevitable. The Peace of the Pyrenees ended twenty-four years of war; France's frontiers had been reinforced, Habsburg expansionism had been checked and Spain's military supremacy ended. Louis could look forward to a future far more secure than had seemed possible in 1643.

Although the peace was very satisfactory for France, it saddled Louis with a wife with whom he had little in common. Marie Mancini was dark, vivacious and beautiful, a fine horsewoman, who could talk intelligently on a wide range of subjects. Marie Thérèse was stolid, plain and boring. Her interests were confined to a superficial, mechanical piety and gambling: being rather slow-witted, she usually lost heavily. She collected little dogs and dwarves: the dogs, it was noted, were treated better. Sluggish and indolent, with a pale complexion which burned in the sun, she found little pleasure in Louis' hunting trips, nor did she share his imperviousness to bad weather and discomfort. She was often ill, especially when pregnant, and had to suffer the indignity of the King's open favour to his mistresses: never very astute, she was usually the last to know of his affairs. She bore her misfortunes stoically, finding consolation in religion, while Louis, mindful of one part of his responsibilities, slept with her at least twice a month: next day she would take communion and pray for children. Her prayers were answered, in part. Of her five children only the Dauphin lived to maturity and he, unfortunately, took after his mother in both looks and intelligence. When she died in 1683 her passing was little noticed. She had lacked the personality to make an impact at court, where she remained something of an outsider. Her marriage had been part of a diplomatic package and she had done her best to do her duty and to produce heirs. If her life was dreary and sometimes unhappy, her expectations were low and she showed little resentment of her fate.[16]

For Louis, marriage did nothing to interrupt his pursuit of women. Marie Mancini would not become his mistress, but others had no such scruples. While his mother lived he showed some restraint. For a time he seemed to be interested in his sister-in-law, Henriette, sister of Charles II. Her husband, Philippe, Duc d'Orléans, had little to offer his wife. Determined that her second son should not become another Gaston, Anne had dressed him as a girl, with ribbons and flounces, and prevented him from competing in any way with his elder brother. Philippe grew up slothful, effeminate and dissipated, fond of make-up, jewellery and handsome young men, but that did not prevent him from fathering several children, or showing a petulant possessiveness towards his wife. (As the King's brother was known as Monsieur, she was called Madame.) While Louis was attracted to Henriette, he had to contend with his brother's jealousy and the watchfulness of both his mother and hers (Henrietta Maria was still at the French court), who feared scandal if the relationship developed. To evade their scrutiny, Louis used a 'decoy', Louise de la Vallière. She came of a minor noble family and was slightly lame and none too bright, so it surprised everyone (not least Louis) when he fell in love with her and acknowledged her as his mistress. She bore him several children, but there were always others eager to supplant her.

The one who succeeded was Françoise-Athénais, Marquise de Montespan. The daughter of a duke, she was socially far more distinguished than la Vallière, as well as blonder, more beautiful and much more intelligent, with a quick wit and a sharp tongue. She was married to a far from complaisant husband, which made the relationship doubly adulterous. It was six years before the Parlement legally separated Mme de Montespan from her husband, enabling her to appear openly as the King's mistress. Until then, la Vallière remained the 'official' mistress. Louis passed through her bedchamber on his way to Mme de Montespan and during the campaigns of 1672–3 the Queen, la Vallière and Montespan travelled in the same coach to admire Louis' military prowess.

As Louis claimed to be the guardian of public morality, his liaison with Mme de Montespan attracted unfavourable comment. He could not take her to Fontainebleau, because it was in the diocese of her uncle, the Archbishop of Sens, who pointedly circulated the Church's canons against adultery to his clergy. Worse was to follow. With age she put on weight and Louis showed an interest in other women. Unable to compete with her rivals by natural means, she resorted to the supernatural, obtaining love philtres from a well-known Parisian quack, Mme Voisin. Mme Voisin, however, became implicated in a wide-ranging scandal involving poison, magic and black masses, by which means some of the cream of Parisian society had sought to win new lovers or to rid themselves of inconvenient spouses. Many of the allegations were probably false, but Louis followed the investigations avidly, until they reached Mme de Montespan, at which point he promptly had them stopped. She remained at court for the rest of her days, but never regained her position as favourite mistress, not because of the poisoning scandal, but because Louis no longer found her attractive: she had become obese and foul-tempered. As Louis entered middle age, he found a more mature and restful companion in Mme de Maintenon.

At the time of Louis' marriage, this succession of mistresses lay in the future. He was twenty-one, vigorous and full of promise. The end of the long Spanish war opened up a wide range of opportunities for reform at home or glory abroad. Meanwhile, Mazarin's tutelage neared its end; he became frail and gouty and prepared for death, which came at last on 9 March 1661. Together with the Queen Mother, he had steered the monarchy through the storms of the Fronde and had prepared Louis for his responsibilities. Convinced that Mazarin's services to the monarchy had been beyond price, Louis revered his memory and applied his precepts in his government. The day after the cardinal died, Louis called together his leading officials. He confessed later to having felt very nervous, but did not show it. He told them that he was taking over the direction of the government. Each minister was to confine himself to his own sphere. No orders were to be sent out without Louis' approval. There was to be no first minister: the King would play the co-ordinating role of the two cardinals. They had dominated the government partly through their own great abilities, partly because their clienteles linked them to key figures in the administration, armed forces and Church, but they had developed their pivotal role only because the King had been unable to exercise it himself.

Now Louis was determined to rule as well as reign: as King his authority and patronage resources were greater than those of even the greatest minister, but he would need a considerable grasp of detail and strength of character to avoid being manipulated by ministers and courtiers, forever pushing their own viewpoints and pressing for favours. How well would Louis cope with these pressures?

Rather than create his own team of ministers, Louis used that assembled by Mazarin: his instinct was always to stand by tried and trusted servants. Few were honoured with the coveted title of 'minister' — usually only three at a time, never more than five. Most served for a long time — there were only seventeen in over fifty years — and died in office: Louis worked them hard. Of the seventeen, only one was a great noble and only two were soldiers. The rest came from noble families with a long tradition of administrative or diplomatic service. They included three of the Le Tellier family (plus a cousin) and five Colberts; the solitary duke, Beauvilliers, had married a Colbert. Government might seem a family affair, but many ministers were highly ambitious, harsh and ruthless. As the limits of their spheres of activity were ill-defined, they often interfered in each other's affairs and argued furiously over policy. The rivalry between Jean-Baptiste Colbert and the Marquis de Louvois (the second of the Le Telliers) was especially acute: both were abrasive and brutal, formidable workhorses intolerant of opposition. Usually, Louis ensured that these rivalries did not breed disruption, but that ministers competed to serve him. Louis slapped down any minister who over-reached himself, but generally he sought to balance ministers (and families) against one another: there was usually at least one Colbert and one Le Tellier in office. Louis also came to consult ministers individually, as well as formally in his councils.[17]

Any doubts about Louis' determination to rule without a first minister were removed by the fall of Nicolas Fouquet, the leading finance minister of the 1650s. Fouquet was charming, flamboyant and relentlessly ambitious, very successful with the ladies. Although he came of a legal family, his knowledge of the financial world was unrivalled: he was adept at securing loans and would lend himself if other sources failed; if many loans were contracted at very high interest, this reflected the fragility of the crown's credit after the Fronde. The high cost of his borrowing, his slipshod accounting methods and his extravagant lifestyle left him wide open to accusations of profiteering and corruption. At the head of his critics was Jean-Baptiste Colbert, who came of an extensive financier family and learned his trade managing Mazarin's vast fortune. As ambitious as Fouquet, Colbert denounced his methods, accumulated evidence against him and plotted his downfall. While Mazarin lived, Colbert's ambitions remained unfulfilled: the cardinal appreciated the benefits of constructive competition between the crown's servants. With Mazarin dead, Colbert saw his chance. He insinuated to Louis that Fouquet wished to become first minister; it may well have been true and Fouquet seemed to go out of his way to give credence to the allegation.

On 18 August 1661 he invited the King and court to celebrate the completion of his new château at Vaux-le-Vicomte, near Melun. The house had been planned and built as an integrated whole, with close collaboration between Fouquet, the architect Le Vau and the painter and designer Le Brun, who was responsible for the décor and furnishings. The gardens, planned by Le Nôtre, were more ordered and geometrical than any yet seen in France — the triumph of human ingenuity over unruly nature, the 'gardens of intelligence'. Over six thousand guests feasted off gold and silver plates, entertained by Lully's music, a play by Molière and a huge firework display, including a whale belching fire.[18]

As a celebration it was magnificent, ostentatious and politically unwise, for it seemed to support Colbert's claim that Fouquet's vast wealth could have come only from embezzling the King's money. Moreover, in outshining the King (who did not have a dinner service for six thousand) Fouquet seemed to advertise his ambitions: only a first minister could entertain on such a scale. Louis was both impressed and affronted. He was later to use the same team to build Versailles, but for the moment he was so furious at Fouquet's presumption that he had to be restrained from having him arrested on the spot. It was not this visit to Vaux which made him decide that Fouquet had to go: he had, indeed, been there before. The crucial point was Fouquet's fortifying Belle-Ile, an island ten miles long off the coast of Brittany. Colbert gleefully accumulated information of building work and stockpiling of munitions on the island: it seemed that Fouquet was preparing an impregnable base in which he could defy the King with impunity. With memories of the Fronde fresh in his mind, Louis was determined to nip such designs in the bud. On 5 September Fouquet was arrested.[19]

At the time, Louis stated that Fouquet had been arrested for acting contrary to his duty. Later he complained that Fouquet 'could not stop his excessive expenses, his fortifications of his château, his decoration of his palaces, the formation of cabals and placing his friends in important places which he secured for them at my expense in the hope of making himself sovereign arbiter of the state.'[20] While Colbert did everything he could to denigrate Fouquet, there can be no doubt that he was ambitious, that he had fortified Belle-Île, that he withheld from the King information about the royal finances and that he was building a clientele like those of the cardinals. He thus posed a threat to the King's declared intention of being his own first minister and had to be removed, and disgraced, in the first great show trial of Louis' personal reign.

As Louis could not admit that Fouquet made him afraid — fear was an ignoble emotion — he was tried before a chamber of justice on charges of treason and financial malpractice. He defended himself with spirit, his evidence embarrassing many members of the social élite — not least his many amorous conquests. He acidly contrasted his impeccable loyalty to the crown with the Frondeur activities of Séguier, the president of the court. Although it was well known that Louis wanted Fouquet dead, the judges found him guilty only of financial malpractice and sentenced him to banishment, to which Louis added perpetual imprisonment at Pinerolo, where he was closely watched by his gaolers for the rest of his days.

From Colbert's point of view, Fouquet's conviction was only the beginning, for the chamber of justice embarked on a lengthy examination of the royal finances. Many financiers were fined, many 'bad' royal debts to financiers were written off and interest payments withheld in what was (in effect) a partial bankruptcy, from which the crown also made one hundred million livres in fines. The chamber of justice has often been seen as cleansing the Augean stables, sweeping away Fouquet's regime, in which crooked financiers got rich obscenely quickly by robbing the taxpayer and the King; in its place was set up an efficient honest regime, run by professional officials under the control of the King's ministers. That was how Colbert wished it to appear, but such a view is somewhat misleading.

It became clear during his trial that Fouquet was never as rich as Mazarin. The cardinal's will decreed that no inventory should be taken of his possessions and Louis ordered that his wishes should be respected: his services to the crown had been, in Louis' eyes, beyond price. In the three years before his death, Mazarin's fortune had grown from about eight to thirty-five million livres — an increase which Colbert, his man of business, would have found difficult to explain. By focusing attention on Fouquet's misdeeds, Colbert avoided awkward questions about the cardinal and himself. The chamber of justice also (in addition to improving the crown's financial position) made possible a major change of personnel in the revenue administration. Many of those condemned had to sell their offices in order to pay their fines; they were replaced by Colbert's clients, kinsmen, friends and associates. The chamber of justice thus served to replace Fouquet's network of financiers with Colbert's.[21]

It is thus misleading to see Fouquet's fall as bringing a change from buccaneering private enterprise to a regime of professional administrators, concerned only to serve the State. The great majority of financiers and tax farmers were always royal officials; many had offices which conferred noble status. This combination of 'public' functions and private investment was inevitable while offices remained venal and tax collection depended on officials using their personal credit to advance money to the crown. Colbert had no objection to tax farms and revenue contracts: the collection of the fines imposed by the chamber of justice was entrusted to a group of financiers in much the biggest contract of the century. All the contractors were Colbert's associates; one had even been fined by the chamber.[22] It would, however, be wrong to dismiss the changes of the 1660s as simply the replacement of one cartel by another. All ministers installed their friends and clients in provincial office: it helped to overcome problems of communication and to bring some cohesion to the administration.

Colbert brought to the royal finances a ferocious determination and high standards of efficiency. He would not tolerate slipshod or fraudulent accounting and sought to rationalize the tax system, reducing exemptions and trying to ensure that more of the burden fell on those able to bear it. He wished to stop members of town governments and provincial estates abusing their power to enrich themselves at the expense of their fellow citizens. He sought to expand the taxable base by promoting trade and industry. Many of his hopes remained unfulfilled. Political timidity and lack of money prevented any serious reduction of tax exemptions or venal offices. The stubborn inertia of businessmen and officials thwarted many of his plans for economic regeneration. The sheer size of France and its administration defeated his efforts at supervision and regulation. Above all, his plans required peace: with the resumption of major wars from 1672, he and his successors were driven back to the expedients of the era of Richelieu and Mazarin; any fleeting hope of financial reform was lost.

Colbert's accession to power did not change the structure of the fiscal system. Revenue officials still doubled as financiers, private individuals still invested in royal revenues. Colbert brought greater order to the system, reducing opportunities for profiteering: officials had to be content with moderate profits, but they could be reasonably sure that the crown would honour its obligations towards them. Circumstances were at first in his favour. He was strongly supported by the King, who expressed a real interest in finance.[23] The coming of peace reduced royal expenditure, the chamber of justice allowed the crown to renege on many of its debts and so reduce the burden of interest. When those circumstances changed, after 1672, the old bad habits revived.

Fouquet's disgrace confirmed that Louis XIV's style of kingship would be very different from his father's: he actually enjoyed the work of government. He could not oversee all of it: there was far too much detail for one man to grasp, even working six to ten hours a day. Some aspects interested him more than others: diplomacy and war were the especial preserve of princes and he had Mazarin's instruction to build upon. Always aware of the need for full information, he constantly pressed his ambassadors and officials for further details. He was also deeply involved with the army and especially with military administration: winning wars depended as much on feeding and equipping France's ever-growing armies as on victory in battle. Michel Le Tellier and his son Louvois turned the French army into the best organized and best supplied in Europe and increasingly brought the generals and senior officers under their control: in place of a confederation of semi-autonomous units they created a truly royal army. Louis showed much less interest in the navy or in domestic administration: his initial enthusiasm for finance did not last and he came to assume that money would be produced, without worrying about where it came from.[24]

As Louis, despite his declared intention, could not supervise the whole range of government, he took the advice of his experts and ministers. To show that he was in charge, he rejected some of the advice he received: one proposal in twenty, according to St Simon. While allowing ministers considerable freedom to argue in private, he crushingly rebuked any who publicly challenged his declared will. In much the same way, he ordered the Parlements to register edicts before remonstrating against them and required provincial estates to vote what he asked at once, without attaching conditions. The intendants' supervisory role was extended, recalcitrant officials were imprisoned or exiled. Slowly and remorselessly, the central government tightened its grip on the localities.

But if Louis was authoritarian, he sought also to be fair. He respected his officials' material interests and sought to avoid extortionate fiscal methods. He encouraged his people to appeal to his justice and set aside one day a week to receive petitions. He tried to realize his ideal, of a ruler at once authoritative and benevolent, providing for his people's every need.[25] At the same time, however, he watched vigilantly for possible disaffection. Spies stalked the royal court, La Reynie, the lieutenant of police, kept a wary eye on Paris and Louvois scanned the mail as it passed through the post office. Such vigilance — like the destruction of Fouquet — suggested that behind Louis' outward self-assurance lay a nagging fear of another Fronde. If so, he never showed it: he was a consummate actor and nowhere was this more apparent than at his court.

By now, the social life of the upper nobility centred on Paris and the court. The dukes and peers, indeed, were expected to live there. As the Duc d'Antin said, they sacrificed liberty, time, health and wealth in attending the court, but as they owed their fortunes to the King they were obliged to show their gratitude. Attendance at court was not just a matter of duty: its social life was the only one that mattered. To live away from court made one not only unhappy, but ridiculous. Wealth was of little use in itself: it provided a way of asserting status and winning esteem within (literally) one's peer group.

Nobles vied to outdo one another in the elegance of their houses, clothes and carriages. Conspicuous consumption and public display were integral features of aristocratic life, just as keeping up with the Joneses is a feature of twentieth-century suburbia. While some ruined themselves in this scramble for self-advertisement, many did not. Most dukes and peers were rich enough to indulge their whims and the court could bring profit as well as expense. The King had a wide range of rewards at his disposal which he distributed with great care, keeping detailed records of what he gave. Nobles who attended assiduously could solicit rewards for themselves, for their clients and (at a price) for others. Places giving frequent access to the King were eagerly sought: that of the first gentleman of the bedchamber changed hands for 800,000 livres in 1675. Moreover, the King recognized an obligation to protect the highest nobility: he bailed out some who fell heavily into debt but most, despite their extravagance, remained very rich.[26]

The growth of the court and court society under Louis XIII had owed more to the growing attractions of Parisian social life than to the actions of the King, who loathed formality and crowds. Louis XIV, with his acting skills and monstrous ego, was ideally fitted to act as the centrepiece of the court and to impose discipline upon it. With his self-control and politeness he oozed dignity. Although he was only five feet four inches tall, high heels and a wig helped to give him the commanding physical presence which his father had lacked and he played out his ceremonial role to perfection. With everyone seeking access to the King and to the bounty which he controlled, there was a risk that court life could degenerate into an unseemly scramble, while many of those at court were young, spoiled and inclined to self-indulgence. As one who sought to set an example to his people, Louis did not wish his court to become a 'brothel' like that of his grandfather and he possessed both the patience and the determination needed to impose order and regularity.

Access to his person was restricted and regulated by a carefully defined daily round and an elaborate code of precedence. This enabled the King to see who was present, or missing; he was forever scanning the faces before him: 'I do not know him' was the ultimate condemnation. As precedence depended not only on rank but also on his personal favour, he could introduce an infinite variety of gradations into the pecking-order: to be chosen to hold the candlestick while the King prepared for bed was a great honour. Courtiers watched like hawks for subtle indications of changes in the balance of favour. Those whose star seemed to be rising (not least potential mistresses) were eagerly courted; those believed to be slipping were ignored. Behind the veneer of ornate politeness, courtiers treated one another as warily as ambassadors of states on the verge of war. 'Society at court', it was said, 'is like a house built of marble. It is made up of very hard and very polished people.'[27]

To modern eyes, there is something a little absurd about the endless bickerings about precedence at court. In the King's presence, only the Dauphin, his wife and children and the princesses of the blood had the right to be seated; in the Queen's, the right was confined to princesses of the blood and cardinals and there were differing arrangements for the other members of the royal family. Sometimes there were scuffles as individuals asserted their alleged right to take a seat. It might seem ridiculous that people should place such importance on apparently meaningless badges of status (although whether they were more meaningless than personalized car number-plates is open to question). It is quite clear, however, that every-body, from Louis downwards, took them seriously. When Mlle de Melun refused to give up her seat to a duchess, Louis was almost speechless with rage: 'Have her removed from here' he spluttered.[28] It was an age which took precedence and status seriously, when peace conferences were held up for weeks on matters of protocol and when there were wars over who should salute whom in the Narrow Seas. In developing the cult of precedence, Louis created a most effective system of management at no cost to himself. 'Nothing moves the well-bred so much', he wrote, 'as distinctions of rank ... it is one of the most visible signs of my power that I can give importance to a person who in himself has none.'[29]

Louis wished to have the nobility dancing attendance on him partly because he could then be sure that they were not making trouble elsewhere, partly because their presence enhanced his prestige. As noble society was geared to conspicuous consumption the King had to outdo them all. The operas, concerts and other entertainments which he arranged were designed not only to amuse the court but also 'to make the lustre of the throne appear more glorious in the eyes of the people'.[30] This was an objective which found its supreme fulfilment at Versailles. When Louis began his personal rule it was a small hunting lodge, used by his father when he wished to escape from the court. Louis liked the site and decided to build a new château there, but then changed his mind, settling for an 'envelope', adding vast new wings to each side and a long gallery (the Hall of Mirrors) to the rear. In the gardens, Le Nôtre tamed nature as he had at Vaux, on a bigger scale and on a far more difficult site. It sloped, but Le Nôtre levelled it. Much of it was marshy — many workmen died of malaria — and it proved very hard to find sufficient water to supply the lakes and fountains which Louis demanded. Eventually Louis decided on a great aqueduct to bring water from the River Eure, fifty miles away. Thirty thousand soldiers laboured for three years, at a cost of eight million livres, only for Louis to abandon the project with the onset of war. Thanks to a vast expenditure of money and an almost limitless supply of conscript labour, the King's dream was at last turned into reality. In 1682 the court and centre of government moved from Paris to Versailles.

At every turn, the palace stressed the power and prestige of monarchy. The siting of the royal apartments on the central axis showed that its life revolved around the King, while everywhere paintings and tapestries celebrated his achievements. Display and formality took precedence over comfort and privacy. The palace was cold, damp and draughty in winter and too hot in summer. The rules of etiquette were rarely relaxed as the King lived out his life in public. Twice a week he held *appartements* where he made himself more accessible than usual and the courtiers amused themselves with dancing, billiards and cards — the gaming table was always a great leveller. When the King wished to relax, he took a select and honoured few to the smaller château of Marly. As he grew older, he visited Paris less and less: only four times in the last fifteen years of his reign and less than once a year even in the 1670s and 1680s. In 1700 he forbade his courtiers (and his son) to visit the capital.[31]

He was not totally isolated from his people. Anyone who was properly dressed could secure admittance to Versailles with little difficulty, but the distance between Paris and Versailles reduced the likelihood of Parisians coming to gaze upon the King who so rarely visited them. Increasingly, his people knew him through his image rather than at first hand. Louis well knew the usefulness of the arts as media of communication and established academies whose purpose was to use them to glorify the monarchy. Opera and drama, painting and sculpture, medals and inscriptions were all subjected to rigid rules and used to spread the cult of the King. Religious services and triumphal arches celebrated Louis' victories; provincial towns were encouraged to erect monuments to his rule; the government press exulted in his achievements.

In the 1660s, the heyday of Versailles lay in the future. Louis was in his prime, revelling in his new-found responsibilities and eager to make his mark in the world. Colbert was bringing order to his finances, Michel Le Tellier and Louvois were creating a formidable army, the institutions of government bowed to the royal will. Abroad, all seemed calm. Spain was only a shadow of her former self. In Germany, many states looked to France for protection against the Emperor. The Dutch, having secured their independence, wished to develop their trade in peace. Even England seemed

12 Mazarin was the archetypal Italian diplomat, polished and ingratiating, a master tactician with a limited awareness of strategy.

13 LEFT One of several versions of the frontispiece to *Eikon Basilike*, which established the image of Charles I as a martyr for monarchy and the Church of England.

14 BELOW Patel's panorama of Versailles in 1668 shows the early stages of the construction of Louis XIV's vast additions to the old château and the laying out of the gardens.

15 OPPOSITE 'The king governs by himself': one of the allegorical and eulogistic paintings with which Louis XIV adorned the Hall of Mirrors at Versailles.

LE ROY
GOVVERNE
PAR LVI MÊME

16 LEFT Marie-Thérèse and the Dauphin, by Mignard. Fine clothes cannot disguise the bovine mediocrity of Louis XIV's wife and son.

17 ABOVE Physically frail, but with a will of iron, William III emerged, in his early twenties, as Louis XIV's most formidable adversary.

The Solemn Mock Procession of the POPE Cardinalls Jesuits Fryers &c through the Citty of London November the 17th 1680

East View of the King's House, and the adjoining Offices as Intended to have been finished by Sir Christopher Wren.

18 LEFT The great pope-burning processions of 1679 and 1680 displayed the full gamut of anti-Catholic stereotypes.

19 BELOW LEFT Charles II's palace of Winchester was built in conscious imitation of Versailles, although Wren added some stylistic flourishes of his own.

20 RIGHT Hawker's portrait of Charles II (*c.*1680) shows the effects of time (and perhaps of debauchery) upon the 'merry monarch'.

21 James II (painted in exile, in 1690) was always happiest when soldiering: a simple, direct and severe man, he found the intricacies and subtleties of politics beyond him.

friendly. For the first time in very many years, the French had little reason to fear foreign attack. Everything seemed to conspire to make Louis' reign happy, for himself and for France. The young King burned to assert himself. He acted decisively in protocol disputes, but his *gloire* demanded something more striking. Increasingly, his attention turned to the rich cities and farm-lands of the Spanish Netherlands.

\*    \*    \*

When Charles I was executed the English monarchy's future seemed not so much bleak as non-existent. It was abolished, along with the House of Lords, and England was declared a republic. Over the next two years the army crushed all vestiges of opposition in the British Isles, putting Charles II to flight at Worcester in September 1651. After a variety of picaresque adventures he fled to France to what seemed likely to be an indefinite exile. There was no likelihood of a successful rising in England and hopes that he might find help on the Continent proved illusory. It seemed that Charles and his companions had no option but to wait for God to open his subjects' eyes. In fact, his position was less hopeless than it seemed. The army was militarily invulnerable, but politically weak. Many of its members saw in its military success a divine mandate to rule — God had shown He was on their side — but most civilians feared and hated it. It was expensive, authoritarian and sometimes ill-disciplined and its élitist republicanism found little support in a mainly monarchist nation. Whereas many soldiers were sectarians or separatists, most civilians were content to attend their parish churches. The differences between soldiers and civilians might not have proved a source of weakness had the army's leader, Oliver Cromwell, been prepared to rule as a godly military dictator. He certainly believed that God had raised him up for His own purposes, but he was usually too humble to take it upon himself to say what those purposes might be.

When Cromwell declared himself Lord Protector, his main priority was to bring about a generally acceptable settlement: but he refused to sacrifice what he saw as the gains of the civil war, above all religious liberty. He hoped to encourage the Presbyterians (moderate Parliamentarians, alienated by Pride's Purge and the King's execution) to return to local government and to Parliament. Many were prepared to serve his regime, but only in order to turn it into something more to their liking. Most had wished to reach agreement with the King on the basis of limited monarchy, which they much preferred to either a republic or a Protectorate: in 1657 Parliament offered Cromwell the crown, which he turned down. Most Presbyterians also stressed the need for an effective national church, to which all had to belong, in order to reimpose theological orthodoxy and moral and social discipline; they were especially worried by the exhibitionism and insubordination of the Quakers. Finally, the Presbyterians wished to be rid of the army, which Cromwell saw as the main guarantor of religious liberty, which would disappear if the Stuarts and the old Church were restored.

Cromwell's hopes of a settlement were doomed to failure because his aims were incompatible with those of the Presbyterians. His elected Parliaments were difficult to manage, even though their membership and competence were restricted: MPs could take their seats only if they swore not to alter the fundamentals of the constitution imposed by the army in 1653. When these restrictions were removed early in 1658, Parliament became so turbulent that Cromwell had to dismiss it. The Presbyterians had greater hopes of his son Richard, who succeeded Oliver as Protector when he died in September 1658, but when Parliament tried to persuade Richard to bring the army under civilian control, the army forced him to dissolve Parliament and, in effect, to abdicate. Without the Presbyterians, the regime's civilian supporters were few and divided, but the failure of a rebellion in August 1659 showed that nothing could seriously challenge the army — provided it remained united. Soon, however, the army in Scotland, under General George Monk, began to denounce its brethren in England; on 1 January 1660 it began to march south.

Monk was a bluff, taciturn career soldier, who had started out as a Royalist. His professional competence won him the respect of Oliver, who put him in command of the forces in Scotland. His habit of chewing his tobacco and saying little convinced many that he possessed great depth and shrewdness; it was difficult to read his mind, but it may be that there were no profound thoughts to be read, that he was keeping his options open and waiting on events. When he entered England the Rump had just returned to power. After much hesitation, on 21 February Monk ordered it to readmit many of the MPs excluded by Pride's Purge. This restored the balance that had existed in 1648, with a majority ready to negotiate with the King. Monk ordered the reconstituted Long Parliament to prepare for elections for a new Parliament (or Convention) and then to dissolve itself. The restoration of monarchy was now inevitable, but its form had yet to be determined. The old Parliament tried to debar Royalists from standing for election or from voting, with a view to securing a Parliamentarian body which would then seek to impose on Charles II conditions as stringent as those put to his father in 1648. The electors thought otherwise. Many Royalists were returned with thumping majorities, while republicans were routed.

The Royalists did not, in fact, win a decisive majority in the Commons, but the Presbyterians' hopes of prescribing conditions for Charles' return were undermined by his Declaration of Breda. This offered reassurance on the points most likely to worry former Parliamentarians. His promise of a general pardon removed fears that they might be charged with treason or otherwise harassed. The knotty problem of the ownership of crown and Church lands, sold off after the civil war, was to be referred to Parliament. Charles promised a liberty to tender consciences and a synod of divines to settle the form of the Church. The army was to receive all its arrears : any soldiers who wished could enter the King's service. Confident that their lives, lands and religion would not be taken away without Parliament's consent, the old Parliamentarians saw little need to impose prior conditions on the King. None of the restrictions they proposed took effect and many Presbyterians rushed to offer him their services.

For Charles II, the transformation of his fortunes was remarkable. A few months earlier, he and his brothers had been living on crumbs of Spanish charity at Brussels (having been expelled from France in 1654, when Mazarin signed a treaty with Cromwell); now everyone wanted to know him. The Dutch, who had earlier declared him persona non grata, feasted him royally at The Hague. He set sail on the *Naseby*, hastily renamed the *Royal Charles*, and landed at Dover on 25 May. There he met Monk, whom he created Duke of Albemarle, and proceeded at a sedate pace towards London. On the 29th (his thirtieth birthday) he entered his capital

with a triumph of above twenty thousand horse and foot, brandishing their swords and shouting with inexpressible joy; the ways strewed with flowers, the bells ringing, the streets hung with tapestry, fountains running with wine ... the windows and balconies all set with ladies; trumpets, music and myriads of people flocking the streets and ways as far as Rochester, so as they were seven hours in passing the City... I stood in the Strand, and beheld it, and blessed God.[32]

The new King made an excellent impression. Tall — about six feet — he combined a regal bearing with an easy charm, a pleasing contrast to his father's stiff diffidence. He was a good listener and an excellent conversationalist, with a ready wit and a smattering of knowledge on many subjects. His temperament seemed well suited to an England tired of the rigours of Puritan virtue. The return of monarchy meant a resurgence of 'the true noble English spirit',[33] a return to normality : to pomp and pageantry, civilian rule, peacetime levels of taxation and a minimum of central interference in the localities. England had been governed in the 1650s by conscientious men, committed to serve the State, but their severity and intrusiveness had been much resented by a population which mostly saw little wrong with 'disorderly' alehouses, maypoles, country sports or the celebration of Christmas.

There was no danger that Charles' regime would prove strenuous : 'He desired nothing else but to be easy himself and that everyone else should be so.'[34] After the privations of exile, he was determined to enjoy being King — not so much the power and responsibility as the opportunities for pleasure. Like Louis XIV, Charles had inherited Henry IV's appetite for women. 'He delivered himself up to a most enormous course of vice without any sort of restraint', wrote Bishop Burnet, '... even a modest whore was unacceptable to him, for studied brutalities were the only things that recommended women long to him.'[35] His court soon became notorious for its licence : unlike Louis, Charles made no attempt to preserve a veneer of propriety. Although he himself rarely got drunk, the drunken japes of his courtiers were widely reported : Pepys heard of two of them 'running up and down all the night with their arses bare through the streets and at last fighting and being beat by the watch and clapped up all night ; and how the king takes their parts'.[36] Such frenetic self-indulgence might be a natural reaction to years of moral and financial austerity, but for many the court's conduct passed all bounds of decency. Pepys was no Puritan, but he was disgusted by much of what he heard : that the talk of the King and his companions 'is so base and sordid that it makes the ears of the very gentlemen of the backstairs ... to tingle'.[37]

The court's public image was thus one of vice, wanton luxury and irresponsibility, but not of dignity. Charles had intended to revive his father's rules, regulating access to the various parts of the court, but this resolution did not last. He 'had so natural an aversion to all formality that ... he could not on premeditation act the part of a king for a moment ... which carried him into the other extreme ... of letting all distinction and ceremony fall to the ground, as useless and foppish.' The Venetian ambassador remarked that he found it impossible to shake off the habits acquired during his years as a private citizen.[38]

Whereas Louis XIV's public persona often hid the private man, Charles preferred to deal with people informally, as one gentleman to another. The ease and wit of his conversation was in marked contrast to his stilted public speeches. As he was unwilling to follow a regular daily round or to impose one on others, his court became disorganized. On certain days anyone could come to watch him dine: Pepys was displeased 'to see my Lord Berkshire waiting at table and serving the king drink, in as dirty pickle as I never saw man in my life'. Charles received ambassadors in his bedchamber which was as chaotic and squalid as the royal table. His beloved spaniels slept there 'where oftentimes he suffered the bitches to puppy and give suck, which rendered it very offensive and indeed made the whole court nasty and stinking'.[39]

As Charles failed to establish either a regular routine or minimal moral standards at his court, it became a jungle where only the fittest survived. Those who succeeded 'will be contented to cog and lie and flatter every man and woman that hath any interest with the persons that are great in favour and can cheat the king'. 'Of all places, if there be hell, it is here — no faith, no truth, no love, nor any agreement between man and wife, nor friends.'[40] Where Louis kept a tight grip on patronage, Charles found it hard to resist importunity, often relying on his ministers to stop grants which he had agreed. His susceptibility made access to his person a great asset: the minor office of squire of the body was worth having because the holder had the King's ear twice a day.[41]

Yet if Charles was vulnerable to importunity, it was not because he had a rosy view of human nature: 'He thinks the world is governed wholly by interest', wrote Burnet, 'and indeed he has known so much of the baseness of mankind that no wonder he has hard thoughts of them.'[42] He believed that his ministers and courtiers cared only for themselves and would readily abandon him if it was in their interest to do so. Like Louis, he feared that his ministers might mislead or manipulate him; unlike Louis, he was not prepared to work hard (except perhaps at foreign policy). His quick intelligence enabled him to grasp the rudiments of a problem, but he would not take the time to accumulate the detailed information that was often vital for successful decision-making. Routine bored him. In council meetings he relieved the tedium by exchanging notes with Lord Chancellor Clarendon. Serious administrators like Clarendon were driven to distraction by his unwillingness to apply himself and his casual irresponsibility. 'His ministers were to administer business to him', wrote the Marquis of Halifax, 'as doctors do physic, wrap it up in something to make it less unpleasant.'[43]

Charles' distrust had serious consequences. It was perhaps not wise for kings to be too trusting, but where there was no trust there could be no loyalty. Charles regarded Clarendon as the architect of the Restoration: he had argued through the long years of exile that Charles should be patient and make no major concessions and that in time he would return. Events had proved him right, yet in 1667 Charles canvassed the Lords to find the Chancellor guilty of treason. This made it clear to his other ministers that Charles would abandon them if he thought it necessary: indeed, when his own safety was at stake, he would sacrifice anyone, no matter how innocent. Despite his sympathy for Catholicism, during the Popish plot he was to advocate more severe measures against Catholics and to order the judges to secure the conviction of men he believed to be guiltless. His attitude contrasted starkly with Louis' loyalty to his ministers or Colbert's terse remark to his subordinates: 'Spare nobody; I shall back you up.'

For a king to control the government without the cohesion provided by mutual trust required more astute judgement than Charles possessed. Despite his fear of being influenced, he was, as Clarendon complained, 'too ... apt to be shaken in those counsels which, with the greatest deliberation, he had concluded by too easily permitting ... men who waited upon him ... to examine and censure what was resolved; an infirmity which brought him many troubles and exposed his ministers to ruin'.[44] His accessibility prevented any minister from gaining a monopoly of credit, for Charles could always hear several viewpoints. This could prove advantageous: he kept contact with 'opposition' politicians via the backstairs, so that they continued to hope that they might win him over and so were not driven to extreme measures. In general, though, his 'humour of hearing everybody against anybody' did as much harm as good because he did not take the necessary pains to weigh the information he received. All too often he ignored the advice of dull drudges like Clarendon, who knew what they were talking about, preferring the amusing, but self-interested, importunities of the body servants, the wits and the women, those whom Clarendon called 'the little people'. Charles claimed that his mistresses had no influence on him. He disliked hearing women talk of business, wrote Clarendon, 'but to that purpose he thought them all made for; however they broke in afterwards upon him to all other purposes' — especially matters of patronage.[45]

Thus despite his distrustfulness Charles was easily led. 'His great dexterity was in cozening himself, by gaining a little one way while it cost him ten times as much another; and by caressing those persons most who had deluded him the oftenest; yet the quickest in the world at espying such a ridicule in another.'[46] He wished to be the great puppet-master, manipulating and balancing, but all too often he failed to make up his mind or was stampeded into short-sighted measures. Superficially clever, he often achieved his immediate ends, but lacked the vision or fixity of purpose to pursue grand political strategies. His unreliability and his ministers' insecurity led to a concentration on short-term expedients: staving off financial and political crises, rather than pursuing long-term goals. None of Charles' ministers had the security or confidence to plan reforms on the scale of those of Colbert or the Le Telliers. Instead, Charles' unreliability and habit of playing one off against another led them to devote as much energy to attacking their 'colleagues' as to doing the King's business. The rivalry which proved creative within Louis' small, stable ministerial team in Charles' court bred factionalism and rapacity, as ministers sought to make all they could out of what might be only a short term in office. Charles' ministers 'rule according to their caprice and for their own private interests, without considering the welfare of the state, acting only for money'.[47]

From such a court it was unlikely that coherent policies would emerge, but this did not necessarily matter. The idea that a regime should have positive aims in all areas of government is a modern one, resting on the assumption that the State can and should bring about change. Colbert's reforms, it is true, presupposed that State direction could stimulate economic growth; a similar belief was emerging among intellectuals and civil servants in England. Most of Charles' subjects, however, would be quite content if he left things as they were: they had had more than enough innovation and intervention over the last twenty years. On some issues, however, definite decisions had to be made, notably in foreign policy and religion. How did Charles tackle these problems?

Before considering this question, one must establish the limits within which he had to operate. He was restored without preconditions, but that did not mean that he could do as he wished. His powers were defined gradually, by the Convention of 1660 and the much more Royalist 'Cavalier Parliament' elected in 1661. Basically, they returned to the position as it had been at the end of 1641, after the abolition of the fiscal methods of the 1630s and the prerogative courts. On the other hand, Parliament dropped its demand for a say in the King's choice of advisers and declared that he should command the armed forces. The 1641 Triennial Act was replaced by a weaker measure, which laid down no minimum length for parliamentary sessions. Parliament abandoned the executive role which it had developed in the 1640s: the King was once more to direct the government. Finally, it agreed that the King should have an income, for life, sufficient to meet his normal peacetime expenses and voted several revenues for that purpose.

Thus at the Restoration Parliament abandoned demands which had in the 1640s seemed essential if royal misrule was to be prevented. Its quarrel had always been with Charles I, not with the monarchy; MPs were ready to give his son the benefit of the doubt. Moreover, the threat from below — from London mobs, upstart soldiers and religious radicals — now seemed more immediate than that from above, from the King and court. MPs believed they needed an effective king to hold down the radical forces which had emerged since 1640: hence measures against 'tumultuous petitioning', hence the reimposition of censorship. MPs cheerfully abandoned their executive role because they had taken it up only in order to defend themselves against the King. Most had never relished it: as country gentlemen who mostly saw their seats as a mark of local prestige or as a way of making useful contacts, they had little interest in the tedious minutiae of government and were glad to hand such time-consuming responsibilities back to the King.

If Parliament wanted Charles to govern, it was not prepared to allow him unlimited power. It ignored his claim that he needed a large standing army; the Convention took charge of paying off the New Model: it had no wish to let the King take over such a formidable force. The Commons were also careful not to grant Charles too much money. When he complained that the revenues granted in 1660-3 brought in less than expected, the Commons made several temporary grants, but voted no more permanent revenues: a king who was always somewhat short of money would have to call Parliament frequently and pay some heed to its wishes. The need to consider Parliament's reaction would also deter ministers from pursuing potentially unpopular policies. Even so, the fact that Parliament gave Charles an independent revenue showed clearly that they wanted him to govern, rather than being a figurehead: nothing would have been easier than to make him wholly dependent on Parliament for money. As it turned out, his permanent revenues eventually brought in much more than expected, so that Charles ended up able to manage without Parliament, without resorting to methods like those of his father.

He had also inherited from the Interregnum a much more effective state apparatus than that of the early Stuarts. His fiscal system was based not on archaic feudal rights or the misuse of the prerogative, but on taxes — customs, excises and land taxes — which were accurately and equitably assessed and efficiently collected. He had a more professional civil service, a much enlarged navy and, despite Parliament's reservations, a small standing army. He still had few paid officials in the localities, until the creation of a royal excise administration in the 1680s; local government and law enforcement still depended on JPs and borough corporations. Such a system, whatever its weaknesses, had, however, worked adequately in the past and commanded general acceptance, so Charles' position was in many respects very favourable.[48]

Charles was not, however, fully aware of this. He came to England as a virtual foreigner. None of his grandparents was English and with his swarthy complexion he looked more Latin than Anglo-Saxon. He had been twelve when the civil war started, so could hardly remember a period of 'normal' government. He lacked Clarendon's deep emotional attachment to the traditional constitution: he had little respect for precedent, so that 'the objections of novelty rather advanced than obstructed any proposition'. Some of those around him 'tell him how neither privileges of Parliament nor City is anything, but his will is all and ought to be so'.[49] Charles told French ambassadors of his admiration for Louis' government and would no doubt have preferred to pay less heed to his subjects' wishes. In an ideal world he might have liked to emulate his French cousin, but there is no evidence that he seriously considered doing so. French ambassadors were surprised that he lacked the will or the energy to change the monarchy, but he saw little reason to do so. He did not wish to be like a Turk, able to have men strangled at pleasure, 'but he did not think he was a king as long as a company of fellows were looking into all his actions and examining his ministers'. 'A king of England that is not a slave to five hundred kings ... is great enough.'[50]

Far from seeking to extend his power, Charles (like his father) saw it as under threat. Bitter experience suggested the English were prone to rebellion and regicide. Historians may argue that the regicides were a tiny few, who achieved their ends due to a fortuitous combination of circumstances, not least Charles I's duplicitous pig-headedness. Charles II, however, was unwilling either to underestimate the strength of his enemies or to blame his father for his own downfall. In 1660 it must have seemed incredible that those who had ruled since Pride's Purge would vanish from the political scene or that most of the New Model would return quietly to civilian life. With hindsight, we can see that that is what happened, but in the early 1660s plots and rumours made both Charles and the old Cavaliers very nervous. Fear underlay both the Cavalier Parliament's concern to build up the powers of the crown and many of Charles' policies. Always watchful for the first signs of another civil war, he viewed criticism or opposition as barely concealed sedition. Acutely conscious of his lack of an effective army, he blamed Parliament for leaving him exposed to his subjects' malice. Conscious of his vulnerability, he tried to conciliate or buy off opposition, which encouraged ambitious politicians to make trouble in Parliament in the hope of being 'taken off' with a place or pension. Sometimes, however, notably on religion, measures which were intended to defuse opposition succeeded only in exacerbating it.

Charles knew his Bible well and liked to discuss theology, but his religious views were somewhat obscure. If he leaned to any church, it was to Catholicism; he may have attended mass in exile, but never did so as King and was received into that church only on his deathbed. He derived little satisfaction from worship and saw the churches in political terms. While implying that the Catholic church had the best claim to authority, he conformed to the Church of England and, when politically necessary, he persecuted the Catholics severely. Experience of the Scots had taught him that Presbyterianism was not a religion for gentlemen and he regarded the sects with patrician disdain : they showed what happened when the poor and ignorant were allowed to read the Bible. He saw religious dissent as politically dangerous : 'He thinks an implicitness in religion is necessary for the safety of government and he looks upon all inquisitiveness into these things as mischievous to the state', wrote Burnet. 'He thinks...that God will never damn a man for allowing himself a little pleasure.... I believe he is no atheist, but that rather he has formed an odd idea of the goodness of God in his mind ; he thinks to be wicked and to design mischief is the only thing God hates and... he was sure he was not guilty of that.'[51]

Two major religious questions needed to be answered at the Restoration. First, while it was clear that there would again be a national, episcopal Church, would the bishops share their power with the parish clergy and would the liturgy be changed to meet the objections of moderate Puritans ? If these conditions were met, many Presbyterians could be brought within the Church. Second, were the sects which had emerged since 1640 to be tolerated or should they be forced to conform to the national Church ? On these points Charles and the majority in the Cavalier Parliament shared similar preconceptions, but reached different conclusions. Both believed that the Presbyterians had started the civil war and were at least indirectly responsible for Charles I's death. The sects were subversive and disobedient ; the Quakers' conduct verged on the anarchic. The old Cavaliers argued that Presbyterians and sectaries were dangerous and should be treated severely. To change the Church in order to accommodate the Presbyterians would be both dangerous and morally wrong. Moderation would be interpreted as weakness and would merely encourage them ; those who would not conform should be — and could be — crushed.

This view rested on the (correct) assumption that nonconformists were a smallish minority : the sectaries probably made up less than ten per cent of the population, while many Presbyterians, seeing order as the first priority, were ready to accept the re-establishment of the Church on traditional lines.

The Earl of Sandwich (once regarded as a Puritan) told Pepys that 'all things would not be well while there was so much preaching and that it would be better if nothing but homilies were to be read in churches'.[52] As for the sects, the Cavaliers would brook no compromise and sought revenge for what they had suffered at their hands.

Charles returned in 1660 assuming that the Presbyterians and sects were much stronger than they were, an impression which Monk sought to reinforce and to exploit. It seemed to him prudent to accommodate the Presbyterians within the Church and to allow toleration to those who did not want to belong to any national Church. In this way, he hoped to heal the wounds of the civil war and to fulfil his promise, in the Declaration of Breda, of 'liberty to tender consciences'. (As far as the old Cavaliers were concerned, there was nothing tender about the nonconformists' consciences; they were motivated by pride and disobedience.) He may have hoped that a toleration for the sects might also benefit the Catholics, but the latter would gain nothing from a broadening of the Church to include Presbyterians. All Charles' hopes, however, were thwarted by the Commons' relentless opposition: the old Cavaliers thus made it very clear that Charles had been restored on their terms. The Act of Uniformity of 1662 laid down that, once again, there was to be only one legal form of worship, based on the Prayer Book.

Early in 1663 Charles accepted defeat on the issue of toleration, but his relations with the Commons did not improve, as divisions at court spilled over into Parliament. At first Clarendon was the dominant minister, but younger rivals sought to turn Charles against him. Henry Bennet, Earl of Arlington, was 'the best bred and courtly person his majesty has about him' but was 'rather a subtle courtier than an able statesman, too much regarding every inclination of his master and too little considering his true interest and that of the nation'.[53] Bennet was, at least, an experienced diplomat: the second Duke of Buckingham could offer only some of his father's brilliance and a bewildering penchant for inconsistency:

> A man so various that he seemed to be
> Not one, but all mankind's epitome ...
> But in the course of one revolving moon
> Was chemist, fiddler, statesman and buffoon.

Charles was swept along by his charisma and verve : 'There is no way to rule the king but by briskness, which the Duke ... hath above all men.' If Charles liked him, others did not. French ambassadors dismissed him as irresponsible, while to Burnet he was 'one of the worst men alive, both as to his personal deportment and as to the public'.[54]

Faced with Arlington's subtle insinuation and Buckingham's dazzling wit, Clarendon could offer only proven loyalty and stolid hard work. Long attacks of gout reduced his administrative usefulness and his enemies sought to discredit his conduct at the Restoration, claiming that he had deliberately failed to secure either a sufficient revenue or a standing army.[55] It is most unlikely that Charles could, in fact, have obtained better terms, but such claims may have contributed to Charles' growing irritation at Clarendon's pompous admonitions to apply himself to business and Olympian dismissals of anything smacking of novelty. Yet although Charles chafed under the old man's tutelage and laughed with those who mocked him, he was not easy to dislodge. By keeping him on, Charles maintained a balance among his ministers, while Clarendon was, at times, ready to follow the King's wishes rather than his own.[56] A precarious equilibrium was thus maintained until the end of the Second Dutch War.

Neither Clarendon nor Charles really wanted war in 1665, but they were swept along by the bellicose mood of court and Commons. The war produced few striking successes and ended in humiliation : in 1667 the Dutch sailed up the Medway, burned some of the King's great ships and carried others home in triumph. The Commons had voted nearly four million pounds for the war — a far cry from the paltry subsidies of the 1620s — and expected some return on their money. As the next session approached, panic gripped the court. Some talked of using the army to establish absolutism, but most argued that the Commons had to be appeased. Clarendon's enemies claimed that MPs blamed him for the débâcle and that he must be sacrificed. Charles was persuaded to dismiss him and then, when Buckingham's followers impeached the chancellor, he urged the peers to find him guilty. Not for the last time, Charles allowed himself to be seriously misled about the Commons' mood : MPs were far less hostile to Clarendon than Charles supposed — they certainly did not want him dead at all costs — but the fact that Charles did drove the chancellor into exile.

If Charles believed that Clarendon's departure would reduce the Commons to compliance he was to be disappointed. Buckingham and Arlington wanted to remove the chancellor's followers from office and replace them with their own. They attacked the mishandling of the war, playing on backbench MPs' anger at the Medway fiasco. Buckingham also persuaded Charles to revive his plan to broaden the Church to include the Presbyterians. He claimed that the Commons would now be more sympathetic to toleration and that the Dissenters were the strongest element in the nation, but the Commons remained hostile to Dissent and Charles lacked the nerve to call a new Parliament. With MPs seeking the causes of English failure in the war and resentful of the proposed toleration, the sessions of 1668−9 were turbulent: the harmony of 1660 seemed to have gone for ever. The divisions of the civil wars had been reopened by the disputes over religion and a breakdown in the relations of King and Parliament seemed imminent.

The appearances were deceptive. In the spring of 1670 Charles abandoned his support for Dissent and took the Commons' side in a dispute with the Lords. The Commons spent the day drinking the King's health on their knees in the royal cellar and voted a duty on wines for eight years. The sessions of 1670−1 were the most harmonious of the reign. The Commons passed a new bill against Dissenting meetings and tried constructively to devise a more equitable but accurate system of subsidy assessment, a task which their forebears of the 1620s would not have dared to attempt; since the civil war, MPs and electors had come to appreciate that effective government, and war, had to be paid for. Some watched these developments with alarm: 'The King was never since his coming in,' wrote the old Cromwellian, Andrew Marvell, 'nay, all things considered, no king since the Conquest, so absolutely powerful at home as he is at present. Nor any Parliament, or places, so certainly and constantly supplied with men of the same temper.'[57] The members of this Parliament had always been ready to support strong monarchy, provided their prejudices were respected, but Charles had shrunk from the risks involved in a policy of vindictive Royalism and exclusive Anglicanism. In 1670−1 Charles overcame his reluctance and re-established good relations with the Commons, yet even as he did so he was bringing to fruition policies destined to bring about a major political crisis.

# 7
# Dover and After

By the summer of 1670 the monarchies of both England and France seemed as powerful as they had ever been. Charles was learning to live with a Parliament whose attitude to government was more constructive and sophisticated than that of its early Stuart predecessors. Louis, it seemed, had imposed his authority on the powerful groups of his realm. The nobility congregated at court, the sovereign courts no longer rejected legislation, provincial estates no longer haggled about voting taxes. The intendants subjected local officials and town governments to ever closer scrutiny. Colbert's great legal codes began to bring order and method to the labyrinth of French law. He tried, through the academies, to impose a similar order on the arts and struggled manfully to galvanize France's sluggish economy. At Versailles, Louis was building a palace that would symbolize the grandeur of monarchy.

Some of these signs of strength were perhaps misleading. While Charles depended in part on money from Parliament he would have to confine himself to policies acceptable to the Commons. Louis' assertions of authority drove opposition underground, where it was harder to counter. The size of France and the diversity of its institutions defeated all attempts at standardization before the Revolution. Even so, the contrast with the earlier seventeenth century was striking. If the English King still depended on the consent of the governed, that now seemed easier to obtain, while the French crown seemed at last to be stamping its authority on the diverse groups into which French society was divided. If politics is the art of the possible, both Charles and Louis seemed to be making the most of the possibilities open to them.

It was not to last. On 22 May/1 June 1670 a treaty between the Kings was signed at Dover. The reasons behind the treaty and the consequences of its implementation were to have profound effects on both kingdoms. Never again would either King enjoy the security or optimism of the summer of 1670, for the treaty plunged Europe into a major war which led, seemingly

# The Spanish Succession

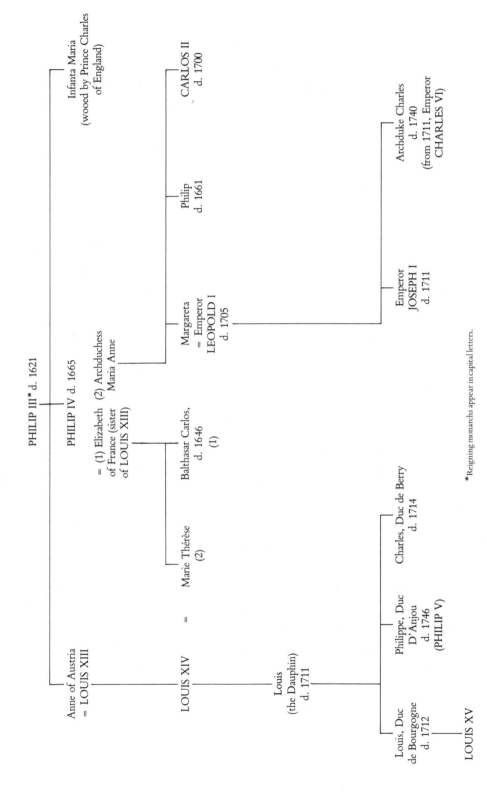

PHILIP III* d. 1621

Infanta Maria
(wooed by Prince Charles
of England)

PHILIP IV d. 1665

= (1) Elizabeth    (2) Archduchess
of France (sister        Maria Anne
of LOUIS XIII)

Margareta
= Emperor
LEOPOLD I
d. 1705

Philip
d. 1661

CARLOS II
d. 1700

Emperor
JOSEPH I
d. 1711

Archduke Charles
d. 1740
(from 1711, Emperor
CHARLES VI)

Balthasar Carlos,
d. 1646
(1)

Marie Thérèse
(2)

Anne of Austria
= LOUIS XIII

LOUIS XIV        =

Louis
(the Dauphin)
d. 1711

Louis, Duc
de Bourgogne
d. 1712

Philippe, Duc
D'Anjou
d. 1746
(PHILIP V)

Charles, Duc de Berry
d. 1714

LOUIS XV

*Reigning monarchs appear in capital letters.

inexorably, to two greater wars. How did it come about?

Louis began his personal rule with France more secure from attack than it had been for centuries. In the Treaty of the Pyrenees in 1659 France gained Roussillon, which pushed the frontier with Spain back to the mountains, and a number of towns which strengthened the vulnerable northern frontier. To the east, the position was complex. Lorraine was a supposedly independent duchy, within which France had acquired sovereignty over the scattered lands of the bishoprics of Metz, Toul and Verdun. Further east, in Alsace, France had jurisdiction over ten major towns and controlled two of the main Rhine crossings (Philippsburg and Breisach), but not the third (Strasbourg). To the south, Franche Comté was still under Spanish rule. The complexity of jurisdictions and the area's strategic sensitivity made any extension of French power there slow and difficult. If the French wanted more effective control to guard against an attack by the Emperor, the neighbouring German states feared that it might lead to French intervention in Germany: the 'gates' on the Rhine could open both ways. For this reason, Mazarin had decided that the eastern frontier could not be secured by military means alone. Playing on the princes' suspicion of Imperial power and greed for French money, he built up the League of the Rhine, an integral part of France's defences.

If neither the northern nor the eastern frontier was wholly secure, France was in little immediate danger of Habsburg attack. If it is over-simplistic to talk of 'the decline of Spain', by the later seventeenth century Spain was feeling the effects of trying to retain an extensive European and American empire from a primitive economic base. The flow of bullion from the New World continued unabated, but the main benefit was now reaped by foreign merchants and financiers.[1] The Madrid government found it increasingly difficult to move money and men to its various territories — not least the Spanish Netherlands — and its confidence had been badly dented by France's great victory at Rocroi and by having to concede Dutch independence in 1648. The days when Spanish aggression threatened France had thus passed. The Austrian branch's main territories were much further away. The Emperor Leopold I claimed rights of suzerainty in Alsace, as over many other parts of Germany, but it seemed unlikely that he would seriously trouble Louis because of the endemic suspicion of the German princes and a growing threat from the resurgent Turkish empire.

It might seem, then, that Louis' assertive foreign policy was unnecessarily aggressive, the product of a lust for *gloire* and territorial expansion, but that would not be entirely true. With hindsight we can say that Spain no longer posed a threat to France, but that was less apparent at the time, while the Austrian Habsburgs were anything but a spent force. Few at first saw Leopold as a great Emperor, but he was to rout the Turks and greatly enlarge the area under his rule; he also reorganized his armies to a point where they could stand comparison with the French. In 1670 this lay far in the future, but experience showed that the Habsburg threat could never be discounted and concern for his northern and eastern frontiers underlay much of Louis' foreign policy. He was also, however, eager to make his mark on Europe. He threatened to make war on Spain after a bloody affray between the followings of the French and Spanish ambassadors in London: only an abject apology from his father-in-law appeased him. Such a flexing of muscles in affairs of honour whetted his appetite for the real thing and he soon found a prize worth seeking in the Spanish succession.

Louis' marriage to his uninspiring spouse opened up some interesting long-term possibilities. By 1661 two of Philip IV's three sons were dead, leaving only Carlos, the ultimate product of Habsburg in-breeding. His protruding jaw, typical of his family, stuck out so far that he was unable to chew his food. He was also mentally retarded and although he married he had no children. Of his two sisters, the elder married Louis and the younger, Margareta, continued the tradition of marriage within the family by marrying Leopold. When Louis married Marie Thérèse in 1659, neither of her surviving brothers had children and both were sickly, so it was possible that one day she would inherit the Spanish empire, or at least claim some part of it. With this in mind, the Spaniards insisted that she should renounce any claim to the succession; Mazarin agreed, but linked the renunciation to the payment of her huge dowry: if it was not paid, her claims would stand. Even if it had been paid (which it was not), it was a moot point whether she could renounce her rights: there were no internationally accepted legal principles governing the inheritance of property.

It could be argued, therefore, that such questions should be settled according to the laws of the various Spanish territories. In parts of the

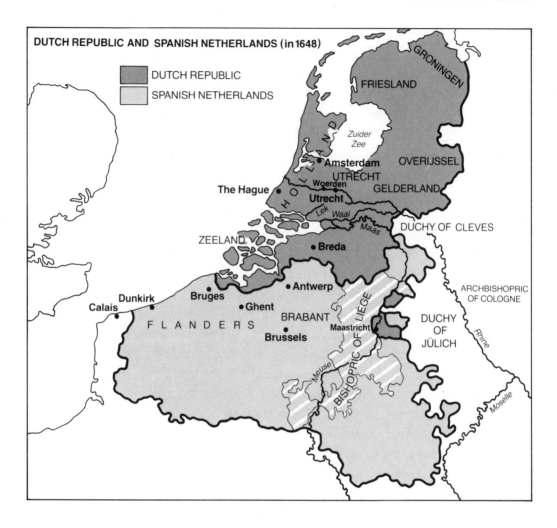

**DUTCH REPUBLIC AND SPANISH NETHERLANDS (in 1648)**

DUTCH REPUBLIC

SPANISH NETHERLANDS

GRONINGEN

FRIESLAND

*Zuider Zee*

OVERIJSSEL

Amsterdam

UTRECHT

Woerden

GELDERLAND

The Hague

Utrecht

*Lek*

*Waal*

*Maas*

DUCHY OF CLEVES

ZEELAND

Breda

Antwerp

ARCHBISHOPRIC OF COLOGNE

Dunkirk

Bruges

Ghent

BRABANT

Calais

F L A N D E R S

Brussels

Maastricht

DUCHY OF JÜLICH

*Rhine*

BISHOPRIC OF LIÈGE

*Meuse*

*Moselle*

Netherlands, the daughter of a first marriage could claim a share of her father's property, even if he had a son by a second. As Carlos was the son of Philip's second wife, as soon as he succeeded his father, in 1665, Louis began to mount a series of claims on behalf of his wife and son. In May 1667 he supported his claims with armed force. His preparations had been thorough and the Spanish forces in the Low Countries offered little resistance to France's formidable military machine. As he progressed from one short-lived siege to another, Louis paraded his soldiers for the delectation of the ladies of the court, the choicest of whom lodged in a sumptuous tent of Chinese silk.

As Louis indulged his fondness for martial posturing, others (notably the Dutch) were dismayed at this show of military strength. It had taken the Dutch eighty years to win their independence of the Spanish crown, which had formerly ruled all of the seventeen provinces of the Low Countries. The Dutch Republic, consisting of the seven northernmost provinces (Zeeland, Holland, Utrecht, Gelderland, Groningen, Overijssel and Friesland), owed its success to a number of factors. On the one hand, Spain had faced huge economic and logistical problems in fighting a major war so far from the mother country. On the other, the Dutch had shown a fierce determination, which owed much to Calvinism, and possessed economic resources out of all proportion to their numbers, thanks to the most advanced trade and shipping in Europe. Geography too was on their side. The Great Rivers (the Maas, Waal and Lek) which ran from east to west across the centre of the Low Countries constituted a formidable defensive barrier, while the two richest provinces were also the most inaccessible: Zeeland consisted of a group of islands and much of Holland had been reclaimed from the sea, so that invading armies could be halted by cutting the dikes and flooding the land.

If the Dutch struggle against Spain was ultimately successful, the 'United Provinces' were rarely united. There was a constant tension between a strong tradition of municipal and provincial autonomy and the need for speedy and decisive action in wartime. To secure the consent of every province in the national Parliament (or States General) and of each major town within each province could be cumbersome and slow. Many argued that only a prince could provide effective leadership and looked to the Republic's greatest princely family, the House of Orange. Each Prince of

Orange was appointed *stadhouder* (or lieutenant) of most of the seven provinces and captain- and admiral-general of the Republic. Such a concentration of power, especially military power, in one man worried those attached to provincial and municipal self-government. Having thrown off the 'tyranny' of Spain, they had no wish to succumb to the 'tyranny' of a home-grown prince. Supporters of the House of Orange denounced those who held such views as parochial and petty-minded, but the 'republicans' (or 'States party' as it was known) had shown during the war with Spain that they could, if necessary, subordinate local to national interests. Moreover, they dominated the major trading towns which paid the bulk of the Republic's taxes, so were in a position to call the tune.

In the 1660s the leader of the States party was Jan de Witt, Grand Pensionary of Holland. (The Pensionary's duties were not easily defined, but he wielded great power at both a provincial and a national level.) The head of the House of Orange was William III, the son of Charles I's daughter Mary, and so the nephew of Charles II. He was born in 1650, at the height of a bitter conflict between his father, William II, and the States party. When William II died suddenly just before his son's birth, his opponents took steps to ensure that the young prince would never occupy the offices of his ancestors, but as William entered his teens there was a growing clamour for his elevation to what many saw as his rightful place in Dutch affairs. De Witt was therefore very perturbed by evidence of Louis' ambitions in the Spanish Netherlands. The Dutch had always regarded France as a useful ally (against Spain) but a dangerous neighbour: having freed themselves from Spanish rule they had no wish to fall under that of France. Moreover, any serious military threat to the republic would intensify the pressure for William's elevation, while a major war would inevitably damage the trade on which the Republic's prosperity depended. De Witt therefore proposed to Louis that they should set up a group of small independent republics in the Southern Netherlands, rather like the Swiss cantons, to act as a buffer between France and the Republic. Louis rejected the proposal: he hoped for more, much more.

De Witt then tried a different approach. Although the victory in the Medway had given the Dutch an advantage in the war with England, they hastily made peace at Breda (July 1667), granting the English better terms than they had reason to expect. Six months later the English, Dutch and

Swedes signed the Triple Alliance. Its ostensible purpose was to force Spain to recognize the claims of Louis' wife and to confirm Louis' title to the towns he had taken, or their equivalent, but Louis was also pressed to be satisfied with his conquests. If either Carlos or Louis refused to comply with these conditions, the allies were to make war on them and (in Louis' case) push France back to the frontiers of 1659.[2]

De Witt's attitude towards the alliance was ambivalent. He hoped that the threat of war would halt Louis' expansionism in the Southern Low Countries, but had no wish to carry out that threat. Not only would war strengthen the case for William's elevation, but de Witt was most reluctant to trust Charles II. Some English diplomats sincerely wanted an anti-French coalition, but it is unlikely that Charles did, although his intentions are difficult to fathom. Louis conducted most of his diplomacy through his ambassadors in the various capitals, to whom he sent detailed instructions. Charles conducted most of his diplomacy in London : one can tell from foreign ambassadors' reports what he told them, but he never set out his views as Louis did in his instructions. One therefore has to try to deduce Charles' intentions from what he said and did, which, as he often said different things to different people, is far from easy : he was a very slippery customer.

Almost as soon as he had signed the Treaty of Breda, Charles approached Louis about a possible alliance. He had several possible motives. He felt bitter at the humiliation in the Medway and burned for revenge. He saw the Dutch as England's main commercial and colonial rivals : he was very interested in ships and navigation, and trade, through the customs, provided a large part of his income. He admired the style of Louis' government and court, whose fashions were imitated throughout Europe, whereas the Dutch leaders were not only republicans, but grubby bourgeois — herring-merchants, usurers, not even gentlemen — yet they kept Charles' nephew, William, out of his hereditary offices. Finally, Charles still worried about his vulnerability to rebellion : he had stressed to an earlier French ambassador that any Anglo-French treaty should include provisions for mutual military help in case of trouble at home.[3] With Parliament so turbulent and Louis' military prowess apparent to all, such an arrangement seemed doubly attractive.

Louis responded promptly to Charles' overtures, so was flabbergasted to hear of the Triple Alliance. Charles claimed that it was de Witt's idea (which it was not) and that it could not harm Louis' interests.[4] Charles may have promoted the Triple Alliance because he felt that, for domestic political reasons, he had to try to curb French expansion, or he may have hoped to encourage Louis to bid more for his friendship. In the event, Louis decided to make peace with Spain, encouraged by a secret treaty with Leopold, which envisaged that, when Carlos died, his lands would be divided between France and the Emperor, with Louis' share including the Netherlands, Franche Comté, Naples and Sicily.[5] Not all Louis' advisers, however, were in favour of waiting for the Spanish Netherlands or relying on a treaty which might later be disavowed. Confident that Spain could offer no serious resistance, his two greatest generals, Turenne and Condé, and his war minister, Louvois, urged Louis to complete the conquest. Others, notably Colbert, Le Tellier and the experienced diplomat Lionne, advised him to be satisfied with what he had gained and to beware of provoking a general coalition against France. The latter argument triumphed: in May 1668 the Treaty of Aix-la-Chapelle confirmed Louis' recent conquests.[6]

Louis was less than satisfied with the treaty. The 'hawks' in France saw it as dishonourable and humiliating: having got the Spaniards at his mercy, it was madness to let them escape. The Dutch exulted at having 'brought peace to Europe',[7] which served only to increase Louis' anger at their presumption and ingratitude: in his eyes, they owed their independence to France. He blamed de Witt for the Triple Alliance and welcomed Charles' proposal for a personal union 'as between one gentleman and another', a proposal which Lionne regarded with great scepticism.[8]

Louis, however, realized that he would never be able to take the Spanish Netherlands until he had removed the possibility of Dutch opposition. To crush the Dutch, he needed to break up the Triple Alliance and so he had to woo the duplicitous Charles II. He was supported in this by Turenne and Louvois, eager for more war. Against this, Lionne argued that Louis had only to wait for Carlos to die and he would secure the Spanish Netherlands anyway, whereas renewed aggression would provoke hostility in Germany, where Mazarin's League of the Rhine was breaking up. Colbert knew that war would ruin his plans for financial reform, which in 1669 still needed another seven to eight years to come to fruition. War, he argued, would harm trade; high tariffs and other economic pressures were the best way to weaken Dutch trade and power. Lionne, however, came to accept the need for war and began to refer to the Dutch in the contemptuous terms *de rigueur* at court. Colbert, after being crushingly rebuked by Louis for opposing his declared will, not only abandoned his opposition to war, but tried with ostentatious zeal to devise ways of paying for it.[9]

On 25 January 1669 Charles introduced a new complication into the negotiations by announcing that he wished to declare himself a Catholic as soon as possible; he asked Louis for military help if his declaration led to a revolt. Louis was embarrassed. As self-styled leader of Catholic Europe he could not express disapproval of Charles' pious intention, but he feared that it would distract Charles from what Louis saw as the first priority, attacking the Dutch. In addition, Charles wished to sign a commercial treaty, before discussing war. As so often, Charles' motives are unclear. He may have felt a fleeting, but genuine, desire to become a Catholic: his only surviving brother, James, Duke of York, was converted at this time. He may have hoped to gain control over the timing of the war, by stipulating that his declaration must come first. Finally, and most plausibly, he may have seen this as a way of extracting a larger subsidy, or a favourable commercial treaty, by playing on Louis' piety. Louis eventually agreed to pay one subsidy for the expenses incurred in announcing his conversion and another for the Dutch war. If Charles received much less than he had asked for, he was promised a substantial sum, paid on terms which Colbert thought far too favourable. Louis also promised him military help in case of insurrection.[10]

When the treaty was finally signed at Dover, Charles agreed that the war should take priority; some said this was at the request of his sister Henriette, who came over to see him, much to the annoyance of her petulant and jealous husband. After a few happy days with Charles, she returned to France and died amid ugly rumours of poison. It is likely that Charles let himself be persuaded, at a price, to agree to something which he had intended from the outset. He now lost his zeal to announce his conversion and busied himself preparing to fight the Dutch. The Kings agreed to wait until 1672, but Louis came to Dunkirk with a great army in the summer of 1671. Thoroughly alarmed, the Dutch mobilized for war, incurring much unnecessary expense. Charles, with brazen duplicity, used the presence of a French army so close to England to extract money from Parliament to strengthen his defences. Meanwhile, French diplomats secured the friendship or neutrality of various German states, so that his attack on the Republic would meet with no obstacles.

Under the treaty, Louis was to provide the land forces while Charles, with some French help, sustained the war at sea. From any joint conquests, England was to receive various islands and towns around the mouth of the Great Rivers. The French strategy was bold and simple. In the spring of 1672 a huge army swept up through the friendly bishopric of Liège, then swung east to cross the Rhine north of Cologne, which rendered nugatory the Dutch defensive preparations further downstream, along the Great Rivers. Within days, the French were at Utrecht and pressing north towards Groningen: five of the seven provinces were at Louis' mercy. The Dutch States General offered to cede all their territories south of the Great Rivers, which would leave them unable to hamper French expansion in the Spanish Netherlands, plus an indemnity of ten million livres. Pomponne, Lionne's successor, urged Louis to accept; Louvois, Turenne and Condé said he should demand an indemnity of twenty-four millions, additional towns and territories, freedom of worship for Dutch Catholics and a mission to Paris each year to thank Louis for giving them peace.

Such demands reflected overweening confidence in France's military superiority and an arrogant contempt for the snivelling bourgeois who ruled the Republic: how could such men hope to compete with kings and nobles? Such arrogance was understandable, but was neither militarily nor politically realistic. The two provinces outside French control, Zeeland and Holland, were the richest and the most difficult to take. Louvois knew that the dikes of Holland had been cut in the past, but did not believe the Dutch would take so desperate a step. In fact, the first sluices were opened even before negotiations began and the water defences grew stronger by the day. More-over, the shock of defeat provoked not abject surrender but rage against the leaders who had allowed it to happen. William III was made *stadhouder* of Holland and Zeeland and captain- and admiral-general and de Witt and his brother were hacked into small pieces by an Orangist mob.[11]

By this time Louis had returned to Paris, confident that the Dutch would see reason and surrender, rather than ruin thousands of acres of rich farmland. Besides, when winter came the waters would freeze and his cavalry would ride to Amsterdam. But the winter of 1672-3 was mild and Louvois' policy of devastation, far from starving the Dutch into submission, hardened their resistance. Louis began to worry that his lines of communication were over-extended. His strategy had depended on speed and on everything going right: it had not. The Dutch had not been crushed; German princes and the Spanish authorities in Brussels were perturbed by France's power and ruthlessness. As neutrals and allies turned against Louis, a contest between the French and Dutch began to escalate into a European war. Still more important in the long run was William's dramatic rise to power. Not yet twenty-two, a hard youth and a stern Calvinism had helped to give him an icy self-control and formidable singleness of purpose. Although he did not instigate the lynching of the de Witts, he did nothing to cool Orangist passions or to disavow those responsible. Cynical and austere, ruthless in his use of power, ferociously loyal to his country and his religion, he was to be Louis' most single-minded and dangerous enemy.[12]

In the spring of 1673 Louis besieged the great fortress of Maastricht. Siege warfare suited him: it depended more on careful preparation than on quick thinking and provided a relatively safe spectacle for onlookers, who on this occasion included the Queen, la Vallière and Montespan, the last-named in the latter stages of pregnancy. A number of foreign volunteers fought with the French army, including Charles' bastard son, the Duke of Monmouth, and a certain John Churchill. The siege's successful outcome owed much to Louis' concern to ensure that his soldiers were properly fed — he appreciated the value of portable bread ovens — and to Vauban, a protégé of Louvois and an engineer of genius, who was to play a prominent part in French strategic thinking.

Taking Maastricht did not, however, alter the fact that the waters barred the way to the great trading towns of Holland, nor did it stem the tide of hostility to France among the Germans, to which Louis responded by looking to his eastern frontier. He occupied, without any excuse, the arch-bishopric of Trier and sent Turenne's army deep into Germany in order to deter Leopold from coming to aid the Dutch: both Louis and Louvois believed firmly in the deterrent effects of force, but (as so often) it proved counter-productive.

Faced with what seemed to be French aggression, German states rushed to the Emperor for protection, encouraging him to join the war. Having abandoned France's traditional strategy of playing the princes off against the Emperor, Louis would now pay the penalty. Both the Spanish authorities in Brussels and Leopold declared war on France; Louis withdrew his forces from the Dutch Republic and prepared to defend himself. Outwardly he remained confident, but he slept badly and had nightmares. Even the capture of Franche Comté in a lightning winter campaign did not alter the fact that he was on the defensive. Despite his capacity for self-delusion and his habit of fudging the record, he must have begun to wish that he had accepted the Dutch terms in 1672. Worried by having to fight on so many fronts and by the occasional irresponsibility of his generals, Louis and Louvois increasingly took over the direction of the war. Strategy on a European scale was too important to be left to soldiers.[13]

Meanwhile, Louis' English ally had problems of his own. Charles offered repeated excuses for delaying the announcement of his conversion; Louis, for whom the Dutch war came first, did not press him. By early 1672 the English fleet was as ready as it would ever be, but before starting the war Charles took a fateful step. He issued a Declaration of Indulgence, which suspended the laws against religious nonconformity, allowing Dissenters to worship in public and Catholics in private. Some of Charles' advisers, notably Buckingham, had always supported toleration for Dissenters, while the limited concession to Catholics could be seen as a gesture towards earning the money Louis had paid for Charles' conversion. Others saw the Declaration as a way of keeping the Dissenters quiet while Charles made war on a Calvinist power.[14]

Despite the Declaration and government attempts to whip up anti-Dutch feeling, the English public had come to see the French as more dangerous than the Dutch: only a resounding success could reconcile it to the war and such success was sadly lacking. While the French army carried all before it, the war at sea was inconclusive and the French naval contingent was accused of half-heartedness. News of the French peace terms — especially freedom of worship for Dutch Catholics — created further alarm. In what was coming to be seen as a religious war, Charles seemed to be taking the wrong side. The English were the more inclined to see the war in denominational terms because of growing fears of Popery (and absolutism) at home. Many complained of the liberty allowed to Catholics by the Indulgence, while

Charles' claim that he could suspend religious laws on his own authority raised the prospect that he might claim to suspend any law he chose. Above all, it was becoming apparent that the Duke of York was a Catholic.

James was very different from Charles: slow-witted, straightforward and loyal, he had inherited his father's habit of thinking in polar opposites: good and evil, right and wrong, loyalty and disloyalty. At one stage he seemed destined for a military career, which would have suited him well: he was conscientious, brave and obedient. Like Charles, he was attracted by the Catholic Church's claim to incontrovertible authority, but Charles never let theoretical preferences override practical considerations. For James, however, the Church's authority answered all questions and stilled all doubts. Unlike his abler and more independently-minded brother, he was willing to submit to the Church's will and found peace and contentment in such submission: it meant that he had no need to trouble his limited mind about the mysteries of life, death and salvation. He derived genuine satisfaction from the Church's rituals, which never meant much to Charles; although he continued to attend Anglican services, he no longer took communion. Eager to appear openly as a Catholic, James was constrained only by obedience to his brother.[15]

The consequences of James' conversion were wideranging. Charles had married Catherine of Braganza in 1662. Pious and inoffensive, she had, like Marie Thérèse, to put up with the indignity of having her husband's leading mistress installed as a personal servant. The Countess of Castlemaine possessed considerable charm and a furious temper; the poor Queen, timid and (at first) speaking little English, was no match for her. Moreover, unlike the fecund Castlemaine, she bore Charles no children. She miscarried twice, perhaps three times, once because she was startled by a pet fox jumping on her bed: on such incidents can the fate of kingdoms turn. Some at court claimed that she was barren and blamed Clarendon for arranging the marriage, so that the offspring of his daughter, who had married James, would inherit the crown. This led to proposals that Charles should divorce the Queen or legitimize his favourite bastard, Monmouth, but Charles would not agree to either. He may have felt, as he said, that his poor wife had suffered enough already. He may have feared that the dashing Monmouth might prove more dangerous as a focus of a 'reversionary interest' than the dim and doggedly loyal Duke of York. He may have believed that to tamper with the succession would weaken the monarchy's prestige and authority; the Stuarts stressed the hereditary element in the divine right of kings far more than the Tudors had done. God, they argued, had both created the monarchy and determined the way it should pass from one king to another.

As Charles would not change the succession, James remained heir presumptive. For Englishmen raised on tales of 'Bloody Mary' and of the cruelties inflicted by Catholic rulers on Protestant subjects, it was a fearful prospect. Moreover, they took it for granted that Popery was inseparable from 'arbitrary government'. 'Papists are enemies', declared one MP, 'not because they are erroneous in religion but because their principles are destructive to the government.' 'Popery in a great measure is set up for arbitrary power's sake,' agreed another, 'they are not so forward for religion.'[16] In Protestant eyes, Catholic kings and priests conspired to keep the people subservient and ignorant: the clergy indoctrinated the laity, the crown protected the Church's interests. Brute force overrode law and justice, Catholics were taught that they were not obliged to keep their word to Protestants, so that under a Catholic king, liberty, property and religion would be in jeopardy. To many, the developments which surfaced in 1672 seemed to form an ominous pattern. Charles joined with the Catholic, absolutist Louis XIV to make war on the Protestant Dutch. His Declaration of Indulgence extended his prerogative and allowed liberty to Catholics. His brother, widely seen as harsh and authoritarian, became a Catholic. He raised additional land forces, later found to include some Catholic officers. This all suggested a great conspiracy to impose Catholicism and absolutism, first on the Dutch and then, with French help, on England.

Looking back, contemporaries saw 1672 as a watershed. Hitherto there had been irritation at the failure of the war of 1665-7 and at Charles' insistence on trying to improve the Dissenters' lot, but he had not seemed to threaten either the constitution or the Protestant religion. Now many believed that the French alliance 'carries the pope in the belly of it'. 'Our jealousies of Popery or an arbitrary government are not from a few inconsiderable Papists here, but from the ill example we have from France.'[17] When Parliament reconvened in 1673, not having met in 1672, the Commons demanded that Charles revoke the Indulgence and assent to a Test Act excluding Catholics from office. Urged on by the French ambassador, Charles agreed, in order to obtain money for the war, but his agreement did not end his people's anxieties. James had resigned his offices rather than take the Test required by the Act, thus proving that he was a Catholic. He went on to marry an Italian princess, Mary Beatrice of Modena. His first wife, who died in 1671, had borne him two daughters, Mary and Anne, both raised as Protestants. If his new Duchess bore him a son, he would presumably be raised as a Catholic and would take precedence over his stepsisters in the succession.

James' remarriage increased the likelihood of a Catholic becoming king. While James had no sons, there would be no 'Popish successor' if Charles outlived his brother, who was only three years younger and seemed less robust than the King. Now a Catholic successor seemed not only possible but probable: Mary Beatrice was only fifteen. News that James had married her (by proxy) drove the Commons to demand that the marriage should not be consummated: an unprecedented interference in the private life of one of the royal family. Charles prorogued Parliament, but Londoners showed their feelings by burning the pope in effigy the night the new Duchess arrived.

Mary Beatrice did not enjoy her first days in England. At one stage destined for a nunnery, she found herself in a strange and barbarous country where the people hated her religion. Her husband was twenty-five years her senior, stern and humourless; like Charles, he had a voracious sexual appetite, which (unlike Charles) made him feel guilty. His new wife was strikingly beautiful, with jet black hair and flashing eyes, but she could never satisfy his needs and numerous women passed up the backstairs to James' apartments; most were so unattractive that Bishop Burnet wickedly suggested that they were given to him by his priests as a penance.

Nevertheless, James proved a kind and affectionate husband and the two became, in most respects, a happy and devoted couple, but in the short run Mary Beatrice's arrival raised a simmering political crisis to boiling point. The Commons refused to vote more money for the war, leaving Charles no choice but to make peace with the Dutch. Louis accepted his decision with good grace; in what was becoming a continental war, England (as a mainly naval power) was of limited use to him. Charles remained benevolently neutral, allowing Louis to recruit troops in Scotland and Ireland and rejecting Dutch and Spanish pleas to join the coalition against France. As the Commons urged him to make war on France, but showed little sign of voting the necessary money, Charles was content to profit from his position as almost the only neutral ruler in Europe. England's trade boomed, boosting his income from customs duties; the revenues granted at the Restoration began to seem less inadequate.

While Charles' financial position improved, Louis' deteriorated, as Colbert's plans for reform went up in cannon-smoke. Like his predecessors, Colbert turned to *affaires extraordinaires*, which brought in ready cash but increased both the crown's indebtedness and the burden on the people. A major revolt in Brittany, sparked off by a new tax on stamped paper, seriously embarrassed a government whose military resources were already fully stretched; a few rebels were executed, the King made a few token concessions. As it turned out, this was to be the last major tax revolt before the Revolution: peasant violence was to turn against landlords rather than the crown,[18] but that did not mean that the burden of taxation was easily borne. The bad old habits denounced by Colbert crept back. Town governments were again allowed to run up debts to meet the King's demands, thus reopening the opportunities for private profit at the public's expense. One could not insist on order and regularity when the crown broke its own rules in order to secure ready money.

Despite these difficulties, Louis' war effort was crowned with considerable, but not unmixed, success. The coalition against him faced many problems. William took time to revitalize the Dutch army. Once the threat to their territory had been removed, with the withdrawal of French forces late in 1673, the Dutch lost much of their enthusiasm for the war, which disrupted trade and necessitated heavy taxation. The Imperial commanders had their initiative tightly restricted by the Vienna government and some were superannuated or dotty. The French had a superior military organization, unified direction and, once on the defensive, internal lines of communication; Vauban strengthened the fortifications of the towns of Alsace and Lorraine. Increasingly, Louis' strategy was coming to depend on an 'iron frontier', a web of heavily fortified towns which would make invasion from the north or east slow and difficult. The more advanced fortifications could also serve as bases for attacks on neighbouring territory, but under Vauban's influence Louis' approach to strategy was becoming defensive; with such a frontier, he would not need to annex the Spanish Netherlands.[19]

By the summer of 1677 Louis was eager for peace. As he took one Flemish town after another, it seemed only a matter of time before his enemies came to terms; he reckoned without William's tenacity and Charles' unpredictability. As French armies promenaded through the Netherlands — even the effeminate Monsieur won a significant engagement — English public opinion became alarmed: if Louis overran the Spanish Netherlands he would control a long stretch of coastline from which he could harass English shipping or mount an invasion. Charles felt he had to take these anxieties seriously. Badly shaken by the furore of 1673−4, he talked often of the danger of rebellion and civil war. Since Clarendon's fall he had had no chief minister. Now he placed increasing reliance on the Earl of Danby, who urged him to return to the 'Cavalier' policies which had worked so well in 1670−1. Danby promoted a religious census, to show the weakness of Dissent and Catholicism, and had the laws against all nonconformity enforced. He pressed Charles to break with France, but the King was reluctant to abandon the one friend who might come to his rescue in case of insurrection. Eventually Danby wore down his opposition. For some years Charles had been on frosty terms with William, but late in 1677 he agreed that William should marry James' elder daughter, Mary.

Mary was fifteen, tall, handsome and serious-minded; William was twenty-seven, short, hook-nosed and asthmatic, with a rasping voice and a limited command of English. As so often with royal marriages, the bride was among the last to know: on hearing the glad news she wept for a day and a half. In time she came to appreciate the warmth behind a cold exterior which owed more to shyness than to innate severity and lavished upon William the affection which he had largely lacked hitherto; he responded with an unswerving devotion. Unlike his uncles, he was essentially monogamous: his relationship with his one mistress was platonic. As with their grandparents, Charles and Henrietta Maria, Mary and William found that a marriage born of transient diplomatic circumstances proved, in human terms, very successful. It was less successful politically. It convinced many Dutchmen that William shared the monarchical ambitions of his predecessors, while many in England believed he had sold out to the court and to Popery. Convinced by William of the need to halt French progress in Flanders, Charles sent Louis an ultimatum: if he did not make peace, giving up some of his recent conquests, England would enter the war on the allied side. Louis rejected these demands — perhaps he thought that Charles was bluffing — so

Charles, reluctantly, prepared for war.

If Charles hoped that the Commons would vote large sums of money for the war they had long called for, he was disappointed. Danby had given the Anglican majority the religious policies it wanted and had persuaded Charles to break with France, but he could not conjure away James' Catholicism. James eagerly supported the war: he liked soldiering and hoped that a successful war would revive his popularity, but his very eagerness aroused suspicion. A large land force was raised to be sent to Flanders and many feared that James might use it to establish absolutism. One wit suggested that the Commons wanted a war but no army, and the court wanted an army but no war. Despite such jests, Louis was shaken by Charles' unaccustomed bellicosity. He stepped up his peace efforts, which ended in the Treaty of Nijmegen, while by a devious manoeuvre leading Charles to spend on keeping up the army the money which Parliament had voted for its disbandment. Charles was indeed left with an army and no war — and no money with which to pay it off.

The terms agreed at Nijmegen in 1678–9 were mostly satisfactory to France. Instead of a jagged jumble, with French and Spanish towns mixed indiscriminately, the northern frontier was now straighter and more defensible. Alsace and Lorraine, where the existing confusion of jurisdictions continued, now became Louis' main concern: not only did he see that international opposition ruled out any conquest of the Spanish Netherlands, but he now regarded the Emperor, not Spain, as the main threat. He had also learned that war on the scale of that of 1672–8 brought unacceptable losses — he was always upset by heavy casualties — and imposed a heavy burden on his subjects: from 1679 he can be found talking of 'the misery of the people'. Louis was, however, far from pleased at the outcome of the war and dismissed Pomponne, the only career diplomat among his ministers and the only consistent advocate of moderation. He was replaced by Colbert's brother, the Marquis de Croissy, Louis' ambassador in London at the time of the Dover treaty and another rude, abrasive personality. One result of this change was that the policies of the next few years kept alive the fears of France aroused by the Dutch War. Meanwhile, the war's financial legacy prevented Colbert from renewing his fiscal reforms.

The Peace of Nijmegen did nothing to reduce Charles' problems. Many of his subjects saw his retaining his army after the treaty as sinister. Amid his many problems he could spare little time for the improbable claims of an eccentric parson and a failed Jesuit novice that there had been a 'Popish plot' to murder him and bring in Popery. He was not alone in refusing to take it seriously : his most vehement critic, the Earl of Shaftesbury, saw it as a ploy to divert attention from the army and the Duke of York, especially as Titus Oates, the chief informant, exonerated James from blame.

Then, on 23 October, Sir Edmund Berry Godfrey, the magistrate who first took down Oates' story, was found murdered. Panic gripped London : everyone feared that a massacre of Protestants was imminent. Fashionable ladies, fearful of Popish assassins, carried daggers bearing the legend 'Remember Justice Godfrey'. Meanwhile, the council ordered the seizure of the papers of those named by Oates. One was Edward Coleman, former secretary to the Duke and Duchess of York, whose papers revealed intrigues with Louis' confessor and other leading Catholics and clearly linked James to the plot. For five years the prospect of a Catholic successor had cast a shadow over English politics. The plot and Coleman's letters brought it to the centre of the stage and provoked an attempt to exclude James from the throne.

# 8
# Zenith and Decline

In 1685 the monarchies of France and England seemed at the zenith of their power. The Peace of Nijmegen interrupted only briefly Louis' acquisition of territory from his weaker neighbours; his gains were confirmed for twenty years in the Truce of Ratisbon (1684). He moved his court to Versailles. Overt opposition to his will disappeared and religious diversity ended with the revocation of the Edict of Nantes in 1685. In England, Charles II defeated the attempt to exclude James from the succession and used the reaction which it provoked to crush his enemies and rule without Parliament. When Charles II died, in February 1685, James succeeded him without a whimper of protest. The most loyal House of Commons of the century voted him all Charles' revenues and more and helped him to crush Argyll and Monmouth's rebellions. Yet these triumphs contained the seeds of their own destruction, seeds sown in the fateful years 1668-73. So long as Louis claimed his 'rights', using a mixture of self-righteous chicanery and deliberate brutality, he could not dissipate the fears he had then aroused among the Dutch and Germans. For the moment, the princes could not oppose him: they needed the backing of the Emperor, who was occupied elsewhere; but their time would come.

In England, James' conversion was to prove his undoing. He owed his accession to the support of the Tories, who were not only monarchists but also Anglicans. They expected him to keep his religion to himself and to protect the interests of the Church of England, but James could not conform to such double standards. His grandfather had allegedly said that Paris was worth a mass, but James would not sacrifice faith to expediency. Successful kingship required an understanding of what was politically possible. Louis, often so acute in domestic affairs, wilfully misunderstood foreign reactions to his policies; James, like his father, did not regard his subjects' opinions as important. Both were to pay the penalty.

When Louis' court moved to Versailles, he entered an environment which he had designed and could control. To the west, Le Nôtre's gardens showed how far human ingenuity could impose order on untidy nature. Even the supposedly natural groves and grottoes were carefully planned and the gardens bristled with ingenious illusions. Within the palace, Louis was forever confronted by images of himself. Often they were symbolic. From his childhood he had been known as the Sun King, the new Apollo, bringing life and warmth to the world; it was an image used to an almost obsessive degree at Versailles, but there were also innumerable images of the King's person, often in stylized form, as in the paintings in the Hall of Mirrors, which purported to chronicle his achievements. Often he appeared as a Roman Emperor, taking personal charge of the government, crossing the Rhine and humbling Dutch, Germans and Spaniards. In contrast to the huge canvases on these subjects were small representations of his bringing order to his finances and reviving French navigation — an indication of his scale of priorities. Never had there been a more single-minded celebration of monarchy and the monarch: in the chapel, completed in 1710, the King alone bowed to the altar; everyone else bowed to the King.

The King's personality dictated not only the setting of the court but its rigorous etiquette and minutely detailed daily round. Louis became more solemn and censorious with age. He took the Church's rituals and rules seriously, partly because he found sumptuousness and order aesthetically pleasing, partly because they instilled into his subjects a certain moral and social discipline. Despite his many mistresses, he was always something of a prude. After 1681, his mistresses were not acknowledged openly; now in his forties, Louis looked for more than beauty in a woman. Despite the constant adulation and his outward self-confidence, he was often lonely and dispirited. His wife was neither attractive nor companionable, his brother was an effeminate poltroon, his son had inherited Marie Thérèse's devastating mediocrity. The only woman in the royal family who combined brains with good looks — Henriette — was dead. Monsieur soon remarried. His new spouse was Elizabeth Charlotte, Princess Palatine (often known as Liselotte), the grand-daughter of Charles I's sister, Elizabeth, and Frederick. She had wit in abundance, but was no beauty. At first she and Louis got on well. She hunted indefatigably and idolized the King: he seemed so much more of a man than her husband; he found her outspoken and amusing. Others were less amused. Determinedly unfashionable, she did not hide her contempt for the artificiality of the court. As a German she was always something of a misfit and she came violently to disapprove of Louis' policies towards the Huguenots and her native land. Louis became cool and she vented her frustrations in innumerable vitriolic letters to her German friends. Liselotte could thus never be the female confidante whom Louis needed, and found in Mme de Maintenon.

The most familiar picture of Maintenon comes from Liselotte and St Simon (the son of Louis XIII's favourite): both knew her in her crabbed old age and hated her. They depicted her as a sour, bigoted hag, instilling into a basically good-natured King her obsessive dislike of innocent pleasure; she filled Versailles with spies who reported on any hint of moral delinquency, so that the court became stiflingly, if superficially, pious and deadly dull. For the last years of the reign, this would be substantially true, but one should not antedate this puritanism or place all the blame on Maintenon. Louis had always been interested in regulating people's private lives, forcing sons to show due respect to their fathers and ordering the Paris authorities to clamp down on vice; he also showed a prurient interest in police reports of scandalous goings-on. He always struggled against his own passions and love of pleasure; he stopped dancing as early as 1669. With age, his struggle became more successful; his public obligation to set an example overcame his affections as a private man. Thus if Maintenon encouraged his outward piety and moral censoriousness, these aspects of his character were already well developed. Her efforts also complemented those of other *dévots* at court, concerned at the spread of vice in French society.

Françoise d'Aubigné, Mme Scarron, was the widow of a minor poet who came to Louis' attention when she took charge of Montespan's children. Of a respectable, but impecunious family, she was widely read, intelligent, handsome and calm. In a world which, at the time of the poisoning scandals, seemed wicked and depraved, she offered an oasis of honesty, gentleness and good sense. If she became Louis' mistress, she did so discreetly, urging him to pay more attention to his Queen: the poor woman was very grateful. When Marie Thérèse died, in 1682, Louis secretly married Mme Scarron, to whom he had given the property at Maintenon by which she became known. He thus legitimated their relationship in the sight of God, without compromising the succession. Although few had any doubts about the nature of their relationship — they talked for hours each day — Louis never acknowledged her as his wife. While meeting his still considerable physical demands, she was to provide him with the solace of a secure and soothing domestic life in the difficult years after 1688.

In moving to Versailles, Louis became more distant from his people. Surrounded by the environment he had created, it was easy to believe that everything could be bent to his will as easily as its stones, plants and fabrics. In theory he devoted one day a week to petitions, but spent much of that day with architects and gardeners, while the petitions were sifted by his ministers. On his rare visits to Paris, the streets were carefully cleared of beggars before he came. Confident of the efficacy of reason and method, and of his ministers' diligence and loyalty, Louis expected government to function predictably and unobtrusively. When he needed money or soldiers for the work at Versailles, they duly appeared. When administrative problems arose, the council would order intendants and other officials to produce dossiers of information, on which to base its decision. If an official or institution appealed against that decision, the council would call for more information, hear the parties concerned and reach a revised decision — only for some local interest to ask it to reconsider. The endless stream of appeals help explain the lack of opposition to the regime : losers could always try again. They were inevitable, given the uncertain boundaries between juris-dictions ; indeed, the crown exploited these uncertainties in order to play one institution against another. The net result of this deliberation and centralization, however, was that decisions were made extremely slowly.

Having issued its orders, the council often found difficulty in having them obeyed. Local officials delayed and equivocated : the intendants tried to make them act, but they could not be everywhere. Besides, intendants spent longer and longer in one province. They put down local roots ; their growing workload led them to appoint subordinates — local men with local interests. The intendants' original role, as the central government's representatives in the localities, was eroded. While decision-making at the centre became clogged with the sheer volume of paperwork, the crown's ability to enforce its will in the provinces still depended on the co-operation of the dominant elements in society, the officials and great nobility. Decision-making at court was not, moreover, as impersonal as it seemed. To succeed in a suit or jurisdictional dispute one needed support in high places. If ministers built up clienteles in order to secure co-operation in the localities, their clients expected them to look after their interests. Provincial governors were no less influential for spending much of their time at court: suitors from their provinces continually applied to them for support and decisions were often influenced more by the balance of favour at court than by the intrinsic merits of the case.[1]

Thus Louis XIV's government was neither as impersonal nor as efficient as it seemed, but France was still governed more effectively than ever before. There were no major popular revolts in the generation after 1675. Taxes were collected, order was maintained, open critics of the regime were punished. This owed much not only to great ministers like Colbert, but also to men of the second rank, like Nicolas de La Reynie, lieutenant of police in Paris. La Reynie's rule reflected the hostility of the King and the *dévots* to deviants of all kinds — whores and Huguenots, gypsies and the insane, beggars and pornographers. They were swept off the streets and incarcerated in houses of correction, notably the General Hospital, where they were subjected to a severe regime intended to turn them into sober, industrious citizens. Idle beggars were flogged, prostitutes had their heads shaved. Moral repression was not La Reynie's only concern: the streets were cleared of obstructions and nuisances, paving and lighting were improved. The city walls were razed to make tree-lined boulevards. All this was achieved on a limited budget, partly by making the Parisians themselves pay for these improvements, but in general Paris was better governed under Louis XIV than ever before.[2]

Such achievements did not occur altogether independently of the King. He set the style of government, stressing the need for regularity and diligence, and chose the ministers who transmitted that style to their subordinates: Colbert worked closely with La Reynie. In time, however, Louis became less and less involved in domestic administration and left the machinery to function without him. He showed little interest in Paris, apart from the juicier bits in La Reynie's reports, provided it caused no trouble. The new building at the Louvre early in the reign owed more to Colbert than the King, who soon lost interest. Thereafter, his only major building project in Paris, apart from the Invalides (a hospital for disabled soldiers), was the Place Vendôme, which was to house the royal academies and ministries and was to contain an equestrian statue of the King large enough for twenty men to dine in the horse's belly. Mansart built the façade, but war came, the money ran out and the scheme was taken over by private developers who turned the square into an exclusive residential development for the super-rich; the academies and ministries were forgotten. As so often, the real beneficiaries of Louis' regime were the magnates and financiers.

By the 1680s that regime, like Charles I's in the 1630s, seemed remote from the nation it ruled. Louis was more efficient and diligent than Charles, but showed the same capacity for ignoring unpalatable realities, as his foreign policy showed clearly. He prided himself on the quality and quantity of his information, but then proceeded, almost wilfully, to misinterpret it. He deduced from reason and experience certain 'maxims of state' about how certain rulers and statesmen would behave in certain circumstances. The maxims showed both knowledge and psychological insight, but came to assume the immutable authority of Holy Writ. Louis applied them inflexibly and ignored information, especially from his ambassadors, which did not fit in with his preconceptions. He believed that rulers were moved more by greed or fear than by principle, so relied on bribes, subsidies and the deterrent effect of brutality, while discounting religion: as he did not take Protestantism seriously, he could not imagine how anyone else could do so. He believed that the Dutch should see Spain, not France, as the main threat to their independence and that German states should fear the Emperor's power more than his own. Reliance on these maxims had led in 1672–3 to a far larger war than he had anticipated, but he did not learn from this, partly because of the influence of Louvois, who shared many of these preconceptions without sharing Louis' extensive knowledge of foreign affairs.

Still more fundamental, however, was Louis' own character: as God had given him such fine judgement, as he had built up the best army and diplomatic corps in Europe, how could he fail? Like Charles I, Louis combined an exaggerated sense of his own abilities with a sublime indifference to the hopes and fears of others. Such egotism was accentuated by the environment which he created at Versailles, but its roots lay within his own character and it was to prove almost as fatal as that of Charles I.

The flaws in his approach appeared in the decade after the Peace of Nijmegen. This left open as many issues as it resolved and Louis and his lawyers were quick to exploit these uncertainties. French courts awarded him sovereignty over all the towns of Alsace, except Strasbourg, and he took possession. Although they failed to concoct even a tenuous claim to Strasbourg, such niceties did not unduly bother Louis and he took it anyway, thus gaining control of a vital Rhine crossing. In the Spanish Netherlands, he claimed and annexed territories which 'depended' on those he had gained in 1678, notably Luxemburg. He may have believed that justice was on his side: others did not, but towns, petty princes and even the Brussels government could not resist the might of France. Such successes reinforced the faith of Louis and his ministers in this combination of legalism and violence: 'I beg you', wrote Louvois, 'not to slacken in your severity and to pursue matters in this case with all possible rigour.'[3] Louis' government exulted in its ability to bully the weak. Furious that Genoa, a neutral state, ignored his order not to allow Spain to recruit troops and fit out galleys there, Louis sent a fleet which destroyed more than half the city and demanded that it send a deputation to Versailles to beg his pardon.

Louis could get away with such conduct because the major powers were otherwise preoccupied. Charles II, unwilling to call a Parliament, could only plead with Louis to show some restraint. The Dutch were busy rebuilding their trade after the war and their foreign policy was hamstrung by the struggle between the States party and the Orangists. The Emperor, meanwhile, faced a fearsome threat from the east. In 1683 200,000 Turkish troops besieged Vienna. It was a critical moment for Christendom: volunteers came from all over Europe to the Imperial army, while the German states had agreed, in 1681, to raise troops to help in the struggle. Louis' response, by contrast, was equivocal: he briefly broke off his siege of Luxemburg, but seems to have hoped that the Turks would crush the Austrian Habsburgs, so that he could replace Leopold as defender of Christendom and, perhaps, as Holy Roman Emperor.[4]

He was doomed to disappointment: a relieving army of Germans and Poles fell on the Turkish hordes and put them to flight. Louis relieved his feelings by pounding uncooperative Flemish towns to rubble and by humiliating the Genoese, while proclaiming his willingness to make peace if his 'rights' were recognized. The Spaniards and the Rhineland states were in no position to argue, while Leopold's main concern was to follow up his victory. In 1684 the Truce of Ratisbon gave Louis possession, for twenty years, of his recent annexations, thus strengthening his frontiers and, apparently, vindicating the policies of violence. With the danger of invasion reduced, Louis could sit back and wait for the King of Spain to die, so that he could grab what Spanish territories he could.

Louis' position was less secure than it seemed. He still did not control one of the 'gates' on the Rhine: Philippsburg, captured by the Emperor in 1676. Moreover, his defences had never depended on fortifications alone, but on the neutrality or goodwill of German states and their age-old suspicion of the Emperor. Louis either failed to appreciate the value of such intangible defences or assumed that the states would not help the Emperor whatever France might do. It was ominous, for him, that the Diet of the Empire had agreed, for the first time in over a century, to raise forces for the Emperor. Moreover, in the years after the Truce of Ratisbon, Leopold drove the Turks eastwards, greatly enlarging his territories. He also, though the French were loath to recognize it, greatly improved the organization and fighting skills of his armies. A time would surely come when German states could look to the Emperor to help them regain what they had lost in 1684 and when Louis would have to face the consequences of his arrogance and brutality. He would also have to reckon with a revived religious fervour among German, and other, Protestants, thanks to his revocation of the Edict of Nantes.

Louis had confirmed the Edict at his accession, but interpreted it as narrowly as he could. If he did not hate the Huguenots, he had no sympathy for their views and was irritated by their refusal to conform to the Catholic Church. Catholic militants described them not as heretics, and so beyond redemption, but as schismatics: erring brethren, led astray by pride and ignorance, who, for the good of their souls, had to be brought within the bosom of the one true Church. This view appealed to Louis, with his limited theological understanding and fondness for uniformity. He believed that schism had once been an understandable response to the clergy's faults, but those faults had now been remedied. He found it hard to forget that in the past Huguenots had rebelled against the crown and was perturbed by stories of their trying to convert Catholics, contrary to the terms of the Edict. The first twenty years of his personal rule saw a piecemeal assault on Huguenot privileges. They were excluded from more and more trades, professions and offices; many of their churches were closed and razed. They were encouraged to become Catholics by offers of pensions, tax concessions and other privileges, notably exemption from having soldiers billeted on them — an approach which illustrates the belief that self-interest played a larger part than principle in human conduct.

It met with considerable success. Many Protestants abandoned their religion, or ceased to practise it openly. Despite the tenacious efforts of its leaders, the Huguenot community was slowly eroded — too slowly for the Catholic militants. The end of the war in 1678 offered the prospect of speedier methods. In 1681, troops were used to convert Huguenots by force in Poitou. The intendant in question was swiftly moved elsewhere, but the results — 30,000 'converts' in a few weeks — were too spectacular to be ignored. In 1685, with a Catholic King in England, the use of troops resumed on a far larger scale. Those who failed to abjure were subjected to violence of every kind, but often whole villages declared themselves Catholic on the news that soldiers were coming. Three to four hundred thousand southern Protestants abjured their religion in the summer of 1685.[5]

As Louis wandered the gilded apartments of Versailles, he may have had little conception of the brutalities of Breton or Norman soldiers against the Huguenots of Béarn or the Cévennes, who barely spoke the same language. He knew enough of war, however, to know what was involved in a punitive expedition or the sack of a town. While he fretted about military casualties, he showed far less interest in the suffering which his soldiers inflicted on civilians. His soldiers served him : he knew them and had obligations towards them, recognized in the Invalides. He knew little of hill shepherds or peasant cultivators, scratching a precarious living from the soil. In his eyes, if the Huguenots suffered, it was their own fault for clinging to their foolish errors : they were, like Germans or Dutchmen, inferior beings (just as the Irish were to many Englishmen). Some Huguenots chose to believe that a basically kindly King was misled by priests and bigots ; some foreign Protestants depicted him as a sadist, revelling in cruelty. In fact, he was pleased that the Huguenot problem was at last being resolved and was little concerned about the methods used ; claims that Maintenon persuaded him to initiate the persecution were probably unfounded.

The revocation marked the final stage of the campaign : it claimed that there was no longer any need for toleration because there were no longer any Huguenots. More prosaically, with so many 'new converts', the fiscal and other privileges they enjoyed were drastically reducing the royal revenue. Forcible conversions continued after the revocation and many refused to abjure. Pastors were allowed to emigrate, provided they left their property and their children, who were to be raised as Catholics. Lay Protestants were forbidden to leave France or to send away any property, but maybe 200,000 left between 1679 and 1710. A large proportion were young men and people with transportable skills: merchants and businessmen, soldiers, sailors and artisans. Many had contacts among earlier generations of refugees, in England, Holland or Germany, but others sought new places to settle. Many travelled great distances: the people of one western village walked to Cadiz. Some prospered, especially the merchants and financiers, who often kept in contact with 'Catholic' friends or relatives in France. Others suffered disappointment, like the wine growers lured by promises of a new life in Prussia, where it proved too cold for vines to grow.[6]

In many respects, the revocation proved a serious error. It failed to eradicate Protestantism: without their privileges, churches and pastors, Huguenots worshipped in their homes and in the fields; they did not come to mass. Many 'converts' remained Protestants at heart; some reverted to their old ways. Militant Catholic officials and priests watched for backslidings and clandestine meetings, but they were too few to monitor the conduct of thousands of people and they had other things to do. After the first surge of persecution, many covert Protestants lived something like a normal life. Not all Catholics were hostile: for many, ties of neighbourliness had always meant more than differences of religion. Louis' ideal of 'one faith, one law, one king' remained only an ideal, while the revocation did him much harm. If the emigration damaged the economy less than was once thought, it provided France's enemies with highly motivated soldiers and sailors. Moreover, at a time when the age of religious wars seemed to have passed, the revocation re-created a sense of Protestant solidarity which was to play a major part in later events.

Between 1678 and 1685 Louis' power seemed to be at its apogee. He arbitrarily added to his territory, crushed the Huguenots and installed himself in the grandest palace in Europe, and yet, like the gardens and paintings at Versailles, much of this appearance of power was illusory. He gained new territories only because the other major powers temporarily lacked the will or the capacity to oppose him; such a conjuncture could not last for ever. Much, moreover, depended on bluff. After Nijmegen Louis reduced his armies and relied on small-scale, concentrated violence to scare his enemies into submission. Internally, little changed: there was no resumption of the reforming spirit of the 1660s; Colbert was old, tired and losing his grip when he died in 1683. The style and grandeur of the monarchy may have developed since the 1660s; the institutional base remained as muddled and shaky as ever. While Louis could avoid major wars, this would not matter, but France was soon to face greater wars than ever before and the government was to creak and crack under the strain.

\* \* \*

The excitement provoked in 1678 by Oates' revelations inspired in Charles II an awful sense of *déjà vu*: he knew well how potent anti-Popery had proved in 1640-2. Despite his impeccable Protestantism, Charles I had been accused of leaning towards Popery 'without which handle it was morally impossible that the ill-affected part of the nation could ever have seduced the rest into a rebellion'.[7] His son spent much time reading histories of the civil war, which reinforced his conviction that he was facing another attempt to use anti-Popery as a pretext for an attack on the very foundations of monarchy.

Both the popular belief in the plot and Charles' fears of republicanism rested on prejudice and misconception, but were not implausible. Godfrey had been murdered, Coleman's letters did show evidence of Popish intrigues, though not those described by Oates. The fears aroused by the plot were, in fact, ambivalent: not only of Popish assassins but also of James, the court and the army. Even the King was not above suspicion: the plot was the more dangerous, said one MP, 'because carried on so in the court that one would think the King had a hand in it. But my allegiance teaches me to pay my duty as an English subject to an English king'.[8]

For his part, Charles had several reasons for comparing his position to that of his father in 1640–2. Again, the King's chief minister was impeached: Danby's credit was ruined by the revelation that he had asked Louis for money in return for making peace, while asking the Commons for money for the war against France. Again, the bishops' right to sit in the Lords was challenged, but only when hearing cases carrying the death penalty. Again,

MPs sought to interfere in the direction of the armed forces, by pressing Charles to remove James' 'creatures'. Again, unable to achieve their aims through normal constitutional channels, opposition leaders appealed to the wider public outside Parliament. Three times in 1679–81 the electorate returned a House of Commons committed to excluding James from the succession. Three times the Commons passed exclusion bills; one was rejected by the Lords, two were lost when Charles dissolved Parliament. In an effort to persuade the Lords and King to agree to these bills, the Commons leaders, as in 1641, sought popular support, using the press (censorship having lapsed), petitions and demonstrations, notably huge parades which burned an effigy of the Pope.

If the Exclusionists' conduct raised echoes of 1640–2, so did their arguments. Faced with Charles' hostility to exclusion, MPs claimed that his words and deeds were dictated by his advisers, implying that he was either a nonentity or 'deranged', not responsible for his actions. While professing respect for his prerogatives, they argued that he should use them in his subjects' best interests, as expressed by the Commons; this could mean that he should do whatever the Commons commanded and appoint to places of trust only men acceptable to the Commons. Such arguments, taken to their logical extreme, would have left Charles a mere figurehead and implied an attack on his personal direction of government akin to that of 1640–2. There were also, however, major differences between the two crises. Charles I's problems owed much to revolts in Scotland and Ireland; his son had to contend only with one minor insurrection in Scotland. Charles I had been totally dependent on Parliament for money after the reforms of 1641; Charles II was able, by the end of 1680, to subsist without further grants from Parliament, thanks to the increased yield of the revenues granted at the Restoration. Charles I lost control of London: riots forced him to agree to Strafford's execution and later drove him out; Charles II never provoked the City's rulers as his father had done, ensured that a majority of aldermen remained loyal and that the City militia remained in the hands of men he could trust.[9] Above all, the threat from the Exclusionists turned out to be less substantial than it seemed.

This was most apparent in the Pope-burning processions which took place on 17 November, the anniversary of Elizabeth's accession, in 1679 and 1680. The tableaux on the floats included the Pope's effigy, with a child dressed as a devil sitting on its shoulder, and the stock figures of anti-Popery: Jesuits with bloody knives, scheming cardinals and winsome nuns, the Pope's 'courtesans'. There were also figures from the plot, headed by Godfrey and his murderers, and opponents of exclusion. Having crossed the City, the Pope was made to kneel before a huge statue of Elizabeth at Temple Bar and was then consigned to the flames; the little devil escaped. The crowds were huge — maybe as large as 200,000 — but, unlike the crowds who had called for Strafford's head, they were good-natured. The pageants were spectacular and there was a lot of free drink, but when the fun was over everyone tottered off to bed, much to the amazement of the French ambassador: it would not have been so at Paris, he said.[10]

This absence of violence highlights the difference between the Exclusion Crisis and that of 1640–2. The Exclusionists, or Whigs as they became known, played on memories of the earlier crisis, trying to create the impression of an overwhelming popular demand for exclusion, in the face of which Charles would have to give in. Their strategy rested largely on bluff: their methods were essentially peaceful, notably pamphlets and petitions. The Commons published their resolutions, Whig politicians denounced their opponents, the Tories, as favourers of Popery and expelled the most outspoken from the Commons, but they stopped short of a wholehearted appeal to 'the people'. As members of the ruling élite, they remembered the outcome of such an appeal in the 1640s: civil war and the 'world turned upside down'. While demanding that the King should do as the Commons asked, they avoided the obvious justification for such a demand: that the Commons derived their authority from the people whom they represented. Such an argument was tainted by its having been used to justify Charles I's execution, and, for aristocrats like the Whig leaders, it smacked too much of democracy for comfort.[11]

The Whig threat to the King's prerogative was thus less serious than it seemed. Those who voted for Whig candidates, signed Whig petitions and cheered as the Pope burned had no intention of resorting to violence; they regarded exclusion as desirable, but were not prepared to bring about civil war in order to achieve it. The emotions aroused by the plot soon cooled. Some of the accused were punished, the new regiments raised in 1678 were disbanded, the threat of Popish massacre receded. The danger of a Catholic successor became, once again, distant and hypothetical: if Charles outlived James, it would never happen. In 1641, by contrast, the threat of massacre, by Strafford's soldiers or Lunsford's cannon, had seemed imminent. Visceral fear had driven respectable citizens to take to the streets in a mood quite different from that of the cheerful and befuddled crowds at the Pope-burnings.

The hollowness of the Whig threat was not, however, apparent at the time. Charles was deeply worried. James urged him to stand firm and not show the weakness that had ruined their father. Charles' inclination, however, was to play one group off against another and to buy time, and it worked. He rejected or evaded demands that would have abridged his prerogatives of calling and dismissing Parliaments at will or controlling the armed forces. He refused to agree to exclusion, which he saw as the first step towards a wide-ranging assault on monarchy; Danby did not suffer Strafford's fate. Where no essential prerogative was involved, Charles made concessions which were often less substantial than they seemed. He ordered the judges to convict some of the alleged plotters. He proposed swingeing new measures against Catholics. He suggested limitations on the powers of a Catholic successor. Above all, whereas his father had refused to take opposition leaders into office, Charles appointed all of them to the privy council, with the most prominent, the Earl of Shaftesbury, as its president. Time was to show that his new councillors exercised little influence, but their appointment served to divide them from their followers; even after they left the council, Charles held out hopes of a deal in secret meetings at Whitehall.

Charles thus played for time, which turned out to be on his side. Anti-Catholic excitement, on which exclusion depended, was sustained with increasing difficulty. When the Lords rejected the second exclusion bill late in 1680, there was no disorder. By now Charles had no financial need for Parliament; just to make sure, he secured a modest subsidy from Louis, who thought Charles' neutrality worth paying for, as he embarked on further aggression in the Netherlands. Charles hesitated, nevertheless, before dispensing with Parliament. His courtiers feared that it would lead to austerity at court and pressed him to come to terms with the Whigs. He therefore summoned yet another Parliament, at Oxford: he remembered how the Commons had adjourned to the Guildhall after his father's attempt on the five members. The Whigs came well armed and escorted and rushed an exclusion bill through the Commons; Charles sent secretly for his robes of state and dissolved Parliament; it had sat for one week. The Whigs, taken by surprise, dispersed in confusion; Charles returned cheerfully to London. Like his father in 1629 he was about to rule without Parliament; unlike his father he was to do so with the support of a large part of the political nation.

In 1640 most of the ruling élite was united in hostility to the Personal Rule, but that unity was destroyed by a growing reaction against the Commons' leaders' radical demands and demagogic tactics. Similarly, in 1678 there was widespread suspicion of the court's intentions and religion, but many moderates and conservatives became worried by the Whigs' conduct. While not happy at the prospect of a Catholic king, they believed it would be unjust to deprive him of his birthright because his religion *might* lead him to act tyrannically, *if* he succeeded. If James were excluded, he would still be King of Scotland and might receive help from foreign princes. Many found William, as a foreigner, unacceptable as an alternative successor, while Monmouth, despite all the pretences of his supporters, was illegitimate.

James, on the other hand, had served valiantly against the Dutch and was regarded as an honourable man, who kept his word: throughout the Exclusion Crisis he promised that, if he became king, he would uphold the interests of the Church of England. The Whigs argued that, faced with the menace of Popery, Protestants should unite and stop persecuting one another. Many Whigs denounced the Church's stress on ceremonies and alleged that the clergy claimed a monopoly of spiritual truth in order to maintain their own power. Anglicans, however, remembered how in 1640−2 the attack on Popery and Laudianism had broadened to embrace episcopacy and the Prayer Book; the old church order had been overthrown and social discipline and conventional morality had been placed in jeopardy. As the Whigs denounced Anglican opponents of exclusion as 'Papists in masquerade', it seemed that anti-Popery was again a cover for an attack on the Church. Respectable Anglicans resented being denounced as 'Papists': yet again, the Whigs were seeking to enflame the ugly passions of the mob. As in 1640−2, most of the ruling élite wished to preserve limited monarchy, the Protestant church and gentry rule, but disagreed on whether the greater threat to the established order came from the court, the Papists and a possible Catholic successor or from the Whigs, the Dissenters and the mob.

The emergence of such a division had provided Charles I with the support to fight a civil war, but by then he had had to leave London, leaving his enemies in control of the government. Charles II was able to reap the benefits of a similar polarization without losing control of the government. He had an adequate income, a modest army and the full might of the State — above all, the law courts; he could thus exploit to the full the conservative backlash against Whiggism. There had been a similar opportunity at the Restoration, when the old Cavaliers burned for revenge, but Charles had not supported them, perhaps because he overestimated the Parliamentarians' strength, perhaps because he wished to heal the wounds of civil war. Now he had no such inhibitions. He had been badly scared by what he saw as a design to deprive him of his powers and even his head, a view apparently confirmed by the discovery of the Rye House Plot, an alleged design to murder James and himself, in 1683. The Whigs, he believed, must be crushed and so he gave wide-ranging support to the Tories in their search for revenge.

By 1681 Charles had aged visibly, perhaps because of the psychological strain of the Exclusion Crisis, perhaps because a stroke, which nearly killed him, had taken a physical toll. His love of ease became greater than ever; his relationship with his most enduring mistress, the Duchess of Portsmouth, changed from one of frenetic passion to one of domesticity. Simple things pleased him. At Newmarket 'he let himself down from majesty to the very degree of a country gentleman. He … went a-hawking in mornings, to cock matches in afternoons (if there were no horse races) and to plays in the evenings, acted in a barn by very ordinary Bartholomew-fair comedians'.[12] He had enjoyed London and its pleasures far more than the first two Stuarts had done. His reign saw a rapid development of aristocratic housing in the fashionable West End. Members of the landed élite brought their families to London for 'the season'. The court and London's many places of pleasure became the centres of a national aristocratic social life, in which Charles, the most charming of kings, played an important role.

As he grew old, however, he spent more time away from London, at Newmarket, Windsor and Winchester. He had devised several plans for a great new palace. He dreamed of demolishing and rebuilding Whitehall. He began to build a huge palace at Greenwich, only to abandon it in 1669: part of his construction was later incorporated in the Naval Hospital. At Winchester, his dreams came close to fulfilment. In September 1682, a few months after Louis moved his court to Versailles, Charles decided to build his own version, overlooking the city. Wren's design, with its emphasis on symmetry and a three-sided courtyard, showed strong signs of French influence and Charles showed as much impatience as Louis to move in. By the time of his death, the work was nearly finished, but James abandoned the palace, no trace of which remains today.[13]

However much Charles wished to remain at his ease, he had to crush the remnants of Whiggery. His vindictiveness in his last years showed that he had been badly shaken. He removed prominent Whigs from the militia, the commissions of the peace and the judiciary, so that the machinery of justice, in the central courts and the counties, was dominated by Tories : the few remaining Whigs went along with their Tory colleagues. The King appointed Tory sheriffs, who chose Tory juries : Whigs accused of political offences stood little chance of acquittal and Dissenters were persecuted more harshly than at any time in the reign. Many were imprisoned ; in some parishes poor relief went only to those who attended church and it was proposed at least once to quarter troops on recalcitrant Dissenters.

While Charles appointed the judges and county JPs, he had little control over the machinery of justice in towns, most of which enjoyed a measure of self-government under their charters. Although Dissenters were supposedly excluded from municipal office under the Corporation Act of 1661, it was laxly enforced and many urban magistrates sympathized with Dissent. In London, popularly-elected Whig sheriffs chose Whig juries, which acquitted Whigs like Shaftesbury, charged with treason in 1681. Charles was furious and set out to break the City's autonomy : why, he asked, should he alone be denied justice ? His law officers challenged the legality of the City's charter, and his judges declared it forfeit. The Lord Mayor and aldermen were now to govern as the King's commissioners ; Charles declared to all and sundry that he was King of London for the first time.[14]

There were similar challenges to municipal autonomy in many provincial towns, where the initiative came, not from the King, but from local Tories. Three general elections had shown the strength of Dissent and Whiggery in many parliamentary boroughs ; to gain control the Tories needed the help of the King and his law courts. Charters were surrendered, either voluntarily or under threat of a legal challenge. If the means used were often devious, the Tories could argue that the Whigs had seldom played fair either. Charles would then issue a new charter which preserved, or even extended, the town's autonomy, but named the first members of the corporation (Tories or complaisant Whigs) and he reserved the right to remove any member of the corporation in future. In this way he could ensure that politically reliable men held municipal office and that the laws against political and religious dissidents were enforced; such changes would also greatly strengthen the Tories' chances in the next parliamentary election, although Charles himself had no intention of calling another Parliament. In the last months of the reign, the government began to take the initiative in confiscating charters, evidence of the growing ascendancy of James and his allies, while Charles subsided into apathy, muttering prophetically that James would not keep his throne for more than three years.[15]

In some ways English government in the early 1680s approximated more closely to French 'absolutism' than ever before. Parliament did not meet for four years, in defiance of the Triennial Act. The legal system was manipulated to harass dissidents; the press was muzzled, even though the censorship legislation had lapsed. A massive purge of municipal corporations helped to produce an overwhelmingly Tory House of Commons in 1685. Charles did not, however, deliberately set out to become 'absolute': his measures were, in his eyes, forced upon him by the Whigs' malevolence. Often the initiative came from the Tories and he sometimes refused to act on their suggestions. Conscious that they might one day have to answer to Parliament, his ministers and law officers were careful to adhere to strict forms of law, while Charles avoided measures so rigorous that they might provoke the Whigs to revolt.[16] Above all, the measures of 1681–4 were designed to benefit the Tories as well as the King. The Tories believed in authority and hierarchy in Church, State and society. Faced with the Whigs' apparent radicalism, they stressed the divine origins of royal authority and the hereditary succession and the impiety of resistance to that authority. They assumed that the King would respect the law and defend the Church: he was morally obliged to do so and, because the law and Church under-pinned his authority, it was also in his own best interests. In the early 1680s it seemed that James shared this view: later the Tories were to realize that they had been gravely mistaken.

On 2 February 1685 Charles suffered another stroke. When it was clear that he was dying, he agreed to James' suggestion that he should send for a priest; he confessed and received the sacrament and extreme unction and died on the 6th. As a king he had been indolent, selfish, unreliable and often irresponsible, but he had kept his throne, which was more than could be said of his father and brother. His lack of zeal and ambition suited the mood of his people: they had had enough of strenuous government in the 1640s and 1650s. The prim diarist, John Evelyn, thought he had many virtues to counterbalance his obvious vices: he was charming and approachable, neither bloody nor cruel. Perhaps the kindest obituary came from Halifax, a minister whom he had not treated very well.

A prince neither sharpened by his misfortunes whilst abroad nor by his power when restored is such a shining character that it is a reproach not to be ... dazzled with it. ... If he loved too much to lie upon his own down bed of ease, his subjects had the pleasure during his reign of lolling and stretching upon theirs. ... Let his royal ashes lie soft upon him and cover him from harsh and unkind censures; which, though they should not be unjust, can never clear themselves from being indecent.[17]

The accession of King James II was greeted with widespread rejoicing. The Whigs were dispirited and discredited: their lamentable showing in the counties, as well as the boroughs, in the 1685 election showed how far public opinion had turned against them. When Parliament met in May, the Commons granted James his brother's revenues, plus temporary grants to refurbish the fleet, pay off the royal debts and put down the two rebellions. Argyll's revolt in Scotland was soon dealt with, but Monmouth's hastily assembled army gave James some anxious moments until it was bloodily routed at Sedgemoor. James showed no mercy to the defeated. He contemptuously refused to spare Monmouth's life and sent the judges to the West Country to punish his followers. At least three hundred were executed; many more were granted to courtiers, who sold them into virtual slavery in the colonies. To modern eyes such severity is repellent, but few protested at the time: to most Tories, the rebels fully deserved their fate, while Monmouth, who had claimed the crown, was by any definition guilty of treason.

By the end of July 1685 James had every reason for satisfaction. He had defeated both the campaign for exclusion and two rebellions, called the most tractable Parliament of the century and secured an ample revenue. He had also increased his army from nine to twenty thousand men, so now had little reason to fear rebellion, yet a little more than three years later he was on his way into exile, his memory execrated by most of his subjects. The causes of his fall, as in any tragedy, lay partly in his own errors and flaws of character and partly in events outside his control and the actions of others — above all, Louis XIV.

\*　　\*　　\*

Unlike his brother, James was diligent and took his administrative responsibilities seriously, but he tended to become preoccupied by details. This need not have mattered greatly. He inherited an able team of ministers, headed by his first wife's brother, Lawrence Hyde, Earl of Rochester, at the treasury, with the Earl of Sunderland as foreign minister. He had little need to fear rebellion and, with his enlarged revenue, his bargaining position in dealing with Parliament was very strong. Had he been content to continue the policies of 1681−4, he would have met with little trouble, but he chose not to do so. This was not because he wished to establish 'absolutism'. Like his father he believed that decision-making was a matter for kings, as advised by their ministers, not for subjects. Like his father, he saw himself as morally obliged to rule according to the law, as interpreted by the judges ; but, like his father, he had a limited grasp of legal technicalities and his view of what the law ought to be often differed from that of most of his subjects.

Charles I had usually misused the law in order to raise money, but James had no need or pretext to do so : his main aim was to advance his religion. God, he believed, had preserved him from the malice of his enemies and so must have a great task which He wished him to do, which could only be to 'establish' Catholicism in England. By this James meant allowing Catholics to worship and proselytize freely and to hold offices on the same terms as Protestants, not imposing Catholicism by force. Not only did he regard the coercion of conscience as immoral, but he saw no need for it. He had found conversion from Anglicanism so natural that he assumed that if others, too, could see Catholicism as it really was they would recognize it as the one true Church. Protestantism, he believed, had survived because of a mixture of pride, misrepresentation, self-interest and fear. Catholics were prevented from worshipping or putting their case by a wide range of penal laws ;

influential laypeople were inhibited from becoming Catholics by the Test Acts, which excluded them from offices and from Parliament. If those laws were removed, James believed that so many people would become Catholics that they would soon — perhaps in as little as two years — become the majority.

Thus rather than leave things as they were, religious zeal impelled James to pursue a legislative programme, the repeal of the penal laws and Test Acts, which was bound to prove controversial. Whereas in France kings could revoke the edicts of their predecessors, Acts of Parliament could be repealed only by Parliament and few converts would trust in the security of a legally questionable repeal. Moreover, after more than ten years of marriage to his second wife, James had no Catholic heir : he assumed that Mary, and William, would succeed him, so any illegal measures in favour of the Catholics would be reversed after his death ; indeed, the more arbitrarily he behaved, the more severely the Catholics would be treated under his successors. He thus had to find an amenable Parliament and at first pinned his hopes on that elected in 1685. At his accession his promise to protect the Church reassured the Tories : 'I know the principles of the Church of England are for monarchy and the members of it have shown themselves good and loyal subjects ; therefore I shall always take care to defend and support it.' He described the Dissenters as seditious and factious.[18] Nevertheless, the Commons (however loyal) made no secret of their hostility to both Dissent and Catholicism, much to James' irritation.

When Parliament reconvened in November 1685, its mood had changed. Evelyn noted in his diary :

The French persecution of the Protestants raging with utmost barbarity.... The French tyrant abrogating the Edict of Nantes...and without any cause on the sudden, demolishing all their churches, banishing, imprisoning, sending to the galleys all the ministers, plundering the common people and exposing them to all sorts of barbarous usage by soldiers sent to ruin and prey upon them.

The Bishop of Valence had claimed 'that God seemed to raise the French king to this power and magnanimous action that he might be in capacity to assist the doing of the same here'. The government newspaper, meanwhile, remained ominously silent about the persecution.[19] Fears that James might imitate Louis were increased by his truculent approach to the new session :

he intended, he said, to keep up the new forces raised in the summer and to retain some one hundred Catholic officers. His attitude provoked even this Parliament to outspoken criticism. Furious at MPs' unreasoning suspicions and aspersions on his honour, James prorogued it on the 20th. It never met again.

In some ways, Parliament's suspicions were unfounded. James' reactions to the revocation were mixed. At first he welcomed the news of mass conversions: he had no fondness for Calvinists and was glad to hear that so many had seen the error of their ways. When he heard of the violent methods used, his enthusiasm became muted. He always denounced religious persecution, although he favoured a firm line against sedition and often equated religious dissent with political mischief-making. His attitude was summed up when he told Trumbull, his ambassador to Paris:

that though he did not like the Huguenots (for he thought they were of anti-monarchical principles) yet he thought the persecution of them was unchristian and not to be equalled in any history since Christianity; that they might be no good men, yet might be used worse than they deserved.[20]

For the most part, however, he kept his disapproval to himself. He accepted that Louis was within his legal rights and that this was a domestic matter, in which he had no right to interfere. He agreed reluctantly to order a collection for the refugees, but intervened in France only in cases involving his own subjects and Trumbull's servants. The French dismissed his representations rudely: a Catholic king, they said, should praise Louis' piety and not fuss over a few insignificant heretics.[21]

The November session of Parliament forced James to rethink his position. He had supported the Church of England, not because he thought it was a true Church, but because of its compatibility with monarchy; now the Anglican Tories had defied him to his face. As James saw it, this departure from their avowed principles of loyalty and obedience absolved him of any obligation towards them. As Catholics were ineligible to sit in Parliament, he would have to have the penal laws and Test Acts repealed by a Protestant Parliament. As he became disillusioned with the Anglicans, he paid more heed to the arguments of the Quaker, William Penn, that Dissenters were not innately hostile to monarchy, but had been provoked into disobedience by Anglican persecution.

In the course of 1686 James came round to the idea of abandoning the Anglicans and appealing to the Dissenters. As they were less numerous than the Churchmen and of far less social and political weight, and as they were debarred by law from worshipping freely and holding offices, James had to use his own power to compensate for their inherent weakness. First, in 1686, the judges ruled that the King could dispense with the penalties of laws when he judged it necessary. To secure this ruling James had to dismiss several judges who thought otherwise, but in itself it was not out of line with past thinking. Kings had often, in the interests of justice, dispensed with the rigours of the law in particular cases, but only after careful investigation of the merits of each case. James used this power sweepingly, to dispense large numbers of Catholics from complying with the Test Acts and congregations of Dissenters from the penalties for nonconformity. His Declaration of Indulgence of April 1687 suspended the penal laws altogether. James apparently felt no need to consult the judges about this: if he could dispense with laws, why could he not suspend them? One seemed to follow logically from the other and, anyway, the suspension was only temporary, pending repeal by Parliament. Others were alarmed: if he could suspend these laws, why not any law he chose? As one judge later declared: 'If this be once allowed of, there will need no Parliament; all the legislature will be in the king.'[22]

The second way in which James extended his powers was in his campaign to pack Parliament. He used the powers granted by the charters of 1681–5 to remove Tories from town corporations and replaced them with Dissenters, although most charters did not in fact allow for this. Many of these Dissenters were obscure, inexperienced and unenthusiastic. Most (especially the more moderate) were prepared to enjoy the liberty which James offered, but not to pay the price he demanded, the repeal of the Test Acts, which would allow Catholics into positions of power. Most Dissenters were strongly anti-Catholic and their resistance to James' blandishments was increased when William and Mary declared that they favoured toleration for all, but not the repeal of the Test Acts. Faced with the coolness of the more influential Dissenters, James was driven to rely on fraud and force. His electoral preparations were never put to the test, but it seems unlikely that he would have secured the election of his chosen candidates or that, if elected, they would have behaved as he wished.[23] If he had succeeded, however, he would have destroyed the Commons' representativeness and made Parliament a rubber-stamp for royal policies, rather like the weaker French provincial estates.

In all this, James did not intend to break the law, but to use his legal powers to the full to achieve ends which, in his eyes, were self-evidently just: as the anti-Catholic laws rested on misrepresentation and blind prejudice, what could be more reasonable than to repeal them? The judges had declared his dispensing power legal: he could not see that he was using it in ways which they had not envisaged. Similarly, he could see no difference between his electoral methods in 1687–8 and those of the Tories in 1681–5. In each case, however, there were substantial differences of degree, not to mention a subjective, or political, element in the interpretation of the law. Many were not prepared to accept the judges' rulings uncritically, especially since they had so obviously been subjected to pressure. The common-law stress on precedent led people to consider the possible implications of James' actions, while anti-Catholic prejudice led them to view those actions in the most sinister light. As they assumed that a Catholic king would try to establish absolutism, James' conduct served to confirm their preconceptions. By 1688 James had alienated the Tories without winning over the Dissenters. In May seven bishops refused to order their clergy to read the Declaration of Indulgence in their churches; James had them tried for seditious libel, but they were acquitted, amid wild rejoicing. Although there was no hint of rebellion, the King, as in 1640, had alienated his subjects to a point where an invasion would find him exposed and vulnerable.

James showed little awareness of his danger, partly because of his confidence that God was with him, partly because of the advice he received, from the Catholic zealots at court and from Sunderland. Ruthlessly ambitious and a compulsive gambler, Sunderland combined a wide knowledge of foreign affairs with a formidable force of character: his sarcasm could reduce even Judge Jeffreys to quaking silence. As his main rivals, notably Rochester, were Anglicans, Sunderland wooed the Catholics and insinuated that all opposition to James' will was fomented by the Tories. Gradually James was persuaded to remove most of his Tory advisers; others stayed away from the council, which came to be dominated by apolitical technocrats and inexperienced Catholics. The court, too, became uncomfortable for Protestants. It was far more decorous and ordered than Charles': although James' sexual appetite remained undiminished, he insisted on an outward show of propriety. He lacked wit or warmth and many found the court dull. Others were put off by the eagerness of the scurrying priests to convert any Protestant they met. When Trumbull returned from Paris, he saw only one face he recognized at the King's lever.[24]

The more the court was dominated by Catholics, the more it became isolated, as Charles I's had been, from the political realities outside. The zealots dismissed opposition as the product of petty intrigue (the only sort of politics they knew about) and told James that if he held firm his power would conquer all. James, who blamed his father's downfall on his abandoning Strafford, found such advice congenial; any sign of weakness could only encourage the 'republicans'. Such an environment bred self-delusion. Having convinced himself that the Dissenters *must* welcome the toleration he offered, James ignored all evidence that they did not, while welcoming addresses of thanks organized by his own servants. Each setback stimulated more extreme, and dangerous, extensions of his powers; each petty triumph was wildly applauded by the zealots. Only Sunderland could see that James' plans would not work, but he could say nothing, for fear of incurring the very charges of obstructionism and faint-heartedness that he had used against the Tories. So James plunged on, buoyed up by a confidence which transcended human reason.

His faith in divine providence was not entirely blind. Late in 1687 the Queen became pregnant for the first time in five years. The zealots proclaimed that she would bring forth a son who (unlike her previous children) would survive: this convinced many Protestants that a boy would be produced, whatever happened. When on 10 June 1688 the Queen indeed gave birth to a son, rumours spread that the baby was not hers, but had been smuggled into the bedchamber in a warming pan. In fact, as so much could hinge on the legitimacy of a royal baby, royal births were invariably attended by a large crowd of courtiers and councillors. On this occasion, most of those present were Catholics, which gave some credence to the rumours of fraud: the wicked Papists would stop at nothing to achieve their ends. One cynic remarked that only if the baby died would people believe that he was the King's son. He nearly did. The doctors insisted that he should not have a wet-nurse — aristocratic ladies did nothing so vulgar as suckle their own young — so he was fed on gruel and canary wine. Louis and the Pope, who at this time agreed on little else, both expressed amazement at the eccentricity of English paediatrics and, as the child became weak, the doctors relented. Put to the breast, the baby grew strong and healthy. Now that God had answered James' prayers for a Catholic heir, he could expect his policies to be continued after his death. The future of English Catholicism seemed bright.

It was not to be. James' fate was to be settled by events outside his own control. For years William had looked forward to the time when Mary would become Queen and he could bring England's resources into his great struggle against France. As James' reign wore on, however, he began to fear that she might be cheated of the succession. It was rumoured that the zealots wanted James to alter the succession; he firmly rebutted any such suggestions. There was the danger that James might provoke another civil war, which could lead to the establishment of another republic, in which case there would be no crown to succeed to. Above all, when the Queen's pregnancy was announced there was the risk that she might produce, or pretend to produce, a son. As his fears grew, William also became perturbed about the possibility of an Anglo-French alliance, like that which had led to the war of 1672. James' relations with the Dutch deteriorated, thanks mainly to the asylum granted to British political exiles in the Republic, while his relations with Louis seemed increasingly intimate. Appearances were deceptive: Louis had a justifiably low opinion of James' abilities and avoided any formal liaison with England: experience showed that such liaisons achieved little and cost him money. Thus, as crisis loomed in 1688, James had the worst of all possible worlds. He had convinced William and the Dutch of his ill-will and that he was closely united with France, but, when the crunch came, Louis did nothing to help him and, indeed, made his predicament worse.

When James became King the Dutch ruling élite was largely weary of war and suspicious of William's ambitions, so paid little heed to his warnings that another French attack on the Republic was inevitable. The persecution of the Huguenots, however, reawakened a dormant sense of Protestant solidarity; it also harmed Dutch trade, as did new tariffs on Dutch goods entering France, so that by 1688 the merchant interest had little to lose from a war. Meanwhile, James' threats and apparent friendship with France lent credence to William's talk of another joint assault, like that of 1672. The States General agreed to build up the army. In late April, six weeks before

James' son was born, William could tell his English contacts that if he was invited to save England and the Protestant religion, he could be ready to come by the end of September. His ability to act on his assurance depended on Louis. The Emperor's recent successes had revived Louis' worries about his German frontier. On the death of the Archbishop of Cologne, who ruled a strategically vital group of territories near the Dutch frontier, Louis tried to secure the election of one of his clients. The election proved inconclusive and was referred to the Pope, whose hostility to France was well-known. Many believed that Cologne would prove the flashpoint for a new European war and the Dutch stepped up their rearmament.

If Louis had poured troops into Cologne, William would not have been able to invade England: the Dutch armies would have had to concentrate on defending their frontiers. When Louis made his move, however, it was a hundred miles further south. In the late summer of 1688 Leopold's armies were besieging Belgrade and Turkish resistance seemed about to collapse. Louis resolved on a move which could both encourage the Turks and strengthen his own defences. He sent orders to besiege Philippsburg, the only major Rhine crossing not under his control. When it fell, his forces poured into Germany, in an effort to force the German states to convert the twenty-year truce into a lasting peace, so that Louis could consolidate his hold on Alsace. Towns which surrendered promptly were spared; those which did not were shelled ruthlessly, while French soldiers exacted 'contributions' for their subsistence. When these methods provoked further resistance, Louis and Louvois increased the level of violence and pressed deeper into Germany. They had not prepared for a major war and expected these blitzkrieg tactics to prove as effective as in 1680-4. They did not.

When William heard of the attack on Philippsburg he can hardly have believed his luck. All summer he had prepared to invade England, knowing a major French attack on Cologne would render it impossible; now he could proceed. James was desolated: having come to accept that William might attack him, he had relied on the French for help, but what little Louis provided proved counter-productive. The French ambassador at The Hague warned the States General that if James were attacked the ties of 'friendship and alliance' between the Kings would oblige Louis to come to his aid; this did nothing to deter the Dutch and gave credence to William's claims. When the invasion fleet sailed, the wind veered to drive it down the Channel and bottled James' ships up in the Thames estuary. On 5 November — symbolic date ! — William's polyglot forces landed at Torbay to find (like the Scots in 1640) that they were seen more as liberators than invaders. William's professed aim, to secure a free Parliament to remedy all ills, was acceptable to Whig and Tory alike. James went through the motions of opposing the invaders, but his resolve soon collapsed. He could not sleep and suffered constant nosebleeds. Having for so long believed that God was with him, everything now seemed to be falling apart : Louis and his own subjects had deserted him, even the prevailing wind had turned against him. When a few officers, including the future Duke of Marlborough, deserted to the enemy, James retreated and started to negotiate.

William's terms were not ungenerous, but James had no intention of accepting them. A free Parliament would demand stiff measures against the Catholics and restrictions on the prerogative which might, James feared, lead to his deposition ; his father's fate was always in his mind and he talked morosely of Richard II, who had been deposed in 1399 and then murdered. Worse still, a Parliament would investigate his son's birth and declare him spurious. Rather than face such humiliations, he chose to flee and reserve his position. By now luck as well as self-confidence had deserted him and it was only at the second attempt that he was able to escape to France. Louis welcomed him graciously, placing St Germain-en-Laye at his disposal ; how far the French King saw himself as morally responsible for James' expulsion we shall never know.

* * *

When James fled to France the war which had already begun in Germany became also the war of the English succession. Louis would restore James, if he could, so England (now under King William III) joined the coalition against France. This war, often known as the war of the League of Augsburg, and the war of the Spanish succession, which followed, had a profound and lasting impact on the two monarchies. In France it became clear that Louis had not solved — indeed, had not really tackled — the State's fundamental financial and administrative problems. In England, two developments came to fruition. On the one hand, the full potential of the strengthened governmental and fiscal system was now realized and England emerged as a major power. On the other, the monarch's personal power went into a long, gradual decline, so that the more powerful state apparatus was controlled, not by the King but by politicians answerable, to a greater or lesser extent, to the electorate.

When William landed in England, Louis had just turned fifty. He still ate hugely and Mme de Maintenon found difficulty in coping with his demands, but his powerful body was starting to show the strain. Some of his teeth had to be pulled, removing part of the jaw and leaving an aperture needing frequent cauterization. He also underwent an operation for an anal fistula, which provoked much obscene ribaldry among his enemies. Louis bore the pain of these operations with the same stoicism that he showed when undergoing the endless enemas and bleedings prescribed by his physicians. It was perhaps a somewhat perverse pride in his ability to withstand pain which made a graphic account of his medical history one of his favourite bedtime books.

It was not only physically that age left its mark. He became ever more intolerant of frivolity and sexual licence, encouraged by the ageing Maintenon. The court was never a place of unmixed virtue : as the King and the *dévots* became more pious, many courtiers — led by younger members of the royal family — became more debauched. Drunkenness was rife, among women as well as men. Maintenon complained of the women's 'senseless immodest dress, their tobacco, their wine, their overeating, their grossness, their laziness'. In the royal academy of music the singers kept becoming pregnant ; in 1706 the Dauphin and the young Duc d'Orléans took some girls from the academy to the Duc de Vendôme's country estate, where they danced naked while the dukes conducted the orchestra. Others preferred more exotic pleasures. Liselotte, who had earlier complained of the court's suffocating piety, bemoaned the prevalence of sodomy and lesbianism and wrote of one man who claimed to have had sexual relations with everything under the sun, except a toad. The court was increasingly polarized, between self-indulgent vice and self-righteous virtue, while Louis' highly formal lifestyle became further and further removed from that of many of his courtiers.[25]

In the great wars of 1688-97 and 1701-13 Louis reaped the fruits of his earlier aggression and cruelty. Victories were few, petty successes were celebrated with extravagant rejoicing, provincial towns were bullied into erecting statues of the King or triumphal arches. Like James, Louis was becoming the dupe of his own propaganda. All intendants and presidents of Parlements were to keep on their desks an official history of the reign in 'medals, emblems and devices'. Just as a gap appeared between the moral ideals and moral reality of the court, so there was a growing disparity between the grandeur and invincibility of the royal image and the decaying body and frequent failures of the royal person. As one defeat followed another, Louis' monumental self-confidence began to crumble. He started each year's campaign full of naïve optimism, only to have his hopes dashed. At Blenheim, in 1704, Marlborough inflicted such severe casualties on the French army that, for the first time, it was too battered to fight.

Other disappointments followed. His son, elder grandson (the Duc de Bourgogne) and elder great-grandson all died within a year in 1711−12. Like James in 1688, Louis began to believe that God had deserted him, not (as James suspected) because of his sins of the flesh, but because of his aggression and brutality. He longed for peace; he was even ready in 1709 to agree to the removal of his second grandson, Philip V, from the Spanish throne, to which he had succeeded in 1700, when Carlos II, much to everyone's surprise, left his throne to Philip in his will. Louis' enemies, however, demanded that he should help to drive Philip out, which Louis' pride, and that of the French, would not allow. By 1715 he was a chastened man, who talked of his people's sufferings and of having loved war too much.[26]

The wars cruelly exposed the weaknesses of French government. The great military machine almost ground to a halt. Armies had to fight, not just around France's frontiers, but in Spain, Italy and Bavaria and suffered unprecedented casualties. They were raised, equipped and supplied with increasing difficulty: in 1709 Louis' top general wrote that officers and men were deserting in order to avoid starvation and prophesied that next year he would be unable to keep an army in the field for more than a few weeks. At the root of these military problems lay shortage of money. Louis' later finance ministers were mostly honest, but less than brilliant; many took on the job reluctantly. Even a financial genius could have done little to overcome the system's weaknesses.

*Affaires extraordinaires* multiplied as never before. Office-holders were squeezed to a point where some had to mortgage their offices. Often corporate bodies, towns or provinces bought newly-created offices, but to raise the money they had either to borrow or to increase the level of taxation. For some, it was too much. Individual peasants and whole villages ceased to cultivate the land because they could not grow enough to meet the taxman's demands. Arrears of taxation mounted, forcing the crown to borrow and to make increasing use of paper money. The king's credit deteriorated, paper money circulated at a discount and financiers demanded ever higher rates of interest. While peasants starved, financiers (and those who invested in them) prospered: in 1708–10, when famine stalked the land, the building of homes for the super-rich continued apace in the Place Vendôme.[27]

Desperate for ready money, Louis at last grasped the nettle of tax exemption. In 1695 he introduced a poll tax, based on gradations of status rather than wealth; it brought in substantial sums, about one third from persons exempt from the taille. It was reintroduced in the war of the Spanish succession and supplemented by the *dixième* (or tenth), the first attempt to tax wealth, both real and personal. It met with howls of rage from the privileged and some, including the clergy and the estates of Languedoc, were allowed to compound for a lump sum. Both the poll tax and the *dixième* came to an end with the peace, but the fact that they were introduced at all was an acknowledgement of the unfairness and inefficiency of the fiscal system.[28] The wars, indeed, showed how far 'absolutism' depended on the consent — or acquiescence — of the French people. The consent might not always be willing — troops were still used to collect taxes — but the war effort became in some senses a national one. This was seen in the growing use of a civilian militia and in Louis' appeal to his people in 1709. His efforts to secure peace, he said, had been thwarted by his enemies' unreasonable demands, which would leave France open to invasion. 'I come to ask for your counsels and your aid in this encounter which involves your safety .... The happiness and well-being of my people has always been and will always be...my most important and serious consideration.'[29]

Apart from exposing France's fiscal weaknesses, the wars showed that one man, even Louis XIV, could not control the government. Even in peacetime the volume of business grew as the State sought to extend its competence. By 1685 Louis did not have time to approve each order that went out in his name and concentrated on great affairs of state (notably foreign policy) and the affairs of private individuals, often raised by petitions. In the great wars, the volume of business grew further and Louis' capacity for it diminished: he became indecisive, forever saying 'I'll see'. He still heard diplomatic reports, but many decisions were reached without him, in his ministers' offices, which were developing subordinate departments, with staffs and records of their own. Ministers increasingly issued orders in their own name: in the peace negotiations of 1711–13, Louis' role was largely nominal, the main burden falling on the Marquis de Torcy. In local government, the growth of business and of paperwork meant that more decisions were made by those on the spot: sovereign courts, provincial estates (now primarily administrative bodies) and intendants, all of whom depended increasingly on their burgeoning flocks of underlings. It was supremely ironical that the King who aspired to control all the workings of government saw it grow so large that he ended up with perhaps less real control than the more able of his predecessors. His attempts at centralization and increased central demands on local government helped to bring about a revival of local autonomy, centred within the royal bureaucracy, rather than in towns or estates.[30]

On 1 September 1715 Louis XIV died, having outlived his son and elder grandson and the ministers and companions of his youth. He was succeeded by his five-year-old great-grandson, Louis XV. In some ways, the edifice of 'absolutism' which he had created was little more than an elaborate façade. The endless confusions among France's institutions remained until they were swept away by the rigorous logic of the Revolution. For all his stress on ruling alone, his government still depended on the co-operation of the powerful elements in society, above all the nobility. Its character had changed: more families owed their rank and wealth to administrative service, while those who chose a military career now did so as servants of the State; the King's reliance on the nobility remained unaffected.

France's was an aristocratic society, dominated by the values of the nobility, which Louis fully shared. He surrounded himself with nobles, protected their interests and rewarded their services. If he treated his subjects more fairly than his predecessors, this owed much to his own sense of justice. If the nobility became less turbulent in his reign, this may have owed something to the discipline imposed at court, but more to a 'civilizing process' that was occurring independently. The nobility still sought wealth and power, ruthlessly and ingeniously, but now did so through court intrigue rather than armed revolt; one could profit more by tapping the golden stream of rewards at court than by preying on the peasantry. The nobility, whether of sword or robe, remained parasitic upon the true producers of wealth, but their methods became more subtle.

Louis, then, never tried to emancipate the crown from its dependence on the privileged orders, while the personal control which he sought to impose proved short-lived, as decision-making became dominated by royal officials. Even the crushing of overt political opposition proved temporary. His last years saw various calls for reform, many emanating from the entourage of the Duc de Bourgogne. Some, notably Vauban, campaigned for a fairer fiscal system; others called for political liberalization, to protect the individual against the State and give the nobility a larger voice in government, as in England. Such calls bore little fruit while Louis lived. After his death the Parlements and other institutions sought to regain their lost political influence, but at the same time used the rhetoric of liberalism to obstruct all proposals for administrative and fiscal rationalization. In the eighteenth century, as the crown struggled to escape from the straitjacket of its archaic fiscal and administrative system, it was shrilly accused of tyranny by those groups for whom reform would mean a loss of income and status. Trapped in a web of archaism and privilege, the crown lurched towards bankruptcy — and the Revolution. It took Robespierre and Napoleon to create a government able to take France into the modern world.

This is not to say that Louis XIV had failed. By the standards of his time his reign was a success and was seen as such. He brought civil war and rebellion to an end: Louis XV's minority was far more peaceful than those of his two predecessors. France's frontiers were, in 1715, far more defensible than those of 1661. All the efforts of Louis' enemies had failed to drive Philip V out of Spain, so, with a Bourbon king in Madrid, there was no longer any need to fear Habsburg encirclement. Above all, Louis established a system of administration which continued to function effectively long after he lost personal control over it. He established standards of professionalism which permeated down from his ministers and were perpetuated through venality of office: sons were trained for government by their fathers. It was symbolic that, in Louis' last years, the main role in diplomacy was played by Torcy (Croissy's son, Colbert's nephew), who had been trained by the veteran Pomponne, whose daughter he married.

Louis set the machine in motion; it could now function without him, but this could not eliminate its innate weaknesses, from which so many admin-istrators profited. Louis' instinct, unadventurous but realistic, was to make the best use of the institutions at his disposal. Even if he had wished to undertake sweeping reforms, to eradicate venality and tax exemptions would have been slow, costly and politically risky; it would also have needed a long period of peace, which Louis' lust for *gloire* and his enemies' hostility would not have allowed. Thus the French monarchy sailed into the eighteenth century, its superstructure massive and imposing, its hull increasingly rotten, until it foundered on the rocks of the Revolution.

*　　*　　*

While absolutism failed to equip France to meet the ever-increasing demands of eighteenth-century warfare, England, for so long a minor power, went from strength to strength, playing a major role in European wars and accumulating a great colonial empire. Its emergence began while its popula-tion and economic resources were still substantially smaller than those of France, but while the Bourbons plunged ever deeper into the financial mire, British kings mobilized huge sums with seemingly nonchalant ease. How did this come about?

In some ways, the 'English Revolution' of 1640–60 achieved, on a much smaller scale, the sort of transformation later brought about by the French Revolution. The anomalous and inequitable fiscal system inherited from the Tudors was swept away and replaced by one which was much more rational and efficient, on which later generations were to build. William III's average revenue was more than double that of James II and four times that of Charles I, but even that was not enough to pay for the French war, so he resorted to borrowing. Charles II, like his predecessors, had relied heavily on the personal credit of a few great financiers, notably Sir Stephen Fox, who attracted loans from private lenders (including bishops) which he advanced to the King. Under William, the crown's needs became too great to be met by individual financiers. Parliament began to underwrite govern-ment borrowing, voting specific duties for long periods so that lenders were guaranteed their interest. In 1694 the Bank of England began to act as a channel through which the public could lend to the government. As the government's credit was now much stronger than it had been when it depended on the King's word, rates of interest gradually fell, reaching a mere two per cent in the middle of the eighteenth century.[31]

The English system of taxation and borrowing, unlike the French, tapped national wealth fairly and efficiently and rested on consent. Medieval kings had developed representative institutions because they saw that it would be easier to change laws and collect taxes if they had secured at least the semblance of the consent of the governed. During the seventeenth century, French provincial estates and the English Parliament both showed an increasingly constructive and sophisticated attitude towards taxation. Both realized that by co-operating with the crown they could make the tax burden more bearable. Under Charles II, however, the Commons had been reluctant to vote money which might be used to promote Popery and absolutism. In 1689, and in 1702, there was little real disagreement about the need for war against France, to prevent a return to Catholic rule. As in the 1640s, it was in Parliament's interest to raise as much as it could, as quickly as possible : national needs overrode sectional interests. The land tax commissioners, appointed by Parliament, tried to apportion the burden fairly ; there was no need for *affaires extraordinaires*, or the other devious methods used in France.

It was not only financially that the English State grew stronger. The army and navy were greatly expanded for the French wars. Although there was vocal opposition in 1697 to keeping a large standing army, that opposition waned after 1713. With the decline in the King's personal power, an army no longer seemed a potential instrument of absolutism but a useful addition to the machinery of order. The Riot Act of 1716 allowed soldiers to fire upon rioters if, after due warning, they refused to disperse. Meanwhile, the administration grew in size and professionalism, thanks partly to the ideals of service to the State developed in 1642–60, but more to the practical pressures of war from 1689 ; more officials were needed to collect new taxes and for military and naval administration, which opened up lush new pastures of patronage, which could be used for political ends. Meanwhile, some of the much larger sums handled by the government might also be used for patronage purposes. It thus proved possible to provide extensive rewards for the ruling élite without a major sacrifice of fiscal and admin-istrative efficiency, while the State's financial resources, coercive powers and ability to buy support all increased substantially in the generation after 1688.

The benefit of the State's enhanced powers was not reaped by the King. In 1689 William and Mary were invited by the Convention Parliament to become King and Queen. No explicit conditions were attached to the offer; William's powers remained virtually the same as those of his predecessors, but he found it difficult to exercise them. This owed less to formal restrictions imposed by Acts of Parliament than to shortage of money. The Commons deliberately denied William an adequate permanent revenue: experience had shown that the Stuarts could not be trusted to rule responsibly, so Parliament had to retain the financial power to make him do so. 'We may date our misery', said one MP, 'from our bounty here. If King Charles II had not had that bounty from you, he had never attempted what he had done.'[32] William was furious at what he saw as the Commons' suspicion and ingratitude, but they were adamant, so he had to make the best use of the revenues he had. Their inherent insufficiency soon paled into insignificance compared with the problems of paying for the war. Forced to pledge his revenues for years in advance, William emerged in 1697 deeply in debt and more than willing to agree to Parliament's voting him an allowance for the civil government (the civil list) and continuing the wartime practice of annual grants for the army and navy.

Parliament now had to meet each year, for several months. As they handled more business, MPs became better informed about the needs of government, which helps explain their more constructive approach to finance, but William's financial dependence imposed serious constraints on his kingship. Occasionally the Commons overtly attached conditions to money bills, but it rarely came to that, as the King and his ministers framed policies which they believed would be acceptable to the Commons. Wise kings had always operated within the limits imposed by the need to maintain the co-operation of their leading subjects; now the need for that co-operation became more obvious and the limits on the king's freedom of action more constricting.

It might seem that the power lost by the king had passed to the Commons, but that was not entirely true. The average MP did not *want* power, or the responsibilities that went with it. Most still respected the king's prerogatives and expected him to govern; some politicians, however, did want power. With the king dependent on money voted by the Commons, if they could win the support of a majority of MPs they could make themselves indispensable and force their wishes on the king. They claimed that only if he followed their advice could they push his measures through Parliament and sought to use the crown's enlarged patronage resources to buy the support of the venal and the uncommitted. A successful politician used his control over the Commons to make the king employ him and follow his advice, and used his influence with the king to maintain his hold on the Commons. This combination of skills found their supreme exponent in that arch political manipulator Sir Robert Walpole, who dominated politics between 1721 and 1742; under William, politicians found things more difficult.

William was nobody's cipher; he had learned how to operate the Dutch political system, which was far more complex than England's, and had come to exercise far greater powers than those inherent in his offices. In England, he maintained control over large areas of policy — foreign affairs, the army and the navy. He tried to keep out of the sordid business of patronage and parliamentary management, relying on intermediaries like the ubiquitous Sunderland. As a result, his ministers, who steered his measures through Parliament, exercised less influence on either policies or appointments than they would have wished.

That William often, but not always, got his own way was not due solely to his own qualities. It was not easy for a politician to create or sustain a majority in the Commons. MPs were not easy to organize or discipline, unless bound together by ties of party. The divisions of Tory and Whig survived the Revolution, but were of limited importance for much of William's reign, when the major issues were those emerging from the war: waste, corruption and the standing army. From around 1700 the old issues of the succession, and Church against Dissent, revived and the politics of the reign of Queen Anne (1702–14) were dominated by the conflict of Whig and Tory. With the Commons polarized into two blocs, it was easier for party leaders to build a secure majority and to use it to force their way into office. In 1708–10 Anne had to employ Whig ministers whom she loathed and to endorse policies and appointments of which she disapproved. The Whigs were swept from power in the elections of 1710 and 1713, so when George I became King in 1714, they took steps to ensure that the electors would not come up with the wrong answer in future. Every ounce of electoral advantage was squeezed from the government's patronage, Whig grandees spent lavishly building an 'interest' in small venal boroughs and by 1722 the Whigs controlled enough boroughs to be sure of a majority in the Commons, however badly they fared in the larger, more open constituencies. Their leaders, while competing among themselves, combined to force their views on the King. 'Ministers', complained George II, 'are the kings in this country.'[33]

This was not, however, entirely true. While the king's personal autonomy had been much reduced, it was not negligible. Ministers might sometimes gang up on a king and stipulate the conditions upon which they would take office (as George II's did in 1746), but in general they treated his wishes with respect. Not only did common politeness require some show of deference towards one whose rank was superior to theirs, but they knew that their power and prosperity depended in large part on his favour: as he had raised them up, so he could cast them down. For ministers, therefore, managing the king depended more on persuasion than on coercion. If George II felt that his ministers acted like kings, this owed as much to his insufficiencies of character as to any innate weakness in the monarchy. His successor, George III, tried, with some success, to reclaim a personal role in decision-making; as late as 1806 he thwarted his ministers' attempt to grant full civil rights to Catholics. By now, however, a monarch's influence depended more on behind-the-scenes manipulation than on explicit use of his, or her, prerogatives.

The very fact that the king now had to exercise power in covert, indirect ways showed that the monarchy's position had been subtly, but profoundly, changed. It might seem, indeed, that the Revolution of 1688 had transferred power from the king to a narrow landed élite, that England (like France) was now ruled by the aristocracy for the benefit of the aristocracy. The potential for a more democratic system had, however, been anaesthetized, not killed. After the bitter religious and political disputes of the Stuart age, the early Hanoverian period was largely innocent of divisive issues and Whig politicians were eager to keep it that way, hastily abandoning policies that were likely to prove electorally damaging. Such blandness could not last indefinitely. With the American and French Revolutions and the growth of industry, new issues divided both the ruling élite and the nation at large. Demands grew for reform and for wider political participation. As the electorate was extended, politicians had to pay more heed to its wishes and to devote more time to influencing its opinions. As public expectations changed, so did the conduct of government and the political system, though never as rapidly or as radically as the more vehement advocates of reform would have wished.

This ability to respond to changing conditions and expectations was not matched in eighteenth-century France. One can perhaps make too much of the kings' remoteness from their people. There was, of course, a huge gulf between the gilded, mannered artificiality of Versailles and the harsh, brutal existence of the poor, between the custom-built, idyllic pastoral scenes in which queens played at being shepherdesses and the lives of real shepherds, shivering with their mangy flocks on bleak hillsides. On the other hand, none of the Georges displayed an unmixed fondness for his people, nor were they universally popular : indeed, some attacks on George III were probably as venomous as anything seen in France. The major differences between the countries lay, not in the kings' characters, but in the political systems over which they presided. The British kings eventually conceded both Catholic emancipation and Parliamentary reform, despite their (unfounded) fears that these would lead inexorably to the demise of Church and monarchy.

By contrast Louis XV and XVI and their ministers tried repeatedly to extricate themselves from the institutional and financial straitjacket bequeathed by Louis XIV. Only by developing a fiscal system which tapped the nation's wealth as effectively as England's could they escape from the ever-growing mountain of debt which threatened the crown with bankruptcy. They were well aware of the need to destroy the fiscal exemptions of the privileged orders and lacked not the will but the power to do so. Again and again, realistic and constructive reforms were thwarted by the Parlements and other privileged bodies, which portrayed any challenge to their narrow corporate interests as an attack on the people's rights. Again and again, citizens rushed to defend the institutions which claimed to protect their liberties ; only in 1789 did they come to appreciate the hollowness of such claims and to turn against those who had preyed upon them for so long.

In France, then, the crown failed to escape from the crushing embrace of the doomed system of privilege and inefficiency and went down with it. By contrast, as Britain moved from Whig oligarchy to mass democracy the monarchy's role remained largely a peripheral issue. While most politically-aware Englishmen expressed an apparently genuine respect for the monarchy, bitter experience of the Stuarts had left them wary of kings who attempted to direct the government in person, as George III found to his cost. However, so long as monarchs avoided an overt political role, they remained popular ; controversy centred on the way ministers used the crown's powers and on their responsibility to the nation at large.

In France, too, support for the monarchy remained widespread. Its abolition in 1793, like that of the English monarchy in 1649, was carried through by a radical, revolutionary minority, but in a world becoming familiar with the concepts of liberalism and democracy, republicanism established far deeper roots in France than in England; it is probable, indeed, that French republicanism was so much stronger precisely because the French monarchy seemed so much more formidable an obstacle to change than its English counterpart. Nevertheless, despite the strength of commitment to the republican and revolutionary tradition in France's cities, the peasant majority remained predominantly monarchist. The restoration of the monarchy in 1815 was widely welcomed. The republican revolution of 1848 found little favour with the electorate and was swiftly followed by the establishment of a quasi-monarchical regime under the Emperor Napoleon III. When this, in its turn, collapsed in the wake of military defeat in 1870, the National Assembly elected in 1871 contained a majority in favour of yet another restoration of monarchy. The Comte de Chambord, the head of the house of Bourbon, declared, however, that he would never adopt the tricolor flag which had become the symbol of France's nationality: he would stand or fall by the white flag and fleur-de-lys of his ancestors. The Assembly, reluctantly, opted for a republic and the monarchy's last chance had gone.

In Britain, the monarchy showed no such rigidity, adapting to changing circumstances; it never became wholly identified with privilege and reaction. Republicanism remained weak: one Labour prime minister remarked that the abolition of monarchy might be desirable, as an ideal, but it was not worth losing an election for. As the monarchy has become predominantly ornamental, it has remained popular, but its prerogatives have never, in fact, been taken away. Theoretically, the Queen still summons and dismisses Parliament and appoints the prime minister; in practice, she follows her ministers' advice and chooses the leader of the party which wins each general election. What will happen if no clear winner emerges from some future election remains to be seen: if the monarch is forced to make what many would see as a political choice, the monarchy's popularity could be substantially reduced.

Why the English monarchy has survived while the French has not is a complex question. Luck and personalities have played a part: neither James

II nor the Comte de Chambord could be accused of an excess of political realism. Two more general points may, however, be suggested. First, while all government rests to some extent on the consent, or acquiescence, of the governed, that consent was much more explicit in England than in France. The king could not tax or make laws without Parliament, which provided a far more effective mechanism for securing consent, at a national level, than anything developed in France. Second, however selfish and narrow-minded England's ruling élite might be, its members showed greater responsibility and public spirit than their French counterparts. England's tradition of local self-government ensured that office-holders' first responsibility was to the local community to which they belonged, whereas in France venality of office separated officials from the rest of the community : indeed, in the last analysis, those officials derived their wealth from fees taken from the pro-' ductive elements in society. Similarly the main concern of English local officials was to maintain harmony, through arbitration and conciliation, and to protect their locality against undue central interference. In France, officials had a vested interest in multiplying lawsuits and in intervening ever more intrusively in local affairs : the more business they created, the greater their profits. English landowners were never slow to invoke the law to protect their property, but they also expected the law to protect individual liberty and property against the State and were prepared, if need be, to tax themselves heavily for the national good.

Thus on the one hand England's ruling élite never developed a system of privileges which marked it off from, and set it against, the rest of society. On the other, the participation of the more prominent of the governed helped to breed an understanding of the problems of government and a willingness to help to solve them. French monarchs and ministers might sneer at their English cousins' need to go cap in hand to Parliament for money, but their need to seek consent led (with the help of the accident of civil war) to the creation of a viable fiscal system. By contrast, the French kings' peremptory rejection of calls for greater political participation helped to sustain a sense of confrontation, between a king harping on his 'absolute' authority and a ruling élite clinging tenaciously to its privileges.

English kings, of course, paid a price for their subjects' co-operation. Their personal power became more and more limited, although it is open to question whether this would have happened as early as the later seventeenth century without the extraordinary political ineptitude of James II. On the other hand, the French kings' great personal powers proved insufficient to free them from the suffocating creeper of privilege, the seeds of which had been sown when their predecessors began to sell offices and to contract out the collection of taxes. Statements that an English king's greatest asset was his subjects' love, or that he was strongest when he ruled as his people wished, were not simply conventional platitudes. They expressed a profound truth about the nature of early modern government : that a monarchy which could win its subjects' consent and adapt to their changing expectations was, in the long run, stronger and more durable than one which could not.

# Select Bibliography

AILESBURY, T. BRUCE, EARL of, *Memoirs*, ed. W.E. Buckley, 2 vols., Roxburgh Club, 1890.

ASHTON, R., *James I by his Contemporaries*, London, 1969.

AYLMER, G.E., *The King's Servants: the Civil Service of Charles I*, London, 1961.

BABELON, J.−P., *Henri IV*, Paris, 1982.

BARRY, J., *Versailles*, London, 1972.

BAXTER, S.B., *William III*, London, 1966.

BIRCH, T., *The Court and Times of Charles I*, 2 vols., London, 1848.

BONNEY, R., *The King's Debts: Finance and Politics in France, 1589−1661*, Oxford, 1981.

BONNEY, R., *Political Change in France under Richelieu and Mazarin*, Oxford, 1978.

BUISSERET, D., *Henry IV*, London, 1984.

BUISSERET, D., *Sully*, London, 1968.

BURNET, G. *History of my own Time*, 6 vols., Oxford, 1833.

CARLTON, C.H., *Charles I: The Personal Monarch*, paperback edn., London, 1984.

CHAMBERLAIN, J., *Letters*, ed. N.E. McClure, 2 vols., Philadelphia, 1939.

CHEVALLIER, P., *Louis XIII*, Paris, 1979.

CLARENDON, E. HYDE, EARL of, *History of the Rebellion*, ed. W.D. Macray, 6 vols., Oxford, 1888.

CLARENDON E. HYDE, EARL of, *Life of*, 3 vols., Oxford, 1827.

CORVISIER, A., *Louvois*, Paris, 1983.

CUST, R.P., 'The Forced Loan and English Politics, 1626−8', unpublished Ph.D. thesis, London, 1984.

DESSERT, D., *Argent, Pouvoir et Société au Grand Siècle*, Paris, 1984.

EKBERG, C.J., *The Failure of Louis XIV's Dutch War*, Chapel Hill, 1979.

ELIAS, N., *The Court Society*, Oxford, 1983.

EVELYN, J., *Diary*, ed. E.S. de Beer, 6 vols., Oxford, 1955.

FLETCHER, A., *The Outbreak of the English Civil War*, London, 1981.

GARDINER, S.R., *History of England, 1603−42*, 10 vols., London, 1883−4.

GOODMAN, G., *The Court of King James*, ed. J.S. Brewer, 2 vols., London, 1839.

GREGG, P., *King Charles I*, London, 1981.

GREY, A., *Debates in the House of Commons, 1667−94*, 10 vols., London. 1769.

GRILLON, P. (ed.), *Les Papiers de Richelieu: Politique Intérieure*, 5 vols. to date, Paris, 1975− .

HALIFAX, G. SAVILE, MARQUIS of, *Complete Works*, ed. J.P. Kenyon, Harmondsworth, 1969.

ISHERWOOD, R.M., *Music in the Service of the King*, Ithaca, 1973.

JAMES I, *Letters*, ed. G.P.V. Akrigg, Berkeley, 1984.

KENYON, J.P., *The Stuart Constitution* 2nd edn., Cambridge, 1986.

KNACHEL, P.A., *England and the Fronde*, Ithaca, 1967.

LABATUT, J.−P., *Les Ducs et Pairs de France au XVIIe Siècle*, Paris, 1972.

LOCKYER, R., *Buckingham*, London, 1981.

LOUIS XIV, *Mémoires for the Instruction of the Dauphin*, ed. P. Sonnino, New York, 1970.

LUBLINSKAYA, A.D., *French Absolutism: The Crucial Phase, 1620–9*, Cambridge, 1968.

MAJOR, J.R., *Representative Government in Early Modern France*, New Haven, 1980.

MALAMENT, B.C. (ed.), *After the Reformation: Essays in Honour of J.H. Hexter*, Manchester, 1980.

METTAM, R.C., *Government and Society in Louis XIV's France*, London, 1977.

MIGNET, F.A.M., *Négociations Rélatives à la Succession d'Espagne*, 4 vols., Paris, 1835–42.

MILLER, J., *James II: A Study in Kingship*, Hove, 1978.

MOOTE, A.L., *The Revolt of the Judges: The Parlement of Paris and the Fronde*, Princeton, 1971.

MOUSNIER, R. *The Assassination of Henry IV*, London, 1973.

MOUSNIER, R., *La Plume, La Faucille et le Marteau*, Paris, 1970.

PAGÈS, G., *Les Institutions Monarchiques sous Louis XIII et Louis XIV*, Paris, 1962.

PARKER, D., *La Rochelle and the French Monarchy*, London, 1980.

PARKER, D., *The Making of French Absolutism*, London, 1983.

PECK, L.L., *Northampton: Patronage and Policy at the Court of James I*, London, 1982.

PEPYS, S., *Diary*, ed. R.C. Latham and W. Matthews, 11 vols., London, 1971–83.

RANUM, O., *Paris in the Age of Absolutism*, New York, 1968.

RERESBY, SIR J., *Memoirs*, ed. A. Browning, Glasgow, 1936.

RICHELIEU, CARDINAL, *Lettres, Instructions Diplomatiques et Papiers d'Etat*, ed. L.–M. Avenel, 8 vols., Paris, 1853–77.

RICHELIEU, CARDINAL, *Testament Politique*, ed. L. André, 7th edn., Paris, 1947.

RULE, J.C. (ed.), *Louis XIV and the Craft of Kingship*, Columbus, 1969.

RUSSELL, C. (ed.), *Origins of the English Civil War*, London, 1973.

RUSSELL, C., *Parliaments and English Politics, 1621–9*, Oxford, 1979.

ST SIMON, DUC DE, *Mémoires*, various editors, 18 vols., Paris, 1977–9 (vols. 1–3, which cover the period 1691 to 1702, are edited by F.–R. Bastide, P. Erlanger and the Duc de Castries respectively).

*Secret History of the Court of James I*, ed. Sir W. Scott, 2 vols., Edinburgh, 1811.

TANNER, J.R. (ed.), *Constitutional Documents of the Reign of James I*, Cambridge, 1930.

TAPIÉ, V.–L., *La France de Louis XIII et de Richelieu*, Paris, 1967.

WILLSON, D.H., *James VI and I*, London, 1956.

WILSON, A., *The History of Great Britain, being the Life and Reign of King James*, London, 1653.

WOLF, J.B., *Louis XIV*, Panther edn., London, 1970.

# Abbreviations

| | |
|---|---|
| *AESC* | *Annales: Economies, Sociétés, Civilisations* |
| Birch (C) | T. Birch, *The Court and Times of Charles I*, 2 vols., London, 1848 |
| Birch (J) | T. Birch, *The Court and Times of James I*, 2 vols., London, 1849 |
| BT | Baschet transcripts of French ambassadors' dispatches, Public Record Office, PRO 31/3 |
| Chamberlain | *Letters of John Chamberlain*, ed. N.E. McClure, 2 vols., American Philosophical Society, Philadelphia, 1939 |
| *CSPD* | *Calendar of State Papers, Domestic* |
| *CSPV* | *Calendar of State Papers, Venetian* |
| *EHR* | *English Historical Review* |
| *ESR* | *European Studies Review* |
| *FHS* | *French Historical Studies* |
| Gardiner | S.R. Gardiner, *History of England, 1603–42*, 10 vols., London, 1883–4 |
| Grillon | P. Grillon (ed.), *Les Papiers de Richelieu: Politique Intérieure*, 5 vols. to date, Paris, 1975– |
| *HGL* | C. de Vic and J. Vaissette, *Histoire Générale de Languedoc*, continued by E. Roschach, 15 vols., Toulouse, 1872–92 |
| *HJ* | *Historical Journal* |
| *HMC* | *Historical Manuscripts Commission* |
| *JBS* | *Journal of British Studies* |
| *King's Works* | *History of the King's Works*, vol. IV (1485–1660), Pt II, ed. H.M. Colvin, J. Summerson, J.R. Hale, M. Merriman, London, 1982; vol. V (1660–1872), ed. H.M. Colvin, J.M. Crook, K. Downes, J. Newman, London 1976 |
| Liselotte | *Letters from Liselotte*, ed. M. Kroll, London, 1970 |
| NS | New Style |
| *P & P* | *Past and Present* |
| PV | Procès-verbaux of the Estates of Languedoc: various copies in departmental archives of the Hérault, Haute-Garonne, Aude and Gard |
| *PWSFH* | *Proceedings of the Western Society for French History* |
| Secret Hist. | Sir W. Scott (ed.), *Secret History of the Court of James I*, 2 vols., Edinburgh, 1811 |
| *TRHS* | *Transactions of the Royal Historical Society* |

# Notes

## 1 INTRODUCTION

1 Studies of the theory of absolutism in France are legion, but see particularly H.H. Rowen, 'Louis XIV and Absolutism' in J.C. Rule (ed.), *Louis XIV and the Craft of Kingship* (Columbus, 1969), pp. 302–15. For England, see J. Daly, 'The Idea of Absolute Monarchy in Seventeenth-Century England', *HJ*, XXI (1978), pp. 227–50; J.P. Sommerville, *Politics and Ideology in England, 1603–40* (London, 1986), especially ch. 1. Dr. Sommerville's interesting and important book unfortunately appeared too late to be used in the writing of this study. It lends support to the view expressed here, that real divisions of principle underlay the political conflicts of early Stuart England and develops the ideas behind these conflicts in a more sophisticated manner than I have done. On the other hand, by concentrating on the theory of absolutism he plays down the difficulties of translating the theory into practice. Moreover, his logic seems at times over rigorous, especially the stark antithesis between 'absolute' and 'limited' monarchy. In strict theory, perhaps, the king's 'absolute' prerogative was incompatible with the subject's 'absolute' right to his liberty and property (Sommerville, pp. 131–41), but that did not prevent people from believing that prerogative and liberty could (and should) be compatible. Moreover, experience suggested that such a belief was not wildly unrealistic. Past monarchs had respected their subjects' rights and had been respected by them in their turn. If the will existed to achieve a balance between the interests of king and people, then it could be achieved. It was the early Stuarts' political ineptitude which made such a balance unattainable and exposed a latent incompatibility which might otherwise never have manifested itself.

## 2 BEGINNINGS

1 See B. Lenman and G. Parker, 'State, Community and Criminal Law' in V.A.C. Gatrell, Lenman and Parker (eds.), *Crime and the Law* (London, 1980), ch. 1; also J.A. Sharpe, 'Enforcing the Law in a Seventeenth-Century English Village' in *ibid.*, pp. 107–9.

2 On this see W.T. MacCaffrey, 'Place and Patronage in Elizabethan Politics' in S.T. Bindoff, J. Hurstfield and C.H. Williams (eds.), *Elizabethan Government and Society: Essays in Honour of Sir John Neale* (London, 1961), ch. 4; J.E. Neale, *The Age of Catherine de Medici* (London, 1963), pp. 145–70; L. Stone, *The Crisis of the Aristocracy* (Oxford, 1965), ch. 8.

3 A. Hassell Smith, *County and Court: Government and Politics in Norfolk, 1558–1603* (Oxford, 1974), chs. 11–13; P. Clark, *English Provincial Society from the Reformation to the Revolution: Kent 1500–1640* (Hassocks, 1977), chs. 7–8.

4 J.E. Neale, *The Elizabethan House of Commons* (London, 1949), p. 349.

5 J. Wormald, 'James VI and I: Two Kings or One?', *History*, LXVIII

(1983), pp. 193–8.

6 R. Ashton, *James I by his Contemporaries* (London, 1969), pp. 4–8 ; Gardiner, I.87 and note ; Chamberlain, I.192.

7 Stone, *Crisis*, ch. 5 ; M.E. James, 'The Concept of Order and the Northern Rising of 1569', *P & P*, no. 60 (1973), pp. 49–83.

8 James I, *Letters*, ed. G.P.V. Akrigg (Berkeley, 1984), p. 201.

9 Wormald, 'James VI and I', passim ; Ashton, *James I*, pp. 10, 63.

10 D.H. Willson, *King James VI and I* (London, 1956), p. 185 ; Chamberlain, I.258–60, II.316.

11 A. Wilson, *The History of Great Britain, being the Life and Reign of King James* (London, 1653), p. 12 ; Ashton, *James I*, p. 10.

12 Sir J. Harington, *Nugae Antiquae*, et. T. Park (2 vols., London, 1804), I.367–70 ; Chamberlain, II.339 ; Willson, ch. 16.

13 Chamberlain, I.469 ; G. Goodman, *The Court of King James*, ed. J.S. Brewer (2 vols., London, 1839), I.168.

14 Ashton, p. 96.

15 Goodman, I.250–1 ; Ashton, pp. 98–100 ; Chamberlain, I.394 (quoted).

16 It is perhaps significant that Carr came to James' notice as the result of an accident ; later favourites were carefully trained and managed.

17 Wilson, pp. 54–5, 83 ; Harington, I.392, 396.

18 Ashton, pp. 10, 64

19 *King's Works*, IV(2), pp. 11–14 ; Ashton, p. 244.

20 James I, *Letters*, p. 204 ; Wilson, p. 97.

21 L.L. Peck, *Northampton : Patronage and Policy at the Court of James I* (London, 1982), p. 24 ; J. Nichols, *The Progresses of James I* (4 vols., London, 1828), IV. 1083 ; Wilson, p. 61.

22 Chamberlain, I.201 ; James I., *Letters*, pp. 246–9.

23 Willson, p. 185 ; James I, *Letters*, pp. 253–4, 318–9.

24 Peck, *Northampton*, pp. 13–22.

25 K. Fincham and P. Lake, 'The Ecclesiastical Policy of King James I', *JBS*, XXIV (1985), pp. 171–82, 186–96 ; James, *Letters*, pp. 216–7, 221, 223.

26 Fincham and Lake, pp. 182–6.

27 B.P. Levack, 'Towards a more Perfect Union' in B.C. Malament (ed.) *After the Reformation : Essays in Honour of J.H. Hexter* (Manchester, 1980), pp. 57–74 ; Gardiner, I.324–39 ; James, *Letters*, p. 254.

28 J.R. Tanner, *Constitutional Documents of the Reign of James I* (Cambridge, 1930), pp. 15–17 ; see also Gardiner, II.66–7.

29 J. Locke, *Two Treatises of Government*, ed. P. Laslett (New York, 1965), pp. 447–8 ; Ashton, pp. 67–8.

30 Gardiner, II.38–42 ; Wilson, p. 47 ; Birch (J), I.99.

31 Tanner, p. 222.

32 Gardiner, II.1–10 ; Tanner, pp. 343–4.

33 Tanner, pp. 260, 262 ; see also Chamberlain, II.301.

34 Ashton, p. 74 ; James, *Letters*, pp. 316–19.

35 R. Doucet, *Les Institutions de la France au XVIe Siècle* (2 vols., Paris, 1948), I.31.

36 See J.R. Major, *Representative Institutions in Renaissance France* (Madison, 1960) ; P.S. Lewis, *Late Medieval France : The Polity* (London, 1968), pp. 328–74.

37 J.H.M. Salmon, *Society in Crisis : France in the Sixteenth Century* (London, 1975), pp. 207–8.

38 G.R. Elton, *The Tudor Constitution* (Cambridge, 1960), p. 15.

39 See the map in D. Buisseret, *Henry IV* (London, 1984), p. 89.

40 P. Chevallier, *Louis XIII* (Paris, 1979), pp. 18–19.

41 Chevallier, p. 21 ; see also J.–P. Babelon, *Henri IV* (Paris, 1982), pp. 858–65.

42 Babelon, p. 877; Chevallier, p. 23.
43 Buisseret, *Henry IV*, pp. 94–6, 101–5; Babelon, p. 950.
44 Babelon, pp. 828–33; O. Ranum, *Paris in the Age of Absolutism* (New York, 1968), pp. 51–65.
45 N. Brett James, *The Growth of Stuart London* (London, 1935), chs. 3–6, 9–10; R. Ashton, *The City and the Court, 1603–43* (Cambridge, 1979), chs. 5–6.
46 R. Mousnier, *The Assassination of Henry IV* (London, 1973), pp. 364–6.
47 See E.H. Dickermann, *Bellièvre and Villeroy* (Providence, 1971); D. Buisseret, *Sully* (London, 1968). For simplicity's sake I shall use the name Sully throughout, although he acquired it only when he became a duke in 1606.
48 R. Bonney, *The King's Debts: Finance and Politics in France 1589–1661* (Oxford, 1981), p. 64 and ch. 1; Buisseret, *Sully*, chs. 3–4; J. Dent, *Crisis in Finance* (Newton Abbot, 1973).
49 G.E. Aylmer, *The King's Servants: The Civil Service of Charles I* (London, 1961), pp. 62–3, 193–5, 233–4.
50 R. Mousnier, *La Vénalité des Offices sous Henri IV et Louis XIII* (2nd edn., Paris, 1971), pp. 232–40, 307–8, 594–605.
51 J.R. Major, *Representative Government in Early Modern France* (New Haven, 1980), pp. 266–94; Buisseret, *Henry IV*, pp. 163–6; M. Greengrass, *France in the Reign of Henri IV* (London, 1984), pp. 108–10; quote from R. Bonney, *Political Change in France under Richelieu and Mazarin* (Oxford, 1978), p. 351.
52 Babelon, pp. 691–704; Buisseret, *Henry IV*, pp. 121–4.
53 Mousnier, *Assassination*, pp. 115–6, 149–58; Greengrass, pp. 81–5.
54 Babelon, pp. 950–3, 958–61.
55 Babelon, pp. 978–85 (quote from p. 980); Mousnier, *Assassination*, pp. 24–6.

3 FACTIONS AND FAVOURITIES

1 Peck, pp. 200–3.
2 Willson, pp. 336, 378–80, 412, 415, 424; *Secret Hist.*, II.2–3. Dr. Wormald's article, 'James VI and I', offers many valuable insights into James' kingship, but I am sceptical about her claim (pp. 190–1) that most conventional accounts perpetuate Weldon's supposed anti-Scottish bias. His 'Perfect Description of Scotland' (*Secret Hist.*, II.75–89) is a series of bad jokes rather than a diatribe of hatred: 'There is great store of fowl too, as foul houses, foul streets, foul linen ...'. His account of James' reign is far from hostile to the Scots, who are seen as less rapacious than the English, while Carr is treated far more favourably than Buckingham: *Secret Hist.*, I.371–3, 391, 394.
3 Chamberlain, I.350, 409, II.113; Peck, pp. 84–8; Gardiner, II.144.
4 See Gardiner, II. 166–86, 331–63.
5 R. Lockyer, *Buckingham* (London, 1981), pp. 16–20.
6 James, *Letters*, pp. 335–40; *Secret Hist.*, I.411–12.
7 Lockyer, p. 22; James, *Letters*, p. 315.
8 Gardiner, III.98, 187; Wilson, p. 147.
9 Chamberlain, II.121; Ashton, p. 241.
10 Gardiner, II.233–48; D. Hirst, 'Revisionism Revised: The Place of Principle', *P & P*, no. 92 (1981), p. 89; Chamberlain, I.532–9.
11 Gardiner, II.249–52, 260–6; James *Letters*, pp. 296–7. Allegations that Northampton was responsible for the failure of the Parliament are not proven: Peck, pp. 210–1.
12 Chamberlain, I.567–8, 581 (quoted), 584, 601–2, II.168, 222, 243, 275, 323, 395.
13 L.L. Peck, 'Corruption at the Court of James I' in Malament, p. 79.
14 L. Stone, *Family and Fortune* (Oxford, 1973), p. 24; Gardiner, IV.2–24; W.R. Scott, *The History of Joint Stock Companies, to 1720* (3 vols., Cambridge, 1910–12), I.173–8.

15 Chamberlain, II.310, see Elton, *Tudor Constitution*, pp. 158–84.
16 James, *Letters*, p. 297; Gardiner, III.191–4, 349; Willson, pp. 309–12; Wilson, p. 47; Birch (J), I.99; Chamberlain, II.213.
17 Gardiner, II.187–91, IV.117–18; Hirst, 'Revisionism', p. 88.
18 Chamberlain, II.151; Peck, 'Corruption', pp. 81–8; Lockyer, pp. 39–50, 65–76, 89–96.
19 C. Russell, *Parliaments and English Politics, 1621–9* (Oxford, 1979), p. 135 and ch. 2.
20 Russell, p. 140.
21 Fincham and Lake, pp. 197–207; N. Tyacke, 'Puritanism, Arminianism and Counter-Revolution' in C. Russell (ed.), *Origins of the English Civil War* (London, 1973), ch. 4; Gardiner, V.225.
22 J.P. Kenyon, *The Stuart Constitution* (2nd edn., Cambridge, 1986), pp. 60–2; Hirst, 'Revisionism', p. 88. For another advocate of change, see P. Lake, 'Thomas Scott and the Spanish Match', *HJ*, XXV (1982), pp. 805–25.
23 R. Cust, 'The Forced Loan and English Politics, 1626–8', (unpublished Ph.D. thesis, London, 1984), pp. 20–2; Birch (J), II.289; Gardiner, IV.268. For the pejorative use of 'popular' and 'popularity' in 1616, see *Cabala, sive Scrinia Sacra* (1691), p. 26; Chamberlain, II.38.
24 Goodman, II.209–10.
25 See Lockyer, pp. 134–64.
26 Gardiner, V.224–5; Lockyer, pp. 194–8, 202, 233.
27 *Secret Hist.*, II.8, 11–12.
28 See Bonney, *Debts*, pp. 80–6; J.M. Hayden, *France and the Estates General of 1614* (Cambridge, 1974).
29 Chevallier, pp. 453–5.
30 C.J. Burckhardt, *Richelieu and his Age: I: His Rise to Power* (London, 1940), pp. 97–8; Chevallier, pp. 159–70, 176–7; Bonney, *Debts*, pp. 92–3.
31 Chevallier, p. 220.
32 See D. Parker, *La Rochelle and the French Monarchy* (London, 1980); A.D. Lublinskaya, *French Absolutism: The Crucial Phase 1620–9* (Cambridge, 1968), ch. 4.
33 V.–L. Tapié, *La France de Louis XIII et de Richelieu* (Paris, 1967), p. 120.

## 4 DECISIONS

1 Chevallier, p. 279.
2 Grillon, I.353.
3 Birch (C), I.365, 369.
4 Chevallier, p. 291.
5 *ibid.*, p. 357.
6 Grillon, IV.27–33.
7 *ibid.*, I.142; Richelieu, *Testament Politique*, ed. L. André (7th edn., Paris, 1947), pp. 279–86.
8 Grillon, I.88–90, 183–6.
9 *ibid.*, I.250, 259–65.
10 See D. Dessert, *Argent, Pouvoir et Société au Grand Siècle* (Paris, 1984).
11 Bonney, *Debts*, pp. 117–9; see also Grillon, I.116–8.
12 Grillon, I.581–91.
13 Lublinskaya, pp. 315–25; Bonney, *Debts*, pp. 133–4.
14 Richelieu, *Testament*, pp. 398–9; Grillon, I.587 and note (0).
15 See the seminal article by G. Pagès, 'Autour du Grand Orage: Richelieu et Marillac, Deux Politiques', *Revue Historique* CLXXIX (1930), pp. 63–97.
16 Tapié, pp. 168–82, 190–2; Parker, *La Rochelle*; Lockyer, pp. 369–402; Grillon, IV.433–4.
17 Chevallier, p. 362.
18 Grillon, V.209–12.
19 *ibid.*, V.429–31, 491–2.
20 *ibid.*, V.260–1.
21 Richelieu, *Testament*, pp. 253–4.
22 The fullest account is in Chevallier, pp. 379–407.
23 Bonney, *Debts*, pp. 155–6; Tapié, p. 222.

24 Bonney, *Debts*, p. 152.

25 Major, pp. 553−5 ; Lublinskaya, p. 226, n.4.

26 Grillon, V.51. For differing views, see Major, pp. 569−71 and chs. 14−15 ; Y.−M. Bercé, *Histoire des Croquants* (Geneva, 1974), pp. 88−9 ; Bonney, *Debts*, p. 145 and n.2 ; Bonney, *Pol. Change*, pp. 348−50 ; Tapié, p. 285.

27 P. Gregg, *King Charles I* (London, 1981), p. 113.

28 See W.J. Jones, *Politics and the Bench* (London, 1971).

29 Gardiner, VII. 138−40, 110 ; see Birch (C), II.18.

30 Birch (C), I.191 ; see also *ibid.*, I.169 ; Lockyer, pp. 463−5.

31 Cust, pp. 207−21 and ch. 3. Dr. Cust's thesis, shortly to be published, raises many important issues and has had an important influence on my view of the 1620s. I am very grateful to him for permission to refer to it.

32 Russell, pp. 17−23 ; see also C. Russell, 'Parliamentary History in Perspective, 1604−29', *History*, LXI (1976), pp. 25−7.

33 Birch (C), I.285.

34 Lockyer, p. 427.

35 *CSPD 1625−6*, p. 275 ; see also *Cabala*, pp. 255−7.

36 J. Rushworth, *Historical Collections* (8 vols., London, 1721), I.225 ; Kenyon, p. 45.

37 *CSPD 1625−6*, p. 354 ; Bishop of Mende to Herbault and to Richelieu, 26 June 1626 NS, BT 63 ; *CSPV 1625−6*, pp. 461−2, 508.

38 *CSPD 1625−6*, p. 369 ; Gardiner, VI. 131 ; Cust, pp. 37−43.

39 *CSPV 1625−6*, p. 528.

40 *CSPD 1625−6*, p. 441, *1627−8*, p. 538 ; Gardiner, VI.227−8.

41 Cust, pp. 83−9 ; Kenyon, pp. 13−14 ; Gardiner, VI.209.

42 Russell, pp. 338−9.

43 Cust, chs. 1−2 ; R. Cust, 'Charles I, the Privy Council and the Forced Loan', *JBS* XXIV (1985), pp. 208−35.

44 *CSPD 1627−8*, pp. 160 (quoted), 171, 277, 359, 379 ; Birch (C), I.238.

45 *CSPD 1627−8*, p.555, *1628−9*, pp. 5−6 ; Birch (C), I.316, 318, 323, 325, 327 ; *CSPV 1626−8*, pp. 559, 605, *1628−9*, pp. 10, 21.

46 Gardiner, VI.122−3, 206−9, 238 ; Cust, pp. 321−2.

47 Gardiner, VI.223−4 ; Birch (C), I.320−1, 350, 372−5 ; *CSPV 1626−8*, p. 584, *1628−9*, pp. 126, 157 ; *CSPD 1628−9*, pp. 49−50 ; see also S.R. Gardiner, *Constitutional Documents of the Puritan Revolution* (3rd edn., Oxford, 1951), p. 209 (art. 6).

48 Russell, pp. 347−59 ; Birch (C), I.374.

49 *CSPV 1628−9*, p. 45 ; Gardiner, VI.231.

50 Gardiner, VI.263, 267.

51 See Russell, pp. 366−8.

52 *CSPD 1628−9*, pp. 84, 95, 142, 153 ; Lockyer, p. 434 ; Birch (C), I.353−4.

53 Gardiner, VI.301−9, 317−20 ; Lockyer, pp. 440−2 ; Russell, pp. 379−82.

54 *CSPV 1625−6*, p. 508, *1626−8*, pp. 144, 305−6, 559, *1629−32*, p. 259 ; Châteauneuf to (? Richelieu), 22 Aug. 1629 NS, BT 66.

55 Birch (C), I.370 ; *CSPD 1628−9*, p. 183 ; Russell, pp. 400−1.

56 Gardiner, *Documents*, pp. 83−99 (quotes from pp. 97, 95).

57 *CSPV 1628−9*, pp. 589−90, *1629−32*, pp. 177−8, 183, 204−5 ; *CSPD 1628−9*, pp. 482, 533.

58 See C. Russell, 'Monarchies, Wars and Estates in England, France and Spain, c. 1580−c. 1640', *Legislative Studies Quarterly*, VII (1982), pp. 210−11.

## 5 CIVIL WAR

1 Gregg, pp. 122−3, 242, 246 ; C.H. Carlton, *Charles I : The Personal Monarch* (London, paperback edn., 1984) pp. 62, 123−5, 129−30 ; Richelieu, *Testament*, pp. 283−3 ; *King's Works*, IV(2), 35.

2 G. Parry, *The Golden Age Restor'd : The*

*Culture of the Stuart Court, 1603–42*
(Manchester, 1981), p. 202 and passim;
*King's Works*, IV(2). 31–5, 114–22,
328–34.

3 I owe these points to a seminar paper by
Mr J.C. Robertson.

4 Birch (C), II.91, 230–1.

5 Gardiner, VII.193; M. van C.
Alexander, *Charles I's Lord Treasurer*
(London, 1975), pp. 146–7; K. Sharpe,
'The Personal Rule of Charles I' in H.C.
Tomlinson (ed.), *Before the English Civil
War* (London, 1983), p. 74. In a letter to
Wentworth about the Irish Parliament he
shows no hostility to Parliaments as
such: C. Petrie (ed.), *Letters of Charles I*
(London, 1935), p. 96.

6 E. Hyde, Earl of Clarendon, *History of
the Rebellion*, ed. W.D. Macray (6 vols.,
Oxford, 1888), I.130; see also Sharpe,
'Personal Rule', p. 59.

7 Carlton, pp. 155–9; Alexander,
pp. 158–9.

8 Clarendon, *History*, I.85; Alexander,
pp. 194–6, 199.

9 Aylmer, pp. 63–4, 233–4.

10 Gardiner, VII.376–7; K.J. Lindley,
*Fenland Riots and the English
Revolution* (London, 1982).

11 Jones, *Politics and the Bench*;
H. Pawlisch, *Sir John Davies and the
Conquest of Ireland: A Study of Legal
Imperialism*, (Cambridge, 1985).

12 Daly, 'The Idea of Absolute Monarchy',
pp. 227–35 (quote from p. 233).

13 Gardiner, VII.245.

14 A. Fletcher, *A County Community in
Peace and War: Sussex 1600–60*
(London, 1975), ch. 4.

15 C. Haigh, 'Puritan Evangelism in the
Reign of Elizabeth I', *EHR* XCII
(1977), p. 47.

16 Sharpe, 'Personal Rule', pp. 75–6.

17 Chevallier, p. 585.

18 Duc de St Simon, *Mémoires*, ed. F.R.
Bastide et al., (18 vols., Paris, 1977–9),
I.43, 49; Grillon, III.304, 447;
Chevallier, pp. 421–45.

19 Tapié, p. 234.

20 *HGL*, XIV.397; PV 17 March 1653.

21 PV 6 Sept. 1641; *HGL*, XIV, 170–1.

22 PV 15 Nov. 1672, 20 Nov. 1655,
26 Nov. 1657.

23 Richelieu, *Lettres, Instructions Diplomatiques et Papiers d'Etat*, ed. L–M.
Avenel (8 vols., Paris, 1853–77), VI.496,
901–2; see also D. Parker, *The Making
of French Absolutism* (London, 1983),
pp.83–5, 91.

24 J.P. Cooper, *Land, Men and Beliefs*
(London, 1983), pp. 101–9.

25 See Bonney, *Debts*, pp. 165–83; G.
Pagès, *Les Institutions Monarchiques
sous Louis XIII et Louis XIV* (Paris,
1962), pp. 128–9; Dessert, passim.

26 See Bonney, *Pol. Change*, chs. 2, 6, 7;
R. Mousnier, *La Plume, La Faucille et
Le Marteau* (Paris, 1970), pp. 185–7.

27 A.L. Moote, *The Revolt of the Judges*
(Princeton, 1971), pp. 6–18, 40–52;
A.L. Moote, 'The French Crown versus
its Judicial and Financial Officials,
1615–83', *Journal of Modern History*,
XXXIV (1962), pp. 148–52; Mousnier,
*Plume*, pp. 46–52, 245–9; P.J. Coveney
(ed), *France in Crisis, 1620–75* (London,
1977), pp. 34–6.

28 Chevallier, p. 466.

29 Richelieu, *Testament*, pp. 218–23,
285–6.

30 Pagès, pp. 80–5; R. Mousnier, 'Les Sur-
vivances Médiévales dans la France du
XVIIe Siècle, *XVIIe Siècle* nos. 106–7
(1975), pp. 63–6; J.–P. Labatut, *Les
Ducs et Pairs de France au XVIIe Siècle*
(Paris, 1972), pp.255–7; N. Elias, *The
Court Society* (Oxford, 1983), passim.

31 Stone, *Crisis*, ch. 5.

32 Labatut, pp. 117–20, 123; Bonney, *Pol.
Change*, pp. 301–4; R. Harding,
'Aristocrats and Lawyers in French
Provincial Government, 1559–1648', in
Malament, pp. 111–4; S. Kettering,
*Judicial Politics and Urban Revolt in
Seventeenth-Century France* (Princeton,
1978), pp. 135–49.

33 M. Foisil, *La Révolte des Nu-Pieds* (Paris, 1970), p. 150.

34 On revolts see especially Bercé, *Croquants* and R. Pillorget, *Les Mouvements Insurrectionnels de Provence entre 1596 et 1715* (Paris, 1975).

35 Bonney, *Pol. Change*, pp. 183–90 and ch. 10; J. Miller, 'Les Etats de Languedoc pendant la Fronde', *Annales du Midi* XCV (1983), pp. 45–6.

36 Tapié, p. 379.

37 Clarendon, *History*, I.93.

38 La Ferté-Imbault, 9 Jan. 1642 NS, BT 73; A. Browning, *Thomas Earl of Danby* (3 vols., Glasgow, 1951), II.379–80; see also T. Bruce, Earl of Ailesbury, *Memoirs* ed. W.E. Buckley (2 vols., Roxburgh Club, 1890), I.205–6; P.A. Knachel, *England and the Fronde* (Ithaca, 1967), p. 42.

39 See Lindley, *Fenland Riots*; K.J. Lindley, 'Riot Prevention and Control in Early Stuart London', *TRHS* 5th Series, XXXIII (1983), pp. 109–26 (esp. pp. 114–5); J. Brewer and J. Styles (eds.), *An Ungovernable People?* (London, 1980), pp. 13–15, 47–8; C.S.L. Davies, 'Peasant Revolts in England and France: A Comparison', *Agricultural History Review* XXI (1973), pp. 122–34; R. Bonney, 'The English and French Civil Wars', *History* LXV (1980), pp. 367–8.

40 Gardiner, VIII. 353–6, IX.73–6, 119–21, 154, 163–4, 173–4; Cooper, p. 106.

41 T.G. Barnes, *Somerset 1625–40* (Oxford, 1961), p. 239.

42 C. Russell, 'Why did Charles I Call the Long Parliament?', *History* LXIX (1984), pp. 375–83; Cooper, pp. 198–9.

43 Gardiner, X.118; La Ferté-Imbault, 9 and 16 Jan. 1642 NS, BT 73.

44 See A. Fletcher, *The Outbreak of the English Civil War* (London, 1981); C. Hibbard, *Charles I and the Popish Plot* (Chapel Hill, 1983). Professor Hibbard shows, in meticulous detail, just how much substance there was behind the allegations of a Popish plot. Quotation from Gardiner, IX. 221.

45 La Ferté-Imbault, 16 Jan. 1642 NS, BT 73; *CSPV 1640–2*, p. 272; V. Pearl, *London and the Outbreak of the Puritan Revolution* (Oxford, 1961), pp. 210–18; J.S. Morrill, 'The Attack on the Church of England in the Long Parliament', in D. Beales and G. Best (eds.), *History, Society and the Churches: Essays in Honour of Owen Chadwick* (Cambridge, 1985), pp. 105–24.

46 Gardiner, X.75; La Ferté-Imbault, 31 Oct 1641 NS, BT 72.

47 Both Fletcher and Morrill see the religious imperative as crucial and rather discount the fear of violence.

48 Gardiner, IX.285.

49 Morrill, 'Attack', especially pp. 122–3; Gardiner, X.105; Fletcher, pp. 174–5.

50 B. Manning, *The English People and the English Revolution* (London, 1976) attempts to examine the role of the people, but weakens his case by insisting on seeing *all* riots as evidence of class conflict and fear of the mob as *the* major source of Royalism.

51 Fletcher, p. 415.

52 Carlton, p. 298; Aylmer, p. 382; J. Morrill, 'The Religious Context of the English Civil War', *TRHS*, 5th Series, XXXIV (1984), p. 169.

53 See J.H. Franklin, *John Locke and the Theory of Sovereignty* (Cambridge, 1978), ch. 2.

54 See especially C. Holmes, *The Eastern Association in the English Civil War* (Cambridge, 1974); J.S. Morrill, *The Revolt of the Provinces, 1630–50* (London, 1976).

55 Carlton, pp. 252, 292.

56 J. Bruce (ed.) *Charles I in 1646* (Camden Society, 1856), pp. 79, 71.

57 Richelieu, *Lettres*, VI. 799, 895–6.

58 See R. Bonney, 'Cardinal Mazarin and the Great Nobility During the Fronde', *EHR* XCVI (1981), pp. 818–33.

59 Bonney, *Debts*, pp. 193–201; Moote,

'The French Crown', pp. 183–4.

60 Moote, *Revolt*, chs. 3–4.

61 Knachel, p.42 ; R. Mousnier, 'The Revolutionary Days in Paris in 1648,' in Coveney, (ed.), *France in Crisis*, pp. 170–81, 188–96.

62 Knachel, pp. 40–2, 46–7 ; A. Lossky, 'France in the System of Europe in the Seventeenth Century', *PWSFH* I(1974), pp. 39–40.

63 Moote, pp. 109–10. Most of the remainder of this chapter owes much to Moote's arguments.

64 Pagès, pp. 13–19 ; Mousnier, *Plume*, pp. 53–5 ; *HGL* XIV.106, 114, 149–52, 157–64, 396–402 ; Pillorget, *Mouvements*, p. 565.

65 See Bonney, *Debts*, pp. 212–17 ; R. Bonney, 'The French Civil War, 1648–53', *ESR*, pp. 76–83.

6 REBUILDING

1 Moote, ch. 10.

2 Bonney, 'French Civil War', pp. 84–92.

3 Bonney, *Debts*, pp. 214, 239–41 and ch. 6.

4 Bonney, *Pol. Change*, pp. 203–13, 228–30.

5 See A.N. Hamscher, *The Parlement of Paris after the Fronde* (Pittsburgh, 1976), esp. pp. 72–5, 82–118 ; Moote, pp. 356–63.

6 Bonney, *Pol. Change*, ch. 15 ; Miller, 'Etats de Languedoc'.

7 J.B. Wolf, *Louis XIV* (London, Panther edn., 1970), pp. 61, 66–7 ; J.C. Rule, 'Louis XIV, Roi Bureaucrate' in Rule pp. 21–4.

8 Louis XIV, *Mémoires for the Instruction of the Dauphin*, ed. P. Sonnino (New York, 1970), pp. 130–1.

9 *ibid.*, pp. 63, 68.

10 *ibid.*, p. 149.

11 Wolf, pp. 17, 108.

12 Louis XIV, *Mémoires*, pp. 101–2 ; Wolf, pp. 107, 128.

13 *Mémoires*, pp. 28–30 ; Wolf, pp. 32–4, 111.

14 *Mémoires*, pp. 169, 245–6 ; St Simon,

II.39–41, 258–9, 358–9 ; A. Corvisier, *Louvois* (Paris, 1983), pp. 284–5.

15 Wolf, p. 151.

16 *ibid.* pp. 361–4.

17 Rule in Rule, p. 27 ; Corvisier, pp. 276–94, 319–23.

18 J. Barry, *Versailles* (London, 1972), pp. 58–61.

19 Wolf, pp. 186–8 ; I. Murat, *Colbert* (Charlottesville, 1984), pp. 49, 61–3. Dessert states (p. 765, n.97) that Fouquet bought Belle-Ile at Mazarin's request, on the understanding that Mazarin would buy it from him later ; it does not follow that the charge that he was fortifying it was baseless.

20 Murat, p. 69 ; Wolf, p. 185.

21 See Dessert, *Argent*, esp. pp. 280–310 ; Dessert, 'Finances et Société au XVIIe Siècle : à propos de la Chambre de Justice de 1661', *AESC* XXIX (1974), pp. 847–82 ; Dessert and J.–L. Journet, 'Le Lobby Colbert', *AESC* XXX (1975), pp. 1303–36.

22 Dessert and Journet, pp. 1308, 1326 and passim.

23 Murat, p. 69.

24 Wolf, pp. 198–211 ; Barry, pp. 126–7.

25 St Simon, I.243 ; Wolf, p. 203 ; Louis XIV, *Mémoires*, pp. 86–7.

26 Elias, passim ; Labatut, pp. 242–3, 256–7, 300–10 ; Wolf, pp. 225–7 ; J. Levron, 'Louis XIV's Courtiers' in R.M. Hatton (ed.), *Louis XIV and Absolutism* (London, 1976), pp. 140–8 ; St Simon, II.23–6, 399–400.

27 Elias, chs. 5–6 ; St Simon, II.251 ; Liselotte, p. 31 ; Barry, p. 148 ; J. Levron, *Daily Life at Versailles in the Seventeenth and Eighteenth Centuries* (London, 1968), p. 52.

28 St Simon, II.358–9.

29 Barry, p. 147.

30 R.M. Isherwood, *Music in the Service of the King* (Ithaca, 1973), p. 249.

31 Ranum, p. 289.

32 J. Evelyn, *Diary* ed. E.S. de Beer (6 vols., Oxford, 1955), III. 246.

33 *Diurnal of Thomas Rugg*, ed. W.L. Sachse (Camden Society, 1961), p. 87.

34 Sir W. Temple, *Memoirs 1672-9* (London, 1692), pp. 273-4; see also R. North, *Examen* (London, 1742), p. 451; G. Savile, Marquis of Halifax, *Complete Works*, ed. J.P. Kenyon (Harmondsworth, 1969), p. 265.

35 G. Burnet, *Supplement to History of His Own Time*, ed. H.C. Foxcroft (Oxford, 1902), p. 142; G. Burnet, *History of My Own Time* (6 vols., Oxford, 1833), I.481.

36 S. Pepys, *Diary*, ed. R.C. Latham and W. Matthews (11 vols., London, 1971-83), IX.335-6.

37 Pepys, V.60.

38 *HMC 5th Report*, p. 199; J. Sheffield, Duke of Buckingham, *Works* (2 vols., London, 1753), II.59; *CSPV 1661-4*, p. 84; Clarendon, *Life* (3 vols., Oxford, 1827), I.504.

39 Pepys, V.112, VII.218; Evelyn, IV.410; Ailesbury, I.87.

40 Pepys, IV.197, VII.228-9.

41 Clarendon, *Life*, III.3; *HMC 5th Report*, p. 154.

42 Burnet, *Supplement*, p. 48.

43 Halifax, p. 256; see also *HMC Heathcote*, p. 48; North, *Examen*, p. 451; Croissy to Louis XIV, 31 Jan. 1669 NS, BT 121.

44 M. Prestwich, *Cranfield* (Oxford, 1966), p. 225; Clarendon, *Life*, II.144; see also Sir J. Reresby, *Memoirs*, ed. A. Browning (Glasgow, 1936), p. 210.

45 Halifax, p. 256; Clarendon, *Life*, III.61; Reresby, pp. 247-8; see also Croissy to Lionne, 7 Feb. 1669 NS, BT 121; Pepys, VIII.183, 356.

46 Buckingham, II.58-9.

47 *CSPV 1659-61*, p. 297; see also J. Miller, *Restoration England: The Reign of Charles II* (London, 1985), p. 97.

48 Miller, *Restoration England*, chs. 2-3.

49 Clarendon, *Life*, III.18; Pepys, V.60.

50 Burnet, *History*, II.1-2; Ailesbury, I.22. See also Pepys, VIII.332; Burnet, I.467-8.

51 Burnet, *Supplement*, p. 50. See also Ailesbury, I.93; Buckingham, II.55-6; Burnet, *History*, I.356, 475.

52 Pepys, I.271.

53 Evelyn, IV.118; Buckingham, II.63.

54 Dryden, 'Absalom and Achitophel', lines 545-6, 549-50; Pepys, IX.361; Burnet, *Supplement*, p. 64.

55 Miller, *Restoration England*, p. 91; Burnet, *History*, I.270-2.

56 I.M. Green, *The Re-establishment of the Church of England 1660-3* (Oxford, 1978), ch. 10.

57 A. Marvell, *Poems and Letters*, ed. H.M. Margoliouth (3rd edn., 2 vols., Oxford, 1971), II.315.

## 7 DOVER AND AFTER

1 H. Kamen, 'The Decline of Spain: A Historical Myth?', *P & P*, no. 81 (1978), pp. 24-50.

2 F.A.M. Mignet, *Négociations Rélatives à la Succession d'Espagne* (4 vols., Paris, 1835-42), II.549-54.

3 *ibid.*, II.509-10, 518.

4 *ibid.*, II.521-3, 544-6, 562-4; H.H. Rowen, *The Ambassador Prepares for War: Arnauld de Pomponne 1669-71* (The Hague, 1957), pp. 22-7.

5 J. Bérenger, 'An Attempted Rapprochement between France and the Emperor' in R.M. Hatton (ed.), *Louis XIV and Europe* (London, 1976), ch. 6, esp. p. 144.

6 Wolf, pp. 270-2; Rowen, p. 27.

7 Mignet, II.644-6, III.5.

8 *ibid.*, III.11; Wolf, p. 275.

9 Rowen, pp. 36, 65, 67-8; P. Sonnino, 'Lionne and the Origins of the Dutch War', *PWSFH* III (1975), pp. 70-2; Sonnino, 'Colbert and the Origins of the Dutch War', *ESR* XIII (1983), pp. 1-11.

10 See J. Miller, *James II: A Study in Kingship* (Hove, 1978), pp. 59-62.

11 Corvisier, pp. 258-9; Wolf, pp. 288-9; S.B. Baxter, *William III* (London, 1966), pp. 75-85.

12 Burnet, *History*, IV.562–7; Baxter, passim.

13 C.J. Ekberg, *The Failure of Louis XIV's Dutch War* (Chapel Hill, 1979), ch.2; Wolf, pp. 296–309; P. Sonnino, 'Louis XIV's "Mémoires pour l'Histoire de la Guerre de Hollande"', *FHS* VIII (1973), pp. 29–50.

14 J. Miller, *Popery and Politics in England, 1660–88* (Cambridge, 1973), pp. 116–7.

15 Miller, *James II*, pp. 57–9 and passim; Burnet, *History*, I.475, II.22–3.

16 A. Grey, *Debates in the House of Commons, 1667–94* (10 vols., London, 1769), VI.330, VIII.158.

17 Grey, IV.128, III.136; Burnet, *History*, II.1.

18 R.C. Mettam, *Government and Society in Louis XIV's France* (London, 1977), pp. 237–43; Ekberg, pp. 175–8; L. Bernard, 'Popular Uprisings under Louis XIV', *FHS* III (1964), pp. 468–74; E. Le Roy Ladurie, 'Révoltes et Contestations Rurales de 1675 à 1788', *AESC* XXIX (1974), pp. 6–22.

19 Ekberg, pp. 116–9; Corvisier, pp. 210–1, 266; Rule in Rule, p. 53.

8 ZENITH AND DECLINE

1 See Mettam, passim.

2 See Ranum; L. Bernard, *The Emerging City: Paris in the Age of Louis XIV* (Durham, N.C., 1970).

3 Corvisier, p. 442.

4 Wolf, pp. 507–10.

5 See E. Labrousse, *'Une Foi, Une Loi, Un Roi': La Révocation de l'Edit de Nantes* (Geneva/Paris, 1985); J. Orcibal, *Louis XIV et les Protestants* (Paris, 1951).

6 See E. Caldicott, H. Gough and J.–P. Pittion, (eds.), *The Huguenots and Ireland — Anatomy of an Emigration* (forthcoming).

7 Halifax, p. 78.

8 Grey, VIII.261.

9 D. Allen, 'The Role of the London Trained Bands in the Exclusion Crisis', *EHR* LXXXVII (1972), pp. 287–303.

10 Browning, *Danby*, II.379–80; Miller, *Popery*, pp. 182–8.

11 B. Behrens, 'The Whig Theory of the Constitution in the Reign of Charles II', *Cambridge Historical Journal*, VII (1941), pp. 42–71.

12 Reresby, p. 259.

13 *King's Works*, V.144–51, 304–13.

14 Barrillon to Louis XIV, 24 June 1683 NS, BT 155.

15 J. Miller, 'The Crown and the Borough Charters in the Reign of Charles II', *EHR* C (1985), pp. 70–84; Miller, *Popery*, pp. 194–5.

16 J. Miller, 'The Potential for "Absolutism" in Later Stuart England', *History* LXIX (1984), pp. 187–207.

17 Evelyn, IV.409–11; Halifax, pp. 265, 267.

18 Miller, *James II*, p. 120; this section is based mainly on the research for that book.

19 Evelyn, IV. 484–7.

20 British Library, Add. MS 52279, fo. 10.

21 For differing views see R.Gwynn, 'James II in the Light of his Treatment of Huguenot Refugees in England', *EHR* XCII (1977), pp. 820–31; J. Miller, 'The Immediate Impact of the Revocation in England' in Caldicott, Gough and Pittion (forthcoming).

22 Miller, *James II*, pp. 156–7, 164–6, 187.

23 *ibid.*, pp. 178–9, 196–7.

24 *ibid.*, p. 173; also J.P. Kenyon, *Robert Spencer, Earl of Sunderland* (London, 1958), chs. 4–6.

25 Wolf, p. 730; Isherwood, pp. 317–18; Liselotte, pp. 45–7, 68–70, 118, 122.

26 Isherwood, p. 157; Wolf, pp. 746–7 and chs. 31–2.

27 Wolf, pp. 691–3; St Simon, II.471–82; Bonney, *Debts*, p. 176, n.5; Dessert, pp. 185–8, 210–9; Bernard, pp. 21–2.

28 P. Goubert, *Louis XIV and Twenty Million Frenchmen* (London, 1970), pp. 201, 261, 319–20; H. Monin, *Essai*

*sur l'Histoire Administrative de Languedoc* (Paris, 1884), pp. 135−50.

29 Wolf, pp. 683−5.

30 *Ibid.*, pp.468−72, 702 ; Rule in Rule, pp. 29, 90 ; R. Lossky, 'Some Problems in Tracing the Intellectual Development of Louis XIV' in Rule, pp. 321−3 and 342, n.11 ; Rule, 'Louis XIV and Colbert de Torcy', in R.M. Hatton and J.S. Bromley (eds.), *William III and Louis XIV: Essays by and for M.A. Thomson* (Liverpool, 1968), ch. 12.

31 C. Clay, *Public Finance and Private Wealth: The Career of Sir Stephen Fox* (Oxford, 1978) ; P.G.M. Dickson, *The Financial Revolution, 1688−1756* (London, 1967).

32 Grey, IX.125 ; see also J. Miller, *The Glorious Revolution* (London, 1983), chs. 2−5 ; C. Roberts, 'The Constitutional Significance of the Financial Settlement of 1690', *HJ* XX (1977), pp. 59−76.

33 See G.Holmes, *The Electorate and the National Will in the First Age of Party* (Lancaster, 1975).

# Index

# VALOIS

Charles, Comte d'Angoulême
(great-grandson of CHARLES V * d. 1380)

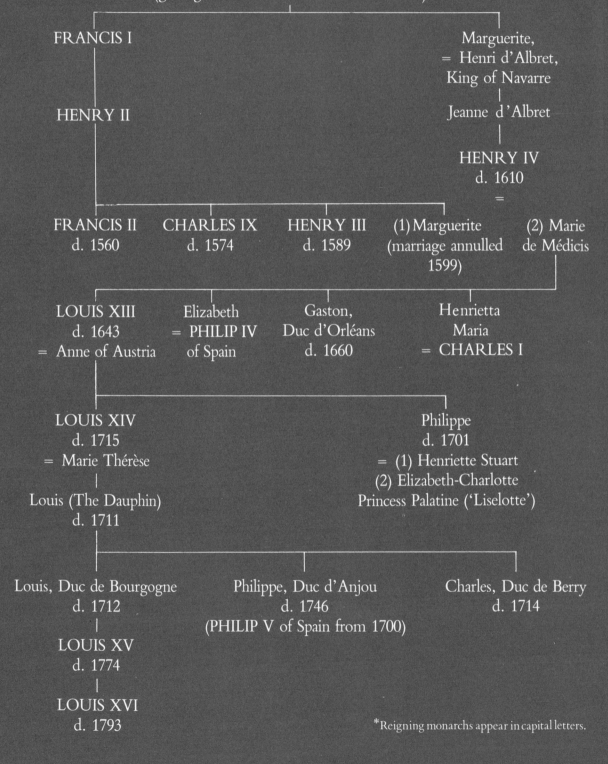

FRANCIS I

Marguerite,
= Henri d'Albret,
King of Navarre

HENRY II

Jeanne d'Albret

HENRY IV
d. 1610

=

FRANCIS II    CHARLES IX    HENRY III    (1) Marguerite    (2) Marie
d. 1560        d. 1574        d. 1589    (marriage annulled    de Médicis
                                          1599)

LOUIS XIII      Elizabeth      Gaston,      Henrietta
d. 1643    = PHILIP IV    Duc d'Orléans    Maria
= Anne of Austria    of Spain      d. 1660      = CHARLES I

LOUIS XIV                        Philippe
d. 1715                          d. 1701
= Marie Thérèse             = (1) Henriette Stuart
                               (2) Elizabeth-Charlotte
Louis (The Dauphin)      Princess Palatine ('Liselotte')
d. 1711

Louis, Duc de Bourgogne      Philippe, Duc d'Anjou      Charles, Duc de Berry
d. 1712                 d. 1746                d. 1714
           (PHILIP V of Spain from 1700)
LOUIS XV
d. 1774

LOUIS XVI
d. 1793                          *Reigning monarchs appear in capital letters.